*Daniel Murphy*
MARTIN BUBER'S PHILOSOPHY OF EDUCATION

# MARTIN BUBER'S
# PHILOSOPHY
# OF
# EDUCATION

*DANIEL MURPHY*

IRISH ACADEMIC PRESS

The typesetting of this book
was output by
Gilbert Gough Typesetting, Dublin for
Irish Academic Press,
Kill Lane, Blackrock, Co. Dublin

BRITISH LIBRARY CATALOGUING IN PUBLICATION DATA
Murphy, Daniel
Martin Buber's philosophy of education.
1. German philosophy. Buber, Martin,
1878-1965 Critical studies
I. Title
193

ISBN 0-7165-2427-9

Printed in Great Britain by
Billing & Sons Ltd, Worcester

*TO MARGARET*

If I had to choose one sentence to summarize the whole message of Buber's life and thought it would be this: 'Let us dare, despite all, to trust.'

*Maurice Friedman*

What gives Buber his imperishable greatness and makes his life symbolic is that he steps forth as this unique man and talks directly to other persons.

*Hans Trub*

I know of no one with a life so rich with intellectual adventures or one who so strongly responded to their challenges as Martin Buber. His greatest contribution was himself, his very being. There was magic in his personality, richness in his soul. His sheer presence was joy.

*Abraham Joshua Heschel*

I remember when I first began reading Buber some commentator referred to people like Gandhi and Schweitzer and Buber as being men of universal faith, people anyone could identify with, and I do believe that in a sense Buber fits that role.

*Father Donnach Moore, S. J.*

He anticipated the freedom from religion, including the institutions of religion, in the name of that to which religion points. This attitude is a reason for Buber's far-reaching influence on the secular world and particularly on the younger generation for which the traditional activities and assertions of churches and synagogues have become largely irrelevant.

*Paul Tillich*

# Contents

# Preface

Martin Buber is best known perhaps as the 'philosopher of dialogue' but he was also a distinguished educator and wrote extensively on various aspects of educational theory and practice. This book looks specifically at his educational philosophy, though it draws on all his intellectual and cultural interests to clarify various issues in his educational thought. With over sixty years experience as an educator, Buber was exceptionally well equipped to write on the subject. He writes, however, not only with his own personal authority but with the full authority of the traditions he represents. They include the three thousand year old Jewish tradition of teaching and learning and the later traditions of Christianity, socialism and existentialism with which he also had deep affinities.

Buber saw education as essentially a dialogue conducted between teacher and learner, and the book seeks to locate his theories within the framework of this all-embracing principle. Deeply disturbed at the disillusionment and cynicism he observed in modern youth, he saw the teacher-learner dialogue as being concerned primarily with the nurturing of hope and a meaning-giving faith. Out of this concern comes his redefinition of the role of the teacher to embrace the specific educational functions of moral, intellectual and cultural formation, as well as the counselling role of the spiritual healer for which he found some compelling precedents in the rabbinic and hasidic traditions of Judaism. As a lifelong socialist he was deeply interested in literacy, seeing it as the key to educability and personal freedom. His ideas provided a philosophical foundation for the theories of Paulo Freire and were implemented with dramatic success in the literacy campaigns of Brazil and Nicaragua. Fundamentally, however, Buber was a *religious socialist* who saw adult education as a means towards the transformation of societies through the process of community renewal.

These are some of the issues explored in the book. There are four main divisions in the work. The first consists of a biographical introduction which reviews Buber's activities as an educator. Two further chapters are devoted to the philosophical and cultural roots of his educational thought. The first is concerned with the evolution of his philosophical anthropology, the second with the specifically Jewish elements in his thought. Four chapters examine the major educational issues on which his work is focussed. They are: the aims of teaching and learning and the nature of the relationships involved in both; the nature of aesthetic creativity and its specific applications in the sphere of linguistic development; the aims and methods of moral and religious education; and finally, the aims and methods of adult and community education. The concluding section explores the implications of these ideas for the education of the future.

There are several people to whom I am indebted for assisting me in the preparation of this work. I would like, firstly, to thank Professor Valentine Rice, Director of the School of Education, and the authorities at Trinity College for granting me sabbatical leave in the Michaelmas term of 1987, during which the final draft of the work was completed. Secondly, I wish to thank the wardens and staffs of Dean Hall, Goldsmiths' College, and London House, University of London for providing me with accommodation during my period of sabbatical leave.

On two visits to Jerusalem I was facilitated by Dr Kalman Yaron, a former student of Martin Buber's, and Director of the Martin Buber Institute of Adult Education at the Mount Scopus Campus of the Hebrew University. I have since corresponded with Dr Yaron and am indebted to him for providing me with photocopies of archival material. I have also corresponded with the late Terence Prittie, author of *Miracle in the Desert* and President of the England-Israel Society, and he has illuminated me on various aspects of Jewish culture. I want to thank them both for their help.

Portions of Chapters 6 and 7 have appeared in *Irish Educational Studies, ATE: Journal of the Association of Teachers of English* and *Studies in Education.* I am grateful to the editorial boards of these journals for allowing me to use this material.I would like to acknowledge the assistance I have received from the staffs of The Library, Trinity College, Dublin, The Senate House and Institute of Education Libraries of The University of London and The Bodleian Library, University of Oxford.

Thanks are due finally to Ms Appie Kennedy-Jonker and Ms Elizabeth Fleeton of the School of Education, Trinity College for typing the manuscript, and to Dr Michael Adams and the staff of Irish Academic Press for guiding the work through its final stages of production.

DANIEL MURPHY
Department of Higher Education and Educational Research,
Trinity College, University of Dublin
February, 1988

# I
# Martin Buber, Educator (1878-1965)
# A Biographical Introduction

## 1 Formative Years, 1878-1898

Martin Mordechai Buber, the only child of middle-class Jewish parents, was born in Vienna on 8 February 1878. In his brief autobiography he recalls two images from his childhood that remained with him throughout his life. The first was his memory of the house in Vienna where he spent his first three years. 'Still today', he writes, 'I see with closed eyes the Danube canal under the house, the sight of which I used to enjoy with a feeling of certainty that nothing could happen to me.'[1] The second was the far more tragic recollection of his parents' separation which occurred when he was three years old. When his mother left home he was sent to live with his grandparents on a large estate near Lvov (Lemberg), the capital city of Galicia. He recalls sitting on the balcony of his grandparents' home with a young girl his grandmother had enlisted to look after him. When they discussed the mystery of his mother's disappearance the girl said to him, 'She will never come back.' To this early experience of 'mismeeting' or 'vergegnung' he attributed his lifelong preoccupation with the nature of human mutuality:

> The house in which my grandparents lived had a great rectangular inner courtyard surrounded by a wooden balcony extending to the roof on which one could walk around the building at each floor. Here I stood once in my fourth year with a girl several years older, the daughter of a neighbour, to whose care my grandmother had entrusted me. We both leaned on the railing. I cannot remember that I spoke of my mother to my older comrade. But I hear still how the big girl said to me: 'No, she will never come back''. I know that I remained silent, but also that I cherished no doubt of the truth of the spoken words. It remained fixed in me, from year to year it cleaved ever more to my heart, but after more than ten years I had begun to perceive it as something that concerned not only me, but all men. Later I once made up the word 'Vergegnung' — 'mismeeting', or 'miscounter' — to designate the failure of a real meeting between men. When after another twenty years I again saw my mother, who had come from a distance to visit me, my wife, and my children, I could not gaze into her still astonishingly beautiful eyes without hearing from somewhere the word 'Vergegnung' as a word spoken to me. I suspect that all that I have learned about the genuine meeting in the course of my life had its first origin in that hour on the balcony[2]

Buber was deeply attached to his grandparents, each of whom he recalls with affection in his autobiography. His grandfather, Solomon Buber, was an eminent scholar who had produced a learned version of the Midrash. He passed on to his grandson both his interest in the Jewish scriptures and his interest in philology. Adele Buber, Martin's grandmother, was a highly cultivated, resourceful, self-educated lady who was well-versed in Jewish and German literature and who managed to combine her cultural interests with a highly active commitment to the management of the large estate on which they lived. To her Buber attributed his reverence for language — for the 'authentic word that cannot be paraphrased' — and for the expressive quality of living speech:

> Among the Jews in the small Galician town where my grandmother grew up the reading of 'alien' literature was proscribed, but for the girls all readings, with the exception of edifying popular books, were held unseemly. As a fifteen year old she had set up for herself in the storehouse a hiding place in which stood volumes of Schiller's 'Die Horen', Jean Paul's book on education, Levana, and many other German books which had been secretly and thoroughly read by her. When she was seventeen years old, she took them and the custom of concentrated reading with her into her marriage, and she reared her two sons in the respect for the authentic word that cannot be paraphrased. The same influence she later exercised on me. I learned even before I was fourteen (at that time I moved into the house of my father and my stepmother) what it means really to express something. I was affected in a special manner by the way that this woman handled the large-size, similarly bound copy-books in which she recorded everyday income and expenditures: in between these entries she registered, after she had spoken them half aloud to herself, the passages which had become important to her out of her readings. Now and then she set down her own comments as well, which in no way imitated the style of the classic but from time to time stated something that she had to reply in intercourse with the great spirits. The same was true of her oral utterances: even when she obviously communicated the conclusion of a reflection, it had the appearance of something perceived. That undoubtedly came from the fact that with her, experiencing and reflecting on experience were not two stages but, as it were, two sides of the same process: when she looked at the street, she had at times the profile of someone meditating on a problem, and when I found her all alone in meditation, it seemed to me at times as if she listened. To the glance of the child, however, it was already unmistakable that when she at times addressed someone, she really addressed him.[3]

Outside his grandparents' home Buber was exposed to a great variety of languages: Yiddish was the main language of the Jewish quarter in Lemberg, Polish was the language of the school he attended when he was ten, and Hebrew was the language of the synagogue. At school he was taught Greek by his tutors; later he acquired a high level of competence in English, French, Italian, Spanish, Latin and Dutch, in addition to German, Hebrew, Yiddish and Polish. Not surprisingly, most of his attention at school was focussed on his linguistic interests:

> I went to school for the first time when I was ten years old. Up till ten I received private tutoring, chiefly in languages, both because of my own inclination and talents and because for my grandmother a language-centred humanism was the royal road to education. The multiplicity of human languages, their wonderful variety in which the white light of human speech at once fragmented and preserved itself, was already at the time of my boyhood a problem that instructed me ever anew. In instructing me it also again and again disquieted me. I followed time after time an individual word or even structure of words from one language to another, found it there again and yet had time after time to give up something there as lost that apparently only existed in a single one of all the languages. That was not merely 'nuances of meaning': I devised for myself two-language conversations between a German and a Frenchman, later between a Hebrew and an ancient Roman and came ever again, half in play and yet at times with beating heart, to feel the tension between what was heard by the one and what was heard by the other, from his thinking in another language. That had a deep influence on me and has issued in a long life into ever clearer insight.[4]

Buber's memories of school were not all as happy as this passage suggests. His description of the gymnasium at Lemberg gives an indication of the isolation experienced by Jewish children amongst the predominantly Christian Poles. 'The atmosphere at the Franz Joseph Gymnasium', he says, 'was that which prevailed or seemed to prevail among the peoples of the Austro-Hungarian empire: mutual tolerance without mutual understanding.' The pupils, he recalls, 'got on well with one another', but the Christians and Jews 'knew almost nothing about each other':

> Before eight o'clock in the morning all the pupils had to be assembled. At eight o'clock the signal bell sounded. One of the teachers entered and mounted the professor's lecturing desk, above which on the wall rose a large crucifix. At the same moment all the pupils stood up in their benches. The teacher and the Polish students crossed themselves; he spoke the Trinity formula, and they prayed aloud together. Until one might sit down again, we Jews stood silent and unmoving, our eyes glued to the floor.
>
> I have already indicated that in our school there was no perceptible hatred of the Jews; I can hardly remember a teacher who was not tolerant or did not wish to pass as tolerant. But the obligatory daily standing in the room resounding with the strange service affected me worse than an act of intolerance could have affected me. Compulsory guests, having to participate as a thing in a sacral event in which no dram of my person could

or would take part, and this for eight long years morning after morning: that stamped itself upon the life-substance of the boy.

No attempt was ever made to convert any of us Jewish pupils; yet my antipathy to all missionary activity is rooted in that time. Not merely against the Christian mission to the Jews, but against all missionarizing among men who have a faith with roots of its own. In vain did Franz Rosenzweig try to win me for the idea of a Jewish mission among the non-Jews.[5]

When he was fourteen years old Buber went to live on his father's estate. He had been visiting the estate periodically since the age of nine. He continued to maintain regular contact with his grandparents. He remembers his father, Carl Buber, as 'a wholly unsentimental man' who was less concerned with the world of books and scholarship than he was 'with genuine human contact'. From his father he learned the importance of interhuman dialogue — the sense of 'active responsible contact that could rise to full reciprocity':

> In a special way the relationship of my father to nature was connected with his relationship to the realm that one customarily designates as the social. How he took part in the life of all the people who in one or another manner were dependent on him: the laborers attached to the estate, in their little houses that surrounded the estate buildings, houses built according to his design, the little peasants who performed service for him under conditions worked out with exact justice, the tenants; how he troubled about the family relationships, about the upbringing of children and schooling, about the sickness and aging of all the people — all that was not derived from any principles. It was solicitude not in the ordinary, but in the personal sense, in the sense of active responsible contact that could rise here to full reciprocity. In the town too my father did not act otherwise. To sightless charity he was fiercely averse; he understood no other help than that from person to persons, and he practiced it. Even in his old age he let himself be elected to the 'bread commission' of the Jewish community of Lemberg and wandered tirelessly around the houses in order to discover the people's real wants and necessities; how else could that take place except through contact![6]

Amongst the peasant people with whom he spent most of his childhood years Buber experienced not only the immediacy of interhuman contact but an extraordinary closeness to the whole world of nature. One of his most moving recollections concerns his attachment to one of the horses on his grandparents' estate. The experience is described in this remarkable passage from the autobiography:

> When I was eleven years of age, spending the summer on my grandparents' estate, I used, as often as I could do it unobserved, to steal into the stable and gently stroke the neck of my darling, a broad dapple-grey horse. It was

not a casual delight but a great, certainly friendly, but also deeply stirring happening. If I am to explain it now, beginning from the still very fresh memory of my hand, I must say that what I experienced in touch with the animal was the Other, the immense otherness of the Other, which, however, did not remain strange like the otherness of the ox and the ram, but rather let me draw near and touch it. When I stroked the mighty mane, sometimes marvellously smooth-combed, at other times just as astonishingly wild, and felt the life beneath my hand, it was as though the element of vitality itself bordered on my skin, something that was not I, was certainly not akin to me, palpably the other, not just another, really the Other itself; and yet it let me approach, confided itself to me, placed itself elementally in the relation of Thou and Thou with me. The horse, even when I had not begun by pouring oats for him into the manger, very gently raised his massive head, ears flicking, then snorted quietly, as a conspirator gives a signal meant to be recognizable only by his fellow-conspirator; and I was approved.[7]

While still a student at the Franz Joseph Gymnasium Buber introduced himself to philosophy, beginning with Kant whom he read when he was fifteen, and Nietzsche whom he discovered two years later. His discovery of Kant's philosophy was bound up with a deep sense of personal isolation and loneliness which caused him to contemplate the problematic nature of existence and especially the problems of temporality and change. Tormented by the question of man's place in the universe and his relation to the realities of time, space, the intemporal and the infinite, he turned to Kant's *Prolegomena to All Future Metaphysics* where he learned that space and time are 'nothing more than formal conditions of our sensory faculty':

Here it must be added above all that at that time the question about time had oppressed me in a far more tormenting fashion than that about space. I was irresistably driven to want to grasp the total world process as actual, and that meant to understand it, 'time', either as beginning and ending or as without beginning and end. At each attempt to accept them as reality, both proved equally absurd. If I wanted to take the matter seriously (and I was ever again compelled to want just this) I had to transport myself either to the beginning of time or to the end of time. Thus I came to feel the former like a blow in the neck or the latter like a rap against the forehead — no, there is no beginning and no end! Or I had to let myself be thrown into this or that bottomless abyss, into infinity, and now everything whirled. It happened thus time after time. Mathematical or physical formulae could not help me; what was at stake was the reality of the world in which one had to live and which had taken on the face of the absurd and the uncanny.

Then a book came into my hand, Kant's *Prolegomena*. In it was taught that space and time are 'nothing more than formal conditions of our sensory faculty,' are 'not real properties that adhere to the things in themselves'' but 'mere forms of our sensory perception'. This philosophy exercised a great quieting effect on me. Now I needed no longer, tormented, to inquire of time a final time. Time was not a sentence hanging over me; it was mine, for it was 'ours'. The question was explained as unanswerable by its nature, but at the same time I was liberated from it, from having to ask it. Kant's present to me at that time was philosophical freedom.[8]

The comfort he found in Kant proved to be transient, however, and, still tormented by the problem of the temporal, he turned to Nietzsche two years later. Nietzsche's philosophy, he recalled, 'not only stirred me up but transported me into a sublime intoxication'. Of Nietzsche's *Thus Spake Zarathustra* (which Buber proposed to translate into Polish) he wrote: 'the book took possession of me, for here a teaching did not simply and calmly confront me, but a willed and able — splendidly willed and able — utterance stormed up to and over me'. This book, he declares euphorically, 'worked on me not in the manner of a gift but in the manner of an invasion which deprived me of my freedom, and it was a long time until I could liberate myself from it.' Nietzsche's notion of a circular flow of time did not, however, provide him with a solution to the mystery of the temporal, though Nietzsche exerted a profound formative influence on his subsequent development as a philosopher:

> Kant had not undertaken to solve the sense-confusing riddle that is set us by the being of time; he completed the philosophical limitation of it in that he made it into a problem of we ourselves being referred to the form of time. Nietzsche, who wanted nothing to do with philosophical self-moderations, set in the place of one of the primal mysteries of time — the manifest mystery of the uniqueness of all happening — the pseudo-mystery of 'the eternal return of the same'. Although the boy of seventeen did not and could not accept this conception, there still took place in his spirit a, so to speak, negative seduction. As he appears to me in my memory, after so many years, — through Kant, who understood time as the form of 'our' perception, the way could open to him to ask the question: 'But if time is only a form in which we perceive, where are "we"? Are we not in the timeless? Are we not in eternity? By that, of course, a wholly other eternity is meant than the circular one which Zarathustra loves as "fatum". What is meant is what is incomprehensible in itself, that which sends forth time out of itself and sets us in that relationship to it that we call existence. To him who recognizes this, the reality of the world no longer shows an absurd and uncanny face: because eternity is. That the entrance to this way long remained closed to me is to be traced to a certain, not insignificant, extent to that fascination by 'Zarathustra'.[9]

At the age of eighteen Buber returned to Vienna and was enrolled as a student at the University. He spent two semesters there and took courses in

German literature, the history of art and philosophy. He found the lectures
— even the 'significant scholarly ones' — generally unhelpful, but enjoyed
seminar discussions. His comments on the seminars point very significantly
to the dialogic conception of the teaching-learning relationship he was to
formulate in later years. 'The regulated and yet free intercourse between
teacher and students, the common interpretation of texts, in which the master
at times took part with a rare humility, as if he too were learning something
new, and the liberated exchange of question and answer in the midst of all
scholastic fluency — all this,' he wrote, 'disclosed to me, more intimately
than anything I read in a book, the true actuality of the spirit as a
"between".'[10] In Vienna he became friendly with the poets, Hugo von
Hoffmanstal and Richard Beer-Hoffmann, and began to study the works of
Goethe, Holderlin and Stefan George. He also developed a deep love of
theatre. In this passage from *Meetings* he indicates the links between his
interest in theatre and his evolving philosophy of dialogue:

> What affected me most strongly, however, was the Burgtheater into which
> at times, day after day, I rushed up three flights after several hours 'posting
> myself': in order to capture a place in the highest gallery. When far below
> in front of me the curtain went up and I might then look at the events of the
> dramatic agon as, even if in play, taking here and now, it was the word, the
> 'rightly' spoken human word that I received into myself, in the most real
> sense. Speech here first, in this world of fiction as fiction, won its adequacy;
> certainly it appeared heightened, but heightened to itself. It was only a
> matter of time, however, until — as always happened — someone fell for
> a while into recitation, a 'noble' recitation. Then, along with the genuine
> spokenness of speech, dialogical speech or even monological (in so far as
> the monologue was just an addressing of one's own person as a fellowman
> and no recitation), this whole world, mysteriously built out of surprise and
> law, was shattered for me — until after some moments it arose anew with
> the return of the over-against.
>
> Since then it has sometimes come to pass, in the midst of the casualness
> of the everyday, that, while I was sitting in the garden of an inn in the
> countryside of Vienna, a conversation penetrated to me from a neighbouring
> table (perhaps an argument over falling prices by two market wives taking
> a rest) in which I perceived the spokenness of speech, sound becoming
> 'Each-Other'.[11]

Following the two semesters at the University of Vienna Buber spent short
periods as a student at the Universities of Leipzig and Zurich. Again he
followed courses in literature, philosophy and the history of art, but he added
some further courses in psychiatry, economics and the natural sciences.
Meanwhile, however, his thoughts were turning towards more active cultural
and political preoccupations.

During a holiday which he spent at his father's estate in the summer of 1898 Buber read Mathias Archer's *Modern Judaism* and became deeply interested in the political and cultural aspects of his own Jewish heritage. In the Autumn he returned to Leipzig and, together with a friend, Aharon Eliasberg, formed a chapter there of the newly founded Zionist movement. Buber represented the chapter at a Zionist convention in Cologne in March 1899. Out of concern for the assimilationist tendencies of the large numbers of emigre Russian Jews crowding into Leipzig, he invited the founder of the movement, Theodor Herzl, to come to Leipzig and provide active support for the work of the movement there. Buber himself wrote several poems on the plight of the immigrant Jews in Eastern Europe and several essays in which he called on Zionists to work for the renewal of Jewish culture.

He was joined in this work by Paula Winkler, a Catholic from Munich whom he had met at a seminar at the University of Leipzig in the summer of 1899. As a child she had witnessed the ill-treatment and abuse meted out to Jews in Bavaria, and remembered these experiences vividly. Buber's address to the Third Zionist Congress in Basle in 1899 left a lasting impression on her. 'A human mouth spoke to me with a wonderful force,' she wrote, 'and my heart stood still.'[12] Shortly afterwards she married Buber, converted to Judaism and enthusiastically espoused the cause of Zionism.

In 1900 Buber moved to Berlin where he addressed several meetings and issued pamphlets on behalf of the Zionist cause. Shortly after his arrival there he was appointed editor of *Die Welt*, the official organ of the Zionist movement. In this role his impact was decisive and it led him into some bitter conflicts with the movement's founder, Theodor Herzl. Buber advocated a broader vision of the Zionist cause than Herzl had articulated. At the Fifth Congress in Basle in 1901 he urged the delegates to work not merely for the political advancement of Jews but for the renewal of Jewish culture as well. He called for the establishment of publishing houses to promote Jewish art, literature, music and philosophy, and proposed that plans be prepared for the founding of a Jewish University in Jerusalem. (At that time Jews were excluded from many European Universities). Buber's proposals were supported enthusiastically by his friend, Chaim Weizmann (later the first President of Israel), but were accepted with great reluctance by Herzl and the more politically minded Zionists.

Buber's intervention at the Congress was a turning-point in the history of the Zionist movement. An immediate result was the founding of Judischer Verlag, a publishing press which was directed by Buber and a colleague, Berthold Feiwel. In 1903 Judischer Verlag produced an important document, under the authorship of Buber, Weizmann and Feiwel, in which plans were outlined for the establishment of the Hebrew University in Jerusalem. It was envisaged that the University would be a centre for the renewal of Jewish culture and a place to which all Jews could come to study their heritage. Shortly after the publication of the document, planning committees for the University were set up in Vienna, Berlin, Paris, London and Brussels. Meanwhile, a new journal, *Der Jude*, was founded in 1903, with Buber and Weizmann as editors. The journal was directed particularly at young Jewish readers and sought to propagate the broad vision of Jewish culture that Buber had been advocating since he joined the Zionist movement.

Throughout his life he would continue to promote an understanding amongst Jews of the richness of their cultural heritage, and would urge them not to identify the cause of Zionism with the narrow goals of a purely political nationalism. His own understanding of that heritage was greatly enriched by his discovery of the treasures of Hasidic Jewish culture in 1904. Ironically, it was through his interests in Christian mysticism that Buber first encountered the works of the Hasidic masters. He was introduced to the Christian mystics, and especially to the writings of Meister Eckhart, by his friend, Gustav Landauer, in 1901. He subsequently undertook some formal studies in Christian mysticism and submitted a thesis on the writings of Jacob Boehme and Nicholas of Cusa for his doctorate at the University of Vienna.[13] By that time, however, he had become deeply critical of the ascetic tendencies of the Christian mystics, and found a radical conflict existed between their world-denying philosophy and the more life-affirming vision of the created universe he was beginning to discover in the Hasidic traditions of Judaism.

Buber had some knowledge of Hasidic Judaism from his childhood years when he attended prayer-meetings with his grandfather at Sadagora and met large numbers of Jewish immigrants, through whom he was introduced to Hasidic legends and myths. It was not, however, until 1904 that he encountered the writings of Israel ben Eliezer (the Baal-Shem-Tov), the first of the Hasidic story-tellers.[14] On reading the life and work of the Baal-Shem-Tov, Buber decided to withdraw from his Zionist activities and to devote himself exclusively to the study of Hasidism for some years. This was the decisive event of his life; he devoted all his energies to the study of the stories and parables of the Hasidic masters and emerged from the experience with a sense of purpose and direction from which he was never deflected. In 1906 he published his first collection of Hasidic stories, *The Tales of Rabbi Nachman*.[15] In this collection he sought not merely to translate the stories of Rabbi Nachman, but to recreate the world of the Hasidim and the events of their everyday lives. 'I had to tell the stories that I had taken into myself from out of myself, as a true painter takes into himself the lives of the models and achieves the genuine images out of the memory formed of them,' he wrote.[16]

All the Hasidic stories that he translated were unified by one recurring theme: the possibility of endlessly apprehending the reality of God through the evidence of his creation. Rabbi Nachman, he said, discovered God in the reeds of the stream, in the horse that bore him into the forest, in the trees and plants, in the mountain-slopes and the valleys. This theme of God's immanent presence in creation is explored again in the second collection that Buber published, *The Legend of the Baal-Shem*,[17] and here one can see emerging also the theme of interpersonal dialogue — the dialogue between man and creation and ultimately between man and God — which would find its mature formulation two decades later in *I and Thou*. The theme is particularly evident in two stories from the collection, 'The Return' and 'From Strength to Strength'. Here also we find one of Buber's favourite metaphors, the image of a narrow ridge with an abyss on either side, which signifies the problematic and hazardous path that man must follow in the course of his life. The essential teachings of the Hasidim are introduced in both collections: the doctrines of *hitlahavut* (the uniqueness of the moment), *avoda* (service to God) and *shiflut* (humility and the authentic affirmation of selfhood). In the figure of the zaddik-rabbi one sees the prototype of Buber's ideal teacher and in the zaddik's relations with his followers the model for the dialogic philosophy of teaching that he set out later in his educational writings. Buber's retelling of these legends contributed significantly to the emergence of a highly distinctive Jewish literature in the twentieth century. Their impact is particularly discernible in the Hebrew novels of S.Y. Agnon and in the Yiddish stories of Isaac Bashevis Singer.[18]

Buber lived mostly in the city of Florence in the five year period he devoted to the study of Hasidic traditions and to the translation of the Hasidic legends. He found excellent opportunities there for developing his theatrical interests. Two essays written at this time, the first on the actress, Eleonora Duse, the second on the actor, Ermette Novelli, indicate the extent of his interest in the theatre and in its particularly intense evocation of the power of interhuman dialogue.[19] He returned to Prague in 1908, renewed culturally and spiritually by his Hasidic studies and determined to lead the Zionist movement towards the ideals he had articulated at the Fifth Congress. He now joined a student movement, the Bar Kochba Union, which was dedicated to the renewal of cultural Zionism and which had attracted a large following of young Jews. He delivered several lectures to the members on the meaning of Jewishness in the twentieth century and on the relevance of Jewish religious traditions. Many of the lectures have since been collected in the anthology, *On Judaism*, under titles such as 'Judaism and Mankind', 'The Renewal of Judaism', 'Jewish Religiosity', 'The Holy Way', 'Myth in Judaism' and 'Herut: On Youth and Religion'.[20] The essays are full of implications for education, and are particularly illuminating on the problems of providing religious education at a time when the formal practice of religion has greatly declined. The Jewish philosopher, Franz Rosenzweig, signifying the importance of these writings, told Buber: 'I am amazed to see to what degree you have become the representative speaker and the advocate of our generations, mine as well as the one after me.'[21]

Much of Buber's thinking on the nature of Jewishness found expression also in *Daniel*, a prose work he completed in 1913.[22] The book anticipates many aspects of his philosophy of dialogue and reflects the growing influence of existentialism on all his work The main theme of *Daniel* is the 'holy insecurity' of man's existence, a theme already anticipated in the Hasidic tales. The work is made up of five dialogues conducted between Daniel and his friends. They deal, respectively, with the nature of personal affirmation, the problem of reality, the nature of meaning, the polarities of evil and good, and the ideal of unity in being. All five themes are drawn together in the inclusive theme of realization, i.e. the notion that man realizes his destiny through the love of the world, by which ultimately he comes to love God. There is considerable comment in *Daniel* on the concept of drama as enacted dialogue, a theme which Buber had already explored in the essays on Eleonora Duse and Ermette Novelli.[23] He was able to develop his dramatic interests in a more concrete fashion when, together with Paul Claudel, he founded the Hellerau Dramatic Union for the production of epic theatre. At the same time he set out his thoughts on the subject of dramatic production in an essay, 'The Space Problem of the Stage'.[24] As well as producing plays at the experimental theatre at Hellerau he assisted in the development of the Dusseldorf Playhouse, and the ideas put forward later in his essay, 'Drama and Theatre',[25] were considerably influenced by his experiences there.

It was at this time an event occurred to which Buber attached immense significance in the evolution of his dialogic philosophy. One day, following his regular period of contemplation, he was visited by a young man called Mehé who asked his advice on various matters that had been troubling him. Buber received him hospitably and responded to his questions. Later when he heard the young man had died ( the circumstances of his death are disputed by Friedman and Hodes),[26] Buber felt he had not been truly present to his visitor and that the young man had unarticulated needs and problems which he failed to detect. He regretted not having penetrated the real nature of the young man's anxieties. Buber subsequently spoke of this event as a 'conversion' that changed the course of his life. He felt he had inadvertently identified the true nature of existential guilt as a condition rooted in the failure to relate authentically. He had failed to respond as a whole person to the need confronting him; by withholding himself he had failed to make real the possibility of genuine dialogue. In his essay, 'A Conversion', he describes how the episode radically changed his understanding of the meaning of the word 'religious' and of the place of religion in human existence:

What happened was no more than that one forenoon after a morning of 'religious' enthusiasm I had a visit from an unknown young man, without being there in spirit. I certainly did not fail to let the meeting be friendly, I did not treat him any more remissly than all his contemporaries who were in the habit of seeking me out about this time of day as an oracle that is ready to listen to reason. I conversed attentively and openly with him — only I omitted to guess the questions which he did not put. Later, not long after I learned from one of his friends — he himself was no longer alive — the essential content of these questions; I learned that he had come to me not casually, but borne by destiny, not for a chat but for a decision. He had come to me, he had come in this hour. What do we expect when we are in despair and yet go to a man? Surely a presence by means of which we are told that nevertheless there is meaning.

Since then I have given up the 'religious' which is nothing but the exception, extraction, exaltation, ecstasy; or it has given me up. I possess nothing but the everyday out of which I am never taken. The mystery is no longer disclosed, it has escaped or it has made its dwelling here where everything happens as it happens. I know no fullness but each mortal hour's fullness of claim and responsibility. Though far from being equal to it, yet I know that in the claim I am claimed and may respond in responsibility, and know who speaks and demands a response. I do not know much more. If that is religion then it is just everything, simply all that is lived in its possibility of dialogue. Here is space also for religion's highest forms. As when you pray you do not merely remove yourself from this life of yours but in your praying refer your thought to it, even though it may be in order to yield it; so too in the unprecedented and surprising, when you are called upon from above, required, chosen, empowered,sent, you with this mortal bit of life are referred to, this moment is not extracted from it, it rests on what has been, and beckons to the remainder which has still to be lived, you are not swallowed up in a fullness without obligation, you are willed for the life of communion.[27]

When war broke out in August 1914 Buber faced the prospect of being enlisted in the armed forces, but was exempted on grounds of personal unsuitability for military service. He debated the war issue with his friend, Gustav Landauer, a committed pacifist, and gradually his thoughts turned to the whole question of interhuman conflict and its roots in the sphere of the interpersonal. The problem of resolving conficts between peoples and nations, he felt, pointed in the first instance to the sources of these conflicts in the realm of interpersonal relationships. 'During the First World War,' he wrote, 'it became clear to me that a process was going on which before then I had only surmised. This was the growing difficulty of genuine dialogue, and most especially of genuine dialogue between persons of different kinds and convictions. Direct, frank dialogue is becoming ever more difficult and more rare. . . I began to understand at that time that this is the central question for the fate of mankind.'[28] The first draft of *I and Thou*, which Buber produced in 1916, was the main fruit of these reflections on the nature of interpersonal and intercommunal dialogue.

By this time Buber had moved his family from Berlin to Heppenheim, a little town near the forest of Odenwald in the beautiful Necker valley. This was to be their home until their departure for Palestine in 1938. Buber continued to live on the income from his father's estate for a further eight years, until he was appointed to an academic post at Frankfurt University.[29] Early in 1916 a new opportunity arose for him to continue his work of re-educating German Jews in the cultural traditions of Judaism. In that year he was appointed editor of *Der Jude*, a new organ founded for the dissemination of Jewish ideas. Under Buber's direction the journal published articles on Jewish life and literature by several notable writers. Amongst them were Franz Kafka, Herman Cohen, Hugo Bergman, Franz Werfel and Gustav Landauer. Once again the journal sought to interpret Jewish nationalism in terms of the cultural and spiritual heritage of the Jewish people rather than their political aspirations. In an article which points significantly to his mature thinking on education, Buber proposed that the models held up before Jewish youth should not be heroic figures, such as David or Siegfried, but prophetic figures like Jeremiah who were renowned, not for spectacular actions and achievements, but for their willingness to speak the truth to their people.[30] There were many such articles in the journal. In 'Zion and Youth',[31] an essay published in May 1918, Buber spoke of the importance of developing the community ideal, a theme which profoundly informs his subsequent thinking on adult education. Emerging traces of anti-semitism (claims, for instance, that Jews had not sufficiently supported the war effort) were firmly countered in *Der Jude*, and the paper continued to highlight the situation of Jewish immigrants in Eastern Europe, many of whom were victims of pogroms in Russia and Poland.

At this time also, largely as a result of Landauer's influence, Buber was defining the essential principles of his social philosophy. In doing so he drew heavily on the ideals of the utopian socialists, Proudhon, Kropotkin and Lassalle, though he had found much common ground between Judaism and community socialism in the course of his Hasidic studies. Like Landauer, he rejected the centralistic principles of marxist socialism in favour of a social philosophy devoted to the fostering of community ideals. In his essay, 'The Holy Way',[32] he cited Biblical support for community socialism, while firmly rejecting the centralistic, politically oriented socialism of the marxists. (Initially, he had welcomed the Russian revolution in *Der Jude*, but later rejected both the deterministic orientation of marxism and the totalitarian structures of the new Soviet state). In another essay, 'Herut: On Youth and Religion',[33] he set out the educational implications of his community philosophy (see Chapter 7).

In November 1918 the armistice was signed and peace was restored in Europe. Socialists were active, however, in several German cities and Landauer was organizing workers in Bavaria in opposition to the policies of the new Weimar government. Their activities provoked a violent reaction from the government authorities. Rosa Luxemburg and Karl Liebknecht, both members of the movement, were imprisoned and brutally murdered in Berlin. Landauer, who had delivered memorial addresses at their funerals, continued to organize the Munich workers until they eventually formed a workers' council, with Landauer himself as its head. As a pacifist, he urged his followers to work constructively and peacefully for the creation of socialist communities. However, when government troops marched on Munich, Landauer was arrested, brutally tortured, and finally murdered. Buber was profoundly shocked by his death. In a commemorative essay he describes the martyrdom of Landauer, the pacifist, as being comparable to the crucifixion of Jesus Christ: 'In a church in Brescia', he wrote, 'I saw a mural whose whole surface was covered with crucified men. The field of crosses stretched to the horizon, and on all of them hung men of all different shapes and faces. There it seemed to me was the true form of Jesus Christ. On one of those crosses I see Gustav Landauer hanging.'[34]

Meanwhile, important developments regarding the resettlement of Jews in Palestine were occurring in the aftermath of the Balfour Declaration of 1917. While deeply committed to the resettlement of the Jews in Palestine, Buber saw great potential dangers in the accompanying prospect of alienating the Palestinian Arabs. In *Der Jude* he urged the emigrating Jews to build good relations with their Arab neighbours, and insisted the Yishuv should develop into a true community rather than a purely nationalist state. In the kibbuz movement — which he supported enthusiastically — he saw great possibilities for the furtherance of socialist ideals and for the transformation of community relationships. At a conference in Prague, which was attended by Jews from Palestine and the Diaspora, Buber appealed directly to Jewish youth to ensure that the advancement of Jewish interests in Palestine should involve the simultaneous advancement of the Arab communities.[35] This was a viewpoint he found it necessary to articulate much more forcefully after he went to Palestine himself in 1938.

Buber continued to involve himself in a variety of educational activities in Germany throughout the nineteen twenties and thirties In 1919 he helped to found the Judische Volksheim, an adult education institute in Berlin which catered specifically for Jewish immigrants. In the same year he hosted a conference in Heppenheim on the theme, 'The Renewal of the Essence of Education', and delivered a paper on his concept of the folk high school.[36] About this time also he met two German educators, Elisabeth Rotten and

Karl Wilker, with whom he founded a pedagogic journal, *Das Werdende Zeitalter*, the main objective of which was to examine the nature of the relationship between teacher and pupil. The aims of the journal (which were printed inside its cover) included a declaration that points unmistakably to the direction that Buber's thinking on education would follow later. 'Education', they declared, 'is for us not an occasion that concerns merely the relation of the older to the younger generation. The readiness for opening up of the brother-soul in each human being is for us the great attempt, touching all aspects of human togetherness, to establish a decisively changed relationship of man to man.'[37] In 'The Task',[38] a paper published in the journal in 1922, Buber describes education as 'an opening up', as a dialogue in which teacher and pupil engage as partners, each contributing actively to the unfolding process in which they are reciprocally engaged. Both in its language and its conception of the educational relationship in terms of dialogue, the paper anticipates Buber's mature formulation of his educational philosophy in the paper he delivered at the Heidelberg Conference on Creativity in 1925.[39]

Meanwhile, Buber was joined in another adult education venture by his friend, the philosopher, Franz Rosenzweig. Buber and Rosenzweig had first met in 1914, but did not work closely together until 1921. They now came together at the Fries Judisches Lehrhaus, an academy for Jewish students at Frankfurt, where they offered courses on various aspects of Judaism. Rosenzweig had already published *The Star of Redemption*,[40] in which he applied the principles of existentialist philosophy to the traditional doctrines of Judaism. Some highly innovative teaching methods were adopted at the Frankfurt Lehrhaus. Seminar discussion was the normal method of teaching, and discussion was concentrated on the close reading and interpretation of texts — methods which Buber was to use very profitably in subsequent ventures in adult education in Palestine. With Rosenzweig also Buber embarked on one of the major enterprises of his life, the translation of the Hebrew Bible into German. Though he suffered a paralysis of the limbs in 1921, Rosenzweig contined to work on this project with Buber for the remaining eight years of his life. In their translation they sought particularly to reproduce the idioms of Hebrew speech. By seeking to capture what they described as 'the presentness of the spoken word' they hoped to promote a genuine encounter of dialogue between the reader and the scriptural text.[41] In two of Buber's essays, 'The Man of Today and the Jewish Bible' and 'Biblical Leadership'[42] the nature of this dialogue is explored. Both essays hold important implications for the teaching of the scriptures (see Chapter 5). Following Rosenzweig's death, Buber continued to work on the Bible project on his own for a further thirty years.

One of the texts adopted by Buber for discussion with his students at the

Frankfurt Lehrhaus was the draft of *I and Thou*, on which he had then been working for several years. Following lengthy and detailed criticism of the work by the Lehrhaus students, he completed a final draft in 1922 and it was published by Insel-Verlag in Leipzig in 1923. That same year Buber delivered a lecture entitled 'The Psychologizing of the World'[43] to the Psychological Club of Zurich, a major centre for the promotion of Jungian therapy. The paper had a profound impact on the theory and practice of psychotherapy. Buber condemned the objectifying processes then current in psychological theory, which treated human capacities and potentialities as phenomena that could be examined and explained analytically. Arguing that man's being must ultimately be understood in its completeness and totality, he insisted that the wholeness of nature has to be observed relationally, since relationships constitute the fundamental reality of existence. Earlier in an essay, 'The Body and Spirit of the Hasidic Movement',[44] he had put forward the term 'psychosynthesis' (in contradistinction to the Freudian term, 'psychoanalysis') to signify the integrity of human capacities that should be the primary concern of psychologists and therapists. The term was adopted later by his friend, the Italian therapist, Roberto Assagioli, and has since become part of the professional terminology of pschotherapy.

Following the publication of *I and Thou* Buber became deeply involved in the planning of the new Hebrew University in Jerusalem. The essential issue was whether it should follow the conventional European model of a university, or whether it should seek to serve the specific needs of the Yishuv in a more radical fashion. Buber attended a planning conference on this issue in London in 1924. It was decided to follow his advice that an adult education institute be incorporated in the University to promote the study of Jewish culture. Buber undertook to travel to Palestine to assist in the planning of this institute, but he was unable to do so until 1927, two years after the official opening of the Hebrew University.

Meanwhile, he attented the Third International Pedagogical Conference of the International Work Circle for the Renewal of Education, which was held at Heidelberg between 2 and 5 August, 1925. The theme of the Conference was 'The Unfolding of the Creative Powers of the Child", and Buber was invited to deliver the keynote address. In his foreword to the printed version of his paper Buber declared he would seek to 'renew the essence of education.' His colleague, Elisabeth Rotten, reported that his address provoked heated controversy amongst the assembled educators.[45] The paper offers the most substantial statement of his educational philosophy, and is an essential source for an understanding of his thinking on matters such as the relationship between teaching and learning, the nature of creativity, and the fostering and development of individual potentialities. It has since appeared under the title 'Education' in *Between Man and Man*.[46]

Buber continued to work at the Frankfurt Lehrhaus and assisted in the founding of similar institutes to provide adult education for Jews at Stuttgart, Cologne, Mannheim, Wiesbaden, Karlsruhe, Munich, Breslau and Berlin. In 1925 he was appointed to a lectureship in Jewish religious philosophy at the University of Frankfurt. The post had originally been offered to Franz Rosenzweig, who was unable to accept it because of illness. Two years later Buber made his first visit to Palestine. The visit was notable for two events, neither of which was connected with the Hebrew University. Since the University had already been opened two years before his visit, Buber was unable to exercise much influence on its work in the sphere of adult education. He participated, however, in a highly innovative project which was designed to promote his ideas on community education. Together with Albert Einstein, he had supported the founding of the Ben Shemen Youth Village Project by Siegfried Lehmann at Lydda in 1927. The community was organized in accordance with principles advocated by Buber: the study of Jewish culture, the fostering of community values, maintaining good relations with their Arab neighbours etc. The curriculum included courses in Hebrew language and literature, the scriptures, Jewish art, music and history. Significantly, it included studies in Arab culture as well. Large numbers of immigrants came to live in the village and at one time it accommodated more than 600 students. Buber also joined the Covenant for Peace, a group that advocated Jewish-Arab understanding and the creation of a binational state in Palestine. Despite intense opposition to the binational ideal from Jewish nationalists, Buber continued for many years to advocate its merits as an arrangement that held out the best prospect for lasting political stability in Palestine.

Some years before his visit to Palestine, Buber met Florens Christian Rang[47] and had been deeply influenced by his ideas on a possible synthesis between Christianity and socialism. *Die Kreatur*, a new journal Buber founded in 1926, was inspired mainly by Rang's ideas. These were taken up by another Christian philosopher, Leonhard Ragaz,[48] and further promoted in his journal, *Neue Wege*. Buber and Ragaz organized a conference on religious socialism at Heppenheim in 1928. The conference was attended by Paul Tillich who was also at that time interested in Christian socialism. Buber expounded his ideas on the whole subject in 'Three Theses of a Religious Socialism',[49] in which he stressed the interdependence of the spiritual and material aspects of the Jewish and Christian traditions. His contacts with Rang and with Ragaz led to further involvements by Buber in Jewish-Christian dialogue. He began a correspondence on the issue with Albert Schweitzer, which continued for several years and decisively influenced his (Buber's) study of the interpenetration of Judaism and

Christianity in *The Two Types of Faith*.[50] As a further indication of his commitment to the cause of Jewish-Christian understanding, Buber appointed two Christian thinkers as co-editors of *Die Kreatur:* Viktor von Weizsaker, a Protestant psychiatrist, and Joseph Wittig, a former Catholic priest who was married and lived in Heppenheim. The paper published articles on religion, literature, education and psychotherapy. Its contributors included Nikolai Berdyaev, Walter Benjamin, Hugo Bergmann, Margarete Susman and Ludwig Strauss. Amongst the articles published was Buber's long essay, 'Dialogue', in which he provided further elaboration of the philosophy developed in *I and Thou*. (This paper was also included in *Between Man and Man*.)[51]

In November 1926 Buber received an invitation from Hermann Gerson, one of the leading figures in the Jewish youth movement in Germany, to help him establish educational institutes for Jews that would seek to implement Buber's community ideals. Gerson had read Buber's versions of the Hasidic tales, and had been deeply impressed by the ideas on community education that Buber had outlined in a paper, 'Folk Education as our Task',[52] which he delivered at a Zionist conference. The two men met in Heppenheim in January, 1927 and agreed to found a new adult school in Berlin which would adopt policies and methods similar to those of the Frankfurt Lehrhaus. Particular attention was to be given to the Bible, the Hebrew language and the study of religious socialism. In response to a request from Gerson , Buber wrote an essay, 'Why We Should Study Jewish Sources',[53] in which he made an eloquent case for the fostering of an historical vision through education. While Gerson's movement, the Werkleute, was designed for Jews intending to reside in Germany, it was forced, as a result of the policies of the Nazi authorities, to turn its attention eventually to the growing numbers of Jews planning to emigrate to Palestine. Gerson himself left Germany in 1933 and established a Werkleute kibbutz to facilitate German immigrants arriving there.

In the early 1930s there were ominous signs in Germany of the catastrophe that was shortly to befall European Jewry. A boycott of Jewish stores was announced in April 1933, and Jews were dismissed from their posts for failing to support the Nazi movement. Several Jews came to Heppenheim to seek advice from Buber; amongst them was his friend, Einstein, who shortly afterwards emigrated to the U.S. Buber himself, anticipating dismissal, resigned his post at Frankfurt University in October 1933. His son-in-law, the poet Ludwig Strauss, was dismissed from his university post. In the summer of 1933 Buber wrote an essay, 'In the Midst of History',[54] in which he indirectly pointed to Hitler as 'the demon of the hour', intent upon destroying the Jewish race. Shortly afterwards he delivered an address at the Frankfurt Lehrhaus (published as 'The Jew in the World')[55] in which he reflected on the plight of the Jew in Nazi Germany, portraying him as the exile — isolated, homeless and forsaken by his countrymen.

Meanwhile, the Reichsvertretung der deutschen Juden, the body officially responsible for Jewish education, invited Buber to advise it on the development of new policies for the education of Jews. Since Jews were excluded by Nazi regulations from attending state schools, Buber was asked to work out proposals for a schooling system that would cater exclusively for Jewish children. In December 1933 he planned to found an experimental school at Mannheim, with a curriculum in which Jewish culture was to be strongly represented, and proposed it to the Reichsvertretung as a model school for Jews .The project failed, however, because of the difficulty of finding suitable teachers for the school. Buber then proposed that a central office be set up to coordinate the various arrangements made to provide adult education for Jews. As a result, the Central Office for Jewish Adult Education was instituted at Frankfurt. Buber was appointed Director and, in this capacity, engaged himself fully in the difficult task of providing community education for adult Jews during his remaining years in Germany.

Buber convened a Conference on Jewish Adult Education at Herrlingen in May 1934. The participants were given copies of his Heidelberg Address and of Franz Rosenzweig's essay, 'Education and no End'.[56] In his keynote lecture Buber drew heavily on the theories of Bishop Grundtvig, the founder of the Danish folkschools. Later, he issued a paper, 'Education and World View',[57] in which he provided further elaboration on his theories of community education. A companion paper, 'Teaching and Deed',[58] which he delivered at the Frankfurt Lehrhaus, once again emphasized the importance of the historical vision in education, and advocated methods of fostering traditional values and ideals. In yet another lecture, 'The Power of the Spirit',[59] which was delivered also at the Frankfurt Lehrhaus, Buber developed the notion of an all-embracing, organic spirituality. In the lecture he referred pointedly to the neo-paganism of western culture in the twentieth century (an unmistakable reference to Nazism), and urged his listeners to resist it in every way they could. As a result of the lecture — which was attended by several Gestapo officers — Buber was prohibited from lecturing in public from 21 February 1935.

At this time an interesting exchange of views occurred between Buber and the German psychologist, Hans Trub. In 1935 Trub had published an essay, 'Individuation, Guilt and Decision: Beyond the Bounds of Psychology',[60] in which he described a ten-year personal crisis, in the course of which he gradually abandoned his dependence on Jungian psychology for the new 'existential' psychology he discovered through Buber. He attributed the change in his outlook primarily to his personal encounters with Buber and described himself as 'renewed for all time, with my knowledge of the reality of things brought one step nearer the truth.' 'What gives Buber his imperishable greatness and makes his life symbolic', he wrote, 'is that he steps forth as this unique man and talks directly to other persons.'[61] The fruits of this personal conversion were to be seen in Trub's *Psychosynthesis as Psychological Personal Healing Process*,[62] a text now widely used by psychotherapists. Earlier, the philosopher and psychiatrist, Ludwig Binswanger, had also written to Buber describing his admiration for *I and Thou* and its impact on his work as a therapist.[63]

Despite the prohibition on his public activities, Buber continued to urge his fellow Jews to remain steadfast in the face of the threats facing them from the Nazi government. His activities helped to save many Jews from despair in the menacing atmosphere of the late 1930s in Germany. ' The Question to the Single One',[64] a document based on lectures he delivered to German students, was published in 1936 — 'astonishingly', Buber wrote, 'since it attacks the life basis of totalitarianism'.[65] In this work he advised his readers that the only safeguard against collectivist domination would be their determination to withstand the dictates of the crowd and to stand for the truth of their own moral convictions, whatever the consequences of doing so. 'The Question to the Single One', together with a companion paper, 'The Prejudices of Youth',[66] which was based on a lecture delivered to students at Prague in 1937, are essential texts for the study of Buber's ideas on community education.

In these years Buber continued to promote Jewish-Christian dialogue, thereby diminishing, however slightly, some of the impact of the antisemitic prejudice which was then rampant in Germany. His debates with Christian theologians, such as Karl Ludwig Schmidt and Gerhard Kittel, were published in 'The Hour and its Judgement'.[67] Since the mid 1930s, however, his thoughts were directed increasingly towards the inevitable prospect of emigrating to Palestine. His two children, Rafael and Eva, had already gone there; Rafael, his wife, Ruth, and children, Barbara and Judith, to live in a kibbutz near Ain Harod; Eva and her husband, Ludwig Strauss, to join Herman Gerson's Werkleute Kibbutz at Hazorea. Ever since his first visit to Palestine, efforts had been made to provide Buber with a professorship at the Hebrew University. Being heavily involved in educational work in Germany, he was reluctant to emigrate. Eventually, however, he accepted the Chair of Social Philosophy at the Hebrew University and, with his wife, Paula, sailed for Palestine in March 1938.

## 3   Educator in Palestine, 1938-1965
Following his appointment to the Chair of Social Philosophy at the Hebrew University, Buber issued a series of papers in which he sought to elucidate the main principles of his philosophical anthropology. The papers, which

were collectively entitled 'What is Man?', have since been included in his anthology, *Between Man and Man*.[68] In 'What is Man?' he describes the evolution of his philosophical beliefs and examines the decisive influences on his thought. He looks particularly at the impact on his own philosophy of the writings of Kant, Kierkegaard, Nietzsche and Scheler, and shows how the principles of his philosophical anthropology expand into a fully fledged community philosophy, the essential elements of which he subsequently elaborated in *The Knowledge of Man*.[69] His interest in educational theory was further advanced in the same period. At the National Conference of Jewish Teachers of Palestine, which was held in Tel Aviv in 1939, he delivered a major paper on moral education, once again stressing the dialogic and religious orientation of his educational thought. The paper which is entitled 'The Education of Character' has also been published in *Between Man and Man*.[70]

Meanwhile, Buber began to campaign publicly against the terrorist methods being used in Palestine, both against the Arabs and the British authorities, by extremist movements such as the Irgun Zwai Leumi. In July 1938 he published an essay, 'Against Betrayal',[71] in which he called on his compatriots to unite in their opposition to such organizations and to work actively for Jewish-Arab rapprochement — a theme he would advocate fervently for the rest of his life. On the other hand, he challenged the view put forward by Mahatma Gandhi in his paper, *Harijan*, that German Jews should practise *satyagraha*, or peaceful resistance, in the face of Nazi persecution, and he vehemently opposed Gandhi's assertion that the Jews were colonisers in Palestine.[72] In two papers which he co-authored with Judah Magnes, the Chancellor of the Hebrew University, Buber defended the right of Jewish immigrants to purchase land in Palestine and to settle there with their Arab neighbours. The essays are published in *Pointing the Way* under the titles, 'Gandhi, Politics and Us' and 'A Letter to Gandhi'. (The latter is also published under the title, 'The Land and its Possessors', in *Israel and the World*.)[73]

Buber continued to voice his concern at the plight of the Jews living in Nazi occupied territories, though he had little knowledge of the true scale of the horrors that were occurring, until the full tragedy of the Holocaust was revealed at the end of the war. In 'People and Leader',[74] one of the first papers he wrote in the Hebrew language, he condemned the evils of fascist dictatorship, directing his comments specifically at Hitler and Mussolini. In the same period he published a work of Biblical exegesis, *The Prophetic Faith*.[75] In the chapter entitled, 'The God of the Sufferers', he contemplates the mysterious irony of a benign and omnipotent creator presiding over a universe in which mass suffering is an endemic reality. The whole issue of the abuse of power is addressed allegorically in a novel written also against the background of the wartime horrors. The novel, *For the Sake of Heaven*,[76] is based on an Hasidic tale that Buber had discovered several years before. Ostensibly concerned with the lives of Hasidic communities in Napoleonic Europe, it explores a number of moral issues, such as the nature of evil and redemption, within the framework of a vivid and exciting narrative which has justifiably been compared with other contemporary works of Hasidic fiction, such as Agnon's *A Guest for the Night* and Singer's *The Family Moskat*.[77]

Seeing the evidence of increasing tension between the two main communities in Palestine, Buber continued to advocate the bi-national political settlement he had put forward at the Zionist congresses in Germany twenty years before. He called on his fellow Jews to see the Arabs as their partners and, in essays such as 'The God of the Nations and God' and 'The Regeneration of a People', he spoke of the need to build up trust between the two communities.[78] In 'Hebrew Humanism'[79] he condemned chauvinistic nationalism and declared that Jews should foster the true spirit of *humanitas* in their relations with their Arab neighbours. In another essay, 'False Prophets',[80] he compares some of the Jewish leaders to the false prophets of Hezekiah's time, and declares that leaders should always speak the truth to their people, even if, like the prophet Jeremiah, they should suffer rejection for doing so. In the meantime he had been campaigning actively for co-operation between the communities through the League For Arab-Jewish Rapprochement he had set up in 1939. Amongst various proposals he had put before the Mandatory Administration, he asked particularly that population parity be maintained between Jews and Arabs so that a binational settlement could be envisaged. Together with his colleague, Judah Magnes, he set up the Ihud, an organization pledged to oppose the creation of a Jewish state, which was then being advocated by David ben Gurion. In August 1942 the Ihud called for the establishment of a Near Eastern Federation of States which would include the binational state of Palestine. The proposal provoked a storm of opposition within Palestine and amongst Jewish communities abroad.[81] There were calls for Buber and Magnes to resign their posts at the Hebrew University. Important support for the binational principle came, nevertheless, from Albert Einstein, who proposed that it be implemented under U.N. supervision at the Anglo-American Committee of Inquiry on Jews in Palestine in 1946.[82] Further support came from an Arab organization, the Falastin-el-Jedida, which had been formed in 1946, specifically to promote the binational ideal.[83]

However, when the U.N. in 1947 recommended, by a majority vote, that Palestine be partitioned, the binational alternative was not considered by the delegates. As the Arab armies converged on Jerusalem, Buber's predictions on the consequences of creating an Israeli state were tragically realized. He continued to live in Jerusalem throughout the siege and worked on the draft of *The Two Types of Faith*, his study of the interpenetration of Jewish and Christian traditions. The work significantly advanced the cause of Jewish-Christian dialogue, and helped to alleviate the tensions between Jews and Christians in the aftermath of the Holocaust. In these years Buber also brought to completion several years of work on Hasidic folklore, and eventually published two volumes of stories, *Tales of the Hasidim: The Early Masters* and *Tales of the Hasidim: The Later Masters*.[84] Hermann Hesse was one of the many distinguished figures who wrote to Buber praising the collections enthusiastically.[85] Hesse, a Nobel laureate himself, wrote to the Swedish Academy nominating Buber for the Nobel prize, on the strength of his contribution to twentieth century literature through his retelling of the Hasidic legends. The nomination, however, was not successful. (Buber was nominated a second time for the Nobel Prize for Literature in 1961. The signatories included T.S. Eliot, W.H. Auden, Hermann Hesse, Gabriel Marcel, Herbert Read and Ignazio Silone. This nomination was also unsuccessful.)

Another important work on which Buber was occupied during the siege of Jerusalem was *Paths in Utopia*,[86] a theoretical study in which he elucidated his community philosophy and examined the theories of the nineteenth century utopian socialists, Proudhon, Kropotkin and Landauer. The work provides the most complete formulation of his social dialogic and clearly asserts the priority of social over political principles, the issue on which he diverged most fundamentally from Marxist-Leninist theorists. Shortly after the publication of *Paths in Utopia*, he was given a practical opportunity to implement his ideas on community education when he assumed responsibility for the training of adult education tutors at the Hebrew University. (This work is discussed in detail in Chapter 7.)

On his retirement from his Chair at the Hebrew University in 1948, Buber began a series of lecture tours in the U.S. and Europe that greatly extended his influence in the spheres of philosophy, education and psychotherapy. He was invited to lecture at the Jewish Theological Seminary of America in 1948, but had to postpone the tour until 1951. Meanwhile, several important essays on which he had been working for some years, such as 'Religion and Philosophy', 'Religion and Ethics' and 'Religion and Modern Thinking', were translated from the German by Maurice Friedman, and were published in the U.S. to coincide with his lecture tour. The essays were collectively entitled *Eclipse of God*.[87] Buber lectured to audiences at the Universities of Yale, Columbia, Chicago and Wisconsin. At the Jewish Theological Seminary he met Abraham Joshua Heschel, author of *God in Search of Man* and *A Passion for Truth*,[88] and at Princeton he met his old friend, Albert Einstein. He also met R.M. Hutchins, with whom he subsequently debated various aspects of educational theory.[89]

On his return to Israel Buber was awarded an honorary doctorate by the Hebrew University. Three persons only, Einstein, Magnes and Weizmann, had been accorded this honour before him. He completed a Biblical drama, *Elijah*,[90] and a major paper on the anthropology of art, 'Man and his Image Work'.[91] At the end of 1953 he published 'Prophecy, Apocalyptic and the Historical Hour',[92] an important paper on the nature of the historical process. The following year he wrote an essay to commemorate the eightieth birthday.of his friend, Albert Schweitzer. Entitled 'A Realist of the Spirit',[93] the essay describes Schweitzer as a doctor who sought to heal body and soul in their totality and thereby exemplified the true meaning of psychosynthesis. 'The spiritualized conception of redemption regained for Schweitzer its basic meaning, that of the factual salvation on earth of the whole human being', Buber wrote. 'But bound up with all this in addition,' he said, 'is Schweitzer's philosophy, the leading idea of which is reverence for human life. The concept', he said, 'refers us once more to the body-soul totality of the individual living man as that which is to be actively honored and helped.'[94]

In 1956 Lesklie H. Farber invited Buber to deliver the William Alenson White Memorial Lecture at the Institute for Psychiatric Medicine in Washington. Farber, a leading figure in psychiatric medicine in the U.S. and the Director of the Washington Institute, told Buber his colleagues had found Freudian psychology of little assistance in their treatment of schizophrenics. He suggested that Buber explore the relevance of his anthropology for the treatment of mental illness. He particularly asked that Buber consider the links between his dialogic philosophy and the interpersonal psychiatry of Harry Stack Sullivan, the founder of the Washington Institute. Buber delivered four major lectures to the assembled psychiatrists; they have since been published under the titles 'Distance and Relation', 'Elements of the Interhuman', 'What is Common to All' and 'Guilt and Guilt Feelings'.[95] In the latter Buber attempted a fundamental reconception of the nature of guilt in terms of its roots in the sphere of interpersonal relationships. He told his audience: 'When the therapist recognizes an existential guilt of his patient, he cannot show him the way to the world, which the latter must rather seek and find as his own personal law. The doctor can only conduct him to the point from which he can glimpse his personal way or at least its beginning. But in order that the doctor shall be able to do this, he must also know about the general nature of the way, common to all great acts of conscience, and about the connection that exists between the nature of existential guilt and the nature of this way.'[96]

At the end of his tour Buber conducted an important seminar with psychiatrists at the University of Michigan. The high point of the proceedings was a formal dialogue between Buber and Carl Rogers which took place before an audience of four hundred people. The text of the dialogue, together with the texts of the four lectures, have been published in *The Knowledge of Man*.[97] Buber returned to the U.S. for another lecture tour in the Spring of 1958, his eightieth year. He addressed the American friends of Ihud on the meaning of Zionism, and stressed the importance of building good relations between Arabs and Jews. The address was published later under the title, 'Israel and the Command of the Spirit'.[98] With his wife, Paula, he left New York in June , travelling first to Zurich and thence to Venice. Paula Buber suffered a heart attack from which she died on 11 August. She was buried in the Jewish Cemetery in Venice. Buber returned to Israel on 15 August. He wrote a moving tribute to his wife in a preface to a collection of her stories which was published in 1961.[99] Earlier, Paul A Schillp, editor of *The Library of Living Philosophers*, a series of books on leading thinkers of the twentieth century, proposed to devote a volume in the series to Buber's philosophy. Several notable scholars were asked to discuss different aspects of Buber's work, and Buber was invited to reply to their comments. Buber provided some autobiographical reminiscences from his childhood and these were appended to the collected essays in the volume.[100] He contributed also to *Philosophical Interrogations*, a work edited by Sidney and Beatrice Rome, in which he had some lively exchanges with Roberto Assagioli on religious education and with Robert Hutchins on the place of traditional values in education.[101]

Throughout the nineteen fifties Buber was involved in various peace movements attempting to alleviate Cold War tensions and create the conditions for international peace. One of his contributions to the cause of peace was an essay, 'Hope for this Hour',[102] in which he sought to identify the conditions necessary to create trust and promote peaceful dialogue between nations. In 1957, with Eleanor Roosevelt , Martin Luther King and Bishop James Pike, he called for a day of protest against the policy of apartheid in South Africa. The leaders of eighty-three nations supported the protest which took place on 10 December, 1957. Early in 1959 Dag Hammerskjold, then completing his second term as Secretary General of the U.N., wrote to Buber indicating his approval of the views expressed in 'Hope For this Hour'. The two men met at the U.N. in May 1958 and agreed to meet again the following year in Jerusalem. They shared a deep passion for the Psalms and for the Hasidic legends. Hammerskjold, who frequently quoted from Buber's writings in his own speeches, fully endorsed his view that dialogue between nations offered the best prospect for international peace. In June 1959 he wrote a lengthy memorandum to the Nobel Committee in Stockholm, nominating Buber for the Peace Prize. Again, the nomination was unsuccessful. Hammerskjold also undertook to translate *I and Thou* into Swedish, and had secured Buber's approval for the translation shortly before his fatal trip to the Congo in January 1962. A copy of *I and Thou*, together with ten translated pages in Swedish, were found amongst his effects after the fatal plane crash. Ironically, Hammerskjold was himself awarded the Nobel Peace Prize post-humously in 1962.[103]

Buber was active also in various protests against the arms race and campaigned vigorously against the testing of nuclear weapons. In 1961 he joined Pablo Casals, Albert Schweitzer, Bertrand Russell and Francois Mauriac in a protest to President Kennedy against nuclear tests conducted by the American armed forces. He expressed support for the Civil Disobedience Movement led by Martin Luther King and declared, at the height of the Cuban missile crisis, that young people would be morally justified in refusing to take up arms if the U.S. went to war. (For a fuller discussion of Buber's views on these issues see Chapter 7.) He closely associated himself also with the problems of Soviet Jews and spoke on their behalf at a conference in Paris in 1960.[104]

Throughout the 1950s and 60s Buber was deeply involved in political developments in Israel. In 1956 he condemned Israeli soldiers for the killing of forty-seven Arabs in an ambush at Kafr Kassem.[105] He opposed the invasion of the Sinai by French, British and Israeli forces in the same year and issued a paper, 'Israel's Mission to Zion',[106] in which he questioned the policies then being pursued by Ben Gurion. When the historian, Aharon Cohen, was arrested and charged with illegally meeting a Soviet agent at a kibbutz (he had met the agent to secure documents for his research), Buber went to court to testfy in his favour. Aubrey Hodes describes the event in *Encounter with Martin Buber*: 'For nearly three hours he remained there, replying patiently to all the queries levelled at him, his voice clear and unhurried, explaining in an almost fatherly way that a man such as Cohen could not possibly have acted deceitfully in the way the prosecution claimed.'[107] Though sentenced to five years in prison, Cohen was eventually pardoned by the President of Israel, largely as a result of Buber's intervention. On several occasions Buber took up the cause of the Palestinian refugees. In 1958 he submitted a memorandum to Ben Gurion, pleading with him to convene an international conference to deal with the problem. Later, through Ihud, he called on the U.N. to work out a plan with Israel and the Arab states for the resettlement of the refugees.

One of Buber's bitterest clashes with the Israeli government was prompted by the trial of Adolf Eichmann in 1962. Eichmann had been kidnapped by Israeli agents and brought to Israel to stand trial for the murder of thousands of Jews in Nazi concentration camps. Buber argued that Eichmann should not be tried by Jewish judges, since the Jewish people were themselves the victims of his crimes. He suggested that Eichmann be tried by an international tribunal. When his views were ignored, and Eichmann was sentenced to death by an Israeli court, Buber pleaded with Ben Gurion to commute the sentence to one of life imprisonment. He also wrote to *Time* and *Newsweek* magazines,[108] declaring that the state, like the individual, is bound by the Biblical injunction, 'Thou shalt not kill'. Buber was mocked and vilified for his stand in Israeli newspapers,[109] yet he continued to assert his view that the execution was an act of vengeance and, in an interview with the *New York Times*, described it as 'a mistake of historical dimensions'.[110]

He continued to write prolifically, despite the heavy demands of his political activities. He edited the five volume *Israeli Encyclopaedia of Education*,[111] and contributed a major paper himself on 'Adult Education'. In July 1960 he delivered a paper, 'The Word That is Spoken',[112] to the Bavarian Academy of Fine Arts and was awarded the Culture Prize of the City of Munich in recognition of the event. The paper provides the most mature formulation of the principles of Buber's linguistic philosophy. He was the recipient of numerous awards in the last years of his life. In December 1960 he received the Henrietta Szold Prize for his work on education, and, in the following year, was elected to the American Academy of Arts and Sciences. He was awarded the Bialik Prize[113] for his contribution to Jewish studies in December 1961, and, two years later, received the Albert Schweitzer Medal for 'having exemplified the spirit of reverence for life and other tenets of the philosophy of Dr Schweitzer.'[114] Shortly before this he had been made an honorary doctor of medicine by the University of Munster for 'his contribution to the philosophy of patient care.'[115]

Buber's eighty-fifth birthday was celebrated at a special ceremony organized by the Hebrew University in September 1963. Students from the University marched in torchlight procession to his home in the Jerusalem suburb of Talbiyeh. A forest, funded by German admirers, was planted in his honour at Kibbutz Hazorea. Earlier he had been awarded the Erasmus Prize in Holland for his 'contribution to European culture'. Previous recipients of the Prize included Marc Chagall, Karl Jaspers and Oskar Kokoschka. Buber travelled to Amsterdam and received the prize from Queen Juliana and Prince Bernhard in July, 1963. In a tribute Prince Bernhard declared that Buber 'had enriched the spiritual life of Europe with his versatile gifts, for over half a century.'[116] Buber delivered a lecture entitled 'A Believing Humanism',[117] in which he explained the interdependence of humanity and faith, and reiterated his belief that religious faith is rooted in the capacity, distinctive to humankind, to 'enter into encounters with other beings'.

Buber suffered periodically from ill-health in his final years. He contracted chronic nephritis in 1961 and underwent major surgery for cataract problems two years later. He continued to work on his translation of the Bible and attended daily to his vast correspondence. One of his finest poems, 'The Fiddler', which he wrote in the last year of his life, shows the serenity with which he faced the impending prospect of death:

> Here on the world's edge at this hour I have
> Wondrously settled my life.
> Behind me in a boundless circle
> The All is silent, only the fiddler fiddles.
> Dark one, already I stand in covenant with you,
> Ready to learn from your tones
> Wherein I became guilty without knowing it.
> Let me feel, let there be revealed
> To this hale soul each wound
> That I have incorrigibly inflicted and remained in illusion.
> Do not stop, holy player, before then.[118]

Buber had an operation on a broken leg at the Hadassah Hospital in Jerusalem in April, 1965. Some time later his nephritis grew worse and developed into uremic poisoning. He died at his home in Talbiyeh on 13 June 1965, and was buried in the Jewish Cemetery in Jerusalem. Ben Gurion, in a radio tribute, described him as 'a true man of the spirit' and a 'great loss to Israel's spiritual life'.[119] In a graveside eulogy the Prime Minister, Levi Eshkol, said: 'The Jewish people today mourns a luminary and a teacher, a man of thought and achievement who revealed the soul of Judaism with a new philosophic daring. All mankind mourns one of the spiritual giants of the century.'[120] *The New York Times* declared in an editorial: 'Martin Buber was the foremost Jewish thinker of our time and one of the world's most influential philosophers. He was a theological bridge-builder long before ecumenism achieved its present popularity. He served as a kind of patron saint for such towering Christian intellectuals as Paul Tillich, Reinhold Niebuhr, Jacques Maritain and Gabriel Marcel.'[121] Abraham Joshua Heschel wrote in *Newsweek*: 'I know of no one with a life as rich with intellectual adventures or who so strongly responded to their challenges as Martin Buber. His greatest contribution was himself, his very being. There was magic in his personality, richness in his soul. His sheer presence was joy.'[122] Buber's tombstone in the Jewish Cemetery was inscribed with the words, 'Va'ani tamid imakh' ('I am continually with thee'), which were taken from his favourite psalm (Number 73):

> When my soul was embittered,
> When I was pricked in heart,
> I was stupid and ignorant,
> I was like a beast towards thee.
> nevertheless, I am continually with thee;
> Thou dost hold my right hand.
> Thou dost guide me with thy counsel,
> And afterward thou wilt receive me to glory.

# II
# The Quest for a Philosophical Anthropology

It is essential, before considering Buber's educational writings, that an attempt be made to define the methodology of his philosophical and religious thought. The term favoured by Buber himself to encompass the great variety of his intellectual and cultural interests is that of 'philosophical anthropologist'. He referred approvingly in *Between Man and Man* to his teacher, Wilhelm Dilthey, as the 'founder of philosophical anthropology'.[1] Many years later, in a lengthy response to a collection of essays compiled to mark his retirement, he spoke of his own 'philosophizing'[2] as 'essentially anthropological' also. He complained of a failure in western philosophy, beginning with the post-Socratic classical thinkers, and including scholastic, rationalist, idealist and materialist philosophers, to formulate the fundamental questions on which such an anthropology could be founded. Allowing for certain exceptions — notably the pre-Socratic Greeks, Augustine, Pascal and the existentialists[3] — he spoke of a threefold deficiency in western philosophical traditions: firstly, their hierarchical ordering of thought into discrete disciplines, such as ontology, metaphysics and theology; secondly, their isolation of man the knower from the object of his knowledge; and thirdly, their unwillingness to conceive of man as distinctively a non-rational as well as a rational being. He argued vehemently that a philosophy should adopt as its starting-point a wide-ranging mode of enquiry sufficiently expansive to conceive of man in his wholeness and totality, in the questionableness of his existence, and in his concrete relatedness to the world. This is what he understood as the essential function of a philosophical anthropology.

There are two complementary lines of enquiry that must be followed if the origins and development of Buber's anthropological thought are to be explained. It is necessary firstly to examine his critique of the historical progress of philosophy from the classical period to the present time, and secondly, it is necessary to consider his explorations of various religious traditions, and particularly those of his own Jewish heritage. His critique of western philosophy is developed over a wide range of philosophical writings but its main elements are set out in the essays of *Eclipse of God* and *Between Man and Man*. In these essays Buber vigorously defends the view that the primary anthropological problem (i.e. the nature of man)[4] has attained mature formulation only in modern existentialist and phenomenological thought.[5] He mentions Heraclitus of Ephesus[6] as an exception to this, and amongst post-classical philosophers, he mentions Augustine and Pascal, in each of whom he detected incipient signs of anthropological insight. But in fact he gave little attention in these essays either to classical or to medieval philosophies. His analysis of historical trends in philosophy is focussed mainly on the post- Cartesian period, beginning with the critical idealism of Kant and proceeding through discussions of Hegelian idealism and the materialist philosophies of Feuerbach and Marx to a detailed consideration of Kierkgaard, Nietzsche, Heidegger and Sartre. This chapter will chart the progress of this critique by considering, firstly, Buber's discussion of Kantian and Hegelian idealism, and of the materialist philosophies which he regarded as their 'rebellious' by-products; secondly, it will consider his assessments of Kierkegaard and Nietzsche, both of whom significantly influenced his thought, though in widely different ways; and thirdly, it will consider his evaluations of his contemporaries, Heidegger and Sartre. Since it will become apparent in the course of this analysis that the purely philosophical and religious aspects of Buber's thought are closely intertwined, a fourth section will consider the relation between them and their place in the formulation of his anthropological method. This, in turn, will necessitate further examination of the specifically cultural and religious elements which closely complement the philosophical in the evolution of the mature anthropology. Buber, like many contemporary existentialists, has found much inspiration in scripture — in Ecclesiastes, Job and the Psalms, particularly — but he has identified an especially close relationship between existentialism and the revived tradition of Hasidic Judaism. The following chapter will examine how this has come about. Together, these philosophical, cultural and religious elements provide the synthesis on which his educational thought is founded.

## 1   Kant, Hegel Feuerbach and Marx

There are three main sources for a discussion of Buber's analysis of Kant: firstly, 'What is Man'?, his extended essays on the nature and scope of anthropological enquiry; secondly, the essays in *Eclipse of God* which examine the religious aspects of Kantian thought, and are focussed mainly on Kant's unfinished posthumous work; and thirdly, his assessments of the neo-Kantian theology of the Jewish philosopher, Herman Cohen, in which he firmly rejected Cohen's reinterpretations of Judaism in the light of idealist thought. Buber, in his own *Autobiographical Fragments*[7] had, in fact, attributed his philosophical awakening to Kant. He recalled his despairing attempts in his fifteenth year to solve the time-space relation through mathematical and physical formulae and the 'salvation' that came to him as he discovered Kant's explanations of space and time as merely the formal conditions of sensory perception. And in his mature writings he spoke of Kant as the philosopher who had initiated the processes of enquiry that were to culminate in the existentialist anthropologies of the present time. Kant, he said, in *The Critique of Pure Reason*, had identified the four fundamental questions on which all philosophizing must converge: the metaphysical, what can I know?, the ethical, what ought I do?, the religious, what may I hope?, and the anthropological, what is man? Yet he was deeply critical of Kant's treatment of these questions. 'It is remarkable', he writes, 'that Kant's own anthropology, both what he himself published, and his copious lectures on man which only appeared after his death, absolutely fails to achieve what he demanded of a philosophical anthropology.'[8] The question of man's place in the cosmos, his relation to the world of things, his understanding of his fellow-man, his existence as a being who knows he must die — such questions, he claimed, were not seriously taken up in Kant's philosophy.

More specifically, Buber complained of a basic methodological defect in Kant. A legitimate anthropology could not be grounded, he said, on the fragmentation of humanness which the categorial method required. Its essential weakness was its isolation of the knower from the object of his knowledge. Man would have to be envisaged in his *relation* to what he knows, in the concreteness of the relation, it its non-rational as well as its rational aspects; in its problematic nature — these, he argued, were the issues evaded in transcendental philosophy, with its overemphasized rationality, its separate spheres of thought, its objectification and abstraction. Paradoxically, it was in the religious sphere, rather than the philosophical, that Buber seemed to find some basis for agreement with Kant. He pointed to a possible elaboration by Kant, in the posthumous writings, of an anthropology that would embrace man's relation to the unconditioned, the infinite and the absolute. But this was undertaken by Kant solely as a justification for his ethical imperatives and could not provide Buber with the all-embracing framework for a divine-human encounter such as he found later in Kierkegaard. In *Eclipse of God* he described the hopeless struggle by Kant to expand his transcendental philosophy into a theology: 'The posthumous writings', he says 'reveal a scene of incomparable existential tragedy; they are filled with unresolved questions, such as "Is there a God?", "What is God?", and with the perennial tension of reason and faith which could be surmounted only by the typical Kantian compromise — 'To thank Him and to believe Him is an identical act.'[9] He was similarly disenchanted with the neo-Kantian Judaism of Herman Cohen. Cohen had discovered in the Kantian system a reinforcement of the ethical element in prophetic Judaism and rigorously reformulated Jewish belief in accordance with the principles of critical idealism. In his essay, 'Herut: On Youth and Religion',

Buber deplored this intellectualized Judaism: 'Intellectualization, in the making for centuries and accomplished within recent generations, has brought a depressing loneliness to the youth of present-day Europe', he wrote.[10] He condemned Cohen's theology for its conceptualized abstractions, it non-personal character, its lack of concrete, existential relevance: 'God is an idea for Cohen as he was for Kant . . . God's only place is within a system of thought. The system defends itself with stupendous vigour against the living God who is bound to make questionable its perfection, and even its absolute authority . . . Cohen has constructed the last home for the God of the philosophers.'[11] The comment underlines his conviction that only a non-theological, non-logicized meaning would ultimately accommodate his own understanding of the nature of religious reality.

For all the criticism of Kantian thought, it is evident nevertheless that, in pointing to the great residual questions remaining when the categorial analysis of phenomena was complete, Kant had identified the critical issues on which the kind of anthropology envisaged by Buber could be constructed. 'He was the first,' he said 'to understand the anthropological problem critically'; he had grasped 'the fundamental problems' — 'what sort of world is it which man knows? How can man, as he is, in his altered reality, know at all'?[12] The post-critical philosophers, on the other hand, while they had borrowed much from Kant seemed, in Buber's view, to have rejected or evaded the anthropological insights to which he had pointed. The two philosophers to whom most of Buber's comments are directed are Hegel and Marx. While his interest in Hegelian thought — negative though it was — had been encouraged by the early writings of his friend and collaborator, Franz Rosenzweig,[13] and he gave some consideration to its theological implications in *Eclipse of God*, Buber's disillusionment with its highly systematized idealism was fundamental and emphatic. In the philosophy of 'universal reason' he found a more radical abstraction than that of which he had earlier complained in Kant. He spoke of an 'alienation from the anthropological question as has probably never happened before in the history of human thought.'[14] The concrete human person, and the concrete human community, were dispossessed in favour of a generalised concept of reason and a subsuming of individualized humaness into the abstract categories of univeralism. The concept of God, already regarded with some ambivalence by Kant, was further removed in Hegelian thought from the sphere of concrete life or — more importantly from Buber's standpoint — from the sphere of concrete *relation* between individual man and God. 'God', he declared, 'is a spiritual principle for Hegel, accessible only to reason, not to the whole of man as he lives his concrete life.'[15] The absoluteness of the Hegelian *idea* of God precluded the direct, existential relation which Buber eventually defined as the essential identity of the religious relationship.

It was logically consistent for Buber — given the depth of his disenchantment with the systemized character of Hegelian thought — that he should find unacceptable also the dialectical philosophy of history into which the universalized rationalism of Hegel was subsumed. In the theory of a sovereign, logical order in history, and the related theory of progress through a contradiction of ideas, he found an almost total obliteration of the anthropological perspective suggested by Kant. 'Thought', he wrote, 'does not have the power to build up man's real life and the strictest philosophical certainty cannot endow the soul with that intimate certitude that the world which is so imperfect will be brought to its perfection.'[16] The very criterion of historical order — the universalized law of reason — would exclude the alternatives present in specific historical solutions: would indeed nullify the choice that a specific situation offers to man and the freedom which is the fundamental source of his response to it. 'The Hegelian house of the universe is admired, explained and imitated', Buber wrote, 'but it proves uninhabitable. Thought confirms it and the word glorifies it but the real man does not set foot on it.'[17]

Two essays on history in *Pointing the Way* — both suggesting links between Hegelian dialectics and the Pauline theory of history as the divinely ordained process of redemption — indicate the degree to which religion is intertwined with Buber's anthropological questioning. He traces Hegel's 'monological' (as distinct from 'dialogical') theory of history to St Paul's theory of a divine plan for salvation which is manifest in the coming of Christ and accomplished through history in the redemption of man through Christ's sacrifice on the cross. He rejects this apocalyptic version of history as diminishing the individual's freedom — his freedom specifically to effect his destiny: 'Everything here is predetermined, all human decisions are only sham struggles. The future is already present in heaven, as it were, present from the beginning.'[18] The dialogical reciprocity between man and God, which is the essential feature of his own and of the Jewish-prophetic view of history, is diminished, if not totally suppressed, in the theory of history as a divinely ordained process, whether the determining principle is the Pauline plan for redemption or the Hegelian laws of reason.

Buber gives scant attention to Hegelian thought in his philosophical writings. Whereas Kantian idealism marked a positive stage in his pursuit of a fundamental anthropology, his rejection of Hegelianism was unreserved and absolute. It was followed in his review of post-Cartesian philosophy by an analysis of Marxism where he found a further dilution of the essential freedom of historical dialogue, and therefore, a further weakening also of the anthropological perspective introduced by Kant. But he encountered an unexpectedly hopeful diversion from the relentless progression of the

Hegelian dialectic of reason to the materialistic dialectic of Marx in the work of another of his compatriots, the Bavarian philosopher, Ludwig Feuerbach. While it would be easy to exaggerate the extent of Feuerbach's influence on Buber, there is evidence that some passages at least from the former's *Principles of the Philosophy of the Future* had some significance for the subsequent development by Buber of his own philosophy of dialogue. It is necessary therefore to make brief mention at least of the link with Feuerbach.

Feuerbach is commonly regarded as a transitional figure whose work marks the advance from the Hegelian to the Marxist dialectic. He is remembered also for the humanism of *The Essence of Christianity* in which religion is defined as 'the dream of the human mind',[19] and the spiritual is defined as an exclusively human property rather than the means by which man finds a relation with God. While not disputing the general accuracy of this view, Buber found much to commend in Feuerbach: not merely his opposition to the cognitive hierarchicalism of Kant, and the universalized abstractions of Hegel, but his construction of a firm anthropological context for his philosophy. 'The new philosophy', he said, in a reference to Feuerbach's *Principles of the Philosophy of the Future*, 'has as its principle not 'the abolute', that is, the abstract spirit, in short, not reason *in abstracto*, but man's real, whole being.'[20] More importantly, he found in Feuerbach a crude but sound formulation of the philosophy of relation which was later to form the basis of his own dialogic thought. He quotes him on the anthropology of the interhuman: 'The individual man for himself does not have man's being in himself. Man's being is contained only in community, in the unity of man with man — a unity which rests, however, only on the reality of the difference between I and Thou.'[21] The closeness in terminology to Buber's own *I and Thou* is unmistakable; indeed the affinity he felt with Feuerbach may explain the rare extravagance of the language he used to describe this prototypical Thou — 'the Copernican revolution of modern thought' . . . 'an elemental happening just as rich in consequences as the idealist discovery of the I.'[22] And yet, while Feuerbach decisively advanced the progress of anthropological thought, his denial of a potential expansion of the I-Thou into a relationship embracing the human and the divine was, in Buber's view, an unacceptable restriction, a reduction of the anthropological to the sphere of the purely human.

In his critique of Marxism Buber spoke of a social reductionism that was even more limiting than the humanist reductionism of Feuerbach. Marx, he said, had confined the anthropological to the sphere of the social and had conceived of human progress exclusively in terms of social transformation. In *Paths in Utopia* he compared Marx with the utopian socialists whom Marx and his followers rejected: Proudhon, Kropotkin and Buber's close friend, Gustav Landauer. He concedes that Marx, because he had identified the material obstacles hindering human progress, would always have a certain anthropological relevance, but because of its concentration on the material conditions of existence, his philosophy appeared to Buber to effect an even narrower constriction of the anthropological than the humanism he condemned in Feuerbach: 'Conditions of production are what are essential and basic for Marx; they are the point from which he starts and to which he retraces everything; there is no other origin and no other principle for him. Certainly, they cannot be considered, like Hegel's universal reason, as the first and last; sociological reduction means an absolute renunciation of a perspective of being in which there exists a first and a last.'[23] In an essay written — significantly — in 1938 (during the Stalinist purges) Buber spoke of 'a new anthropological dread' and warned of the horrendous consequences of materialist determinism:

> Hegel as it were compulsorily combined the course of the stars and of history into a speculative security. Marx, who confined himself to the human world, ascribed to it alone a security in regard to the future, which is likewise dialectic, but has the effect of an actual security. To-day this security has perished in the ordered chaos of a terrible historical revulsion. Gone is the calm, a new anthropological dread has arisen, the question about man's being faces us as never before in all its grandeur and terror — no longer in philosophical attire, but in the nakedness of existence. No dialectical guarantee keeps man from falling; it lies with himself to lift his foot and take the step which leads him away from the abyss. The strength to take this step cannot come from any security in regard to the future, but only from those depths of insecurity in which man, overshadowed by despair, answers with his decision the question about man's being.[24]

Apart from the anthropological limitations of Marxism, it has within it a basic structural defect which Buber attributed to its implied subordination of society to the state: a subordination, as he shows in *Paths in Utopia*[25] which was explicitly advocated in the Leninist doctrine of political centralism. Buber, in his own socialist writings, proposed a community-based socialism in which small co-operative units, such as the Israeli kibbutzim and moshava, would be the main structures of social reorganization. In this respect, his thinking strongly reflected the Hasidic socialism of the Yiddish speaking communities of Eastern Europe. Hasidic culture, as will be shown in detail presently, was to contribute significantly to his anthropological perspectives. While diverging fundamentally from Marxist socialism on the question of social organisation and on the accommodation of the religious perspective, the Judaic tradition of socialism differed significantly from the Marxist also in its linking of ethical and religious perspectives. While showing a certain sympathy for the transforming vision of Marx himself — 'His exertions to give the right answer are of a thoroughness and scrupulosity worthy of admiration'[26] — Buber could not accept the separation of the ethical and the religious which Marx's philosophy required. In two essays, 'Religion and Ethics' and 'On the Suspension of the Ethical'[27] he traces the historical weakening of the interdependence of the religious and the ethical in recent times to the humanism of Feuerbach and Nietzsche, but especially to the socialist humanism of Marx. With the separation of the ethical and the religious he anticipates a decline that could end in total nihilism. The metaphorical language used in the following passage conveys the depth of his fear:

> Time and again, when I ask well-conditioned young souls, 'Why do you give up your dearest possession, your personal integrity?' they answer me, 'Even this, this most difficult sacrifice, is the thing that is needed in order that . . .' It makes no difference, 'in order that equality may come' or 'in order that freedom may come', it makes no difference! And they bring the sacrifice faithfully. In the realm of Moloch honest men lie and compassionate men torture. And they really and truly believe that brother-murder will prepare the way for brotherhood! There appears to be no escape from the most evil of all idolatry.

## 2   Kierkegaard and Nietzsche

The secular/humanist reductionism critized by Buber in his discussion of Feuerbach and Marx was still the main object of his attention when he came to deal with Nietzsche's existentialist thought. While a strict chronological treatment of nineteenth century philosophy would require a discussion of Kierkegaard in advance of Nietzsche, I am proposing, for the purposes of the present commentary, not to follow that order: firstly because it was through his discovery of Nietzsche in his youth that Buber encountered existentialist philosophy; secondly, because a clear progression is discernible from his rejection of Nietzschean humanism to his highly critical and complex acceptance of the religious emphasis of Kierkegaardian thought. While clearly unhappy with Kierkegaard's supposed renunciation of the world, and particularly with his renunciation of the conjugal relationship, he did, nonetheless, write enthusiastically of the religious dimensions of the Kierkegaardian I-Thou. Kierkegaard's influence on Buber was, in many respects, positive and enduring, while Nietzsche remained for him a transitional figure whose significance was that he marked a certain advance from the idealists and materialists while retaining many of their basic weaknesses.

I have referred earlier, in a discussion of Kant, to Buber's recollections in his *Autobiographical Fragments*[28] of the two philosophers who had 'entrenched directly' on his existence during his fifteenth and his seventeenth year. His interest in the time-space relation to Kant's *Prolegomena* has already been mentioned. He recalls also how Nietzsche's *Thus Spake*

*Zarathustra* transported him into 'a sublime intoxication' — 'took possession of me . . . worked on me not in the manner of a gift but in the manner of an invasion which deprived me of my freedom.'[29] He was attracted particularly by the Nietzschean theory of time. Previously he had accepted the Kantian definition of time as a formal condition of sensory perception. Under Nietzsche's influence, however, he redefined it as an infinite sequence of finite periods, the end phase always turning back to its beginning — an 'infinite return of the same'.[30] This he reformulated yet again in the light of a conflict he detected between the Kantian and Nietzschean positions: 'If time is only a form in which we perceive, where are we?' he asked. 'Are we not in the timeless? Are we not in eternity? . . . a wholly other eternity than the circular one which Zarathustra loves as "fatum".'[31] His eventual formulation had as its core the existential uniqueness of each particular event, a development which, paradoxically, owed more to Nietzsche than to Kant.

Whatever the youthful attractions of *Zarathustra*, Buber's mature estimations of Nietzsche were focussed mainly on the humanist character of his 'will to power' philosophy. He spoke again, as in his critique of Feuerbach, of the absurdity of anthropological explanations drawn solely from the world of nature. There is an untypical spirit of irony in his comments: 'He (Nietzsche) attempts to follow out a thought indicated by Empedocles, but since then never discussed in a genuinely philosophical fashion: he wants to understand man purely genetically, as an animal that has grown out and stepped forth from the animal world'.[32] He spoke of the silencing of the absolute ('God is dead!'), the dispensing with metaphysics and religion, the substitution of the strength- weakness dichotomy for the traditional morality of evil versus good as, in all instances, springing from the humanist premisses of Nietzsche's philosophy and culminating in the horrific 'will- to-power' master morality of the Superman dream. In an essay written in Germany during the late 1930s he exposed the underlying fallacies, the psychological contradictions, the pseudo 'creativity' and the deficient concept of responsibility that were inherent in the 'will-to-power' aspiration: 'Power in itself is evil, no matter who exercises it. It has no persistence but is greed and *eo ipso* cannot be fulfilled, hence it is unhappy in itself and is bound to be the cause of unhappiness in others.'[33] For all that, Nietzsche held a positive significance for Buber too. In 'What Is Man ?' he spoke of a certain pathos in man of which intimations could be found in the writings of Augustine, Kane and Pascal: the pathos of man perceiving in himself something he could not explain from nature. Nietzsche reconceived this pathos, he said, as man faced with the mystery of his being, at the edge of natural being, himself the pre-form of an undisclosed being. But, unlike Augustine, Kant and Pascal he would not invoke, as a further depth for this pathos, the possibility of a realm beyond the natural and the finite. Yet, in

pointing to Man's existence as problematic, Nietzsche decisively advanced
the course of anthropological questioning. Whatever the defects of the
humanist vision and the chaos of the Superman 'ethic', he had, in Buber's
view, at least centralized the essential concern of the anthropologist: 'In
elevating, as no previous thinker has done, the questionableness of human
life to be the real subject of philosophizing he gave the anthropological
question a new and unheard of impulse'.[34]

Buber's interest in Kierkegaard was a great deal more complex. He was
profoundly drawn to the Kierkegaardian relation of existential faith, to his
concern for the wholeness of man and for personhood, to his sense of the
potentiality and, above all, the problematic nature of human existence — of
these aspects of Kierkegaard's thought Buber strongly and whole-heartedly
approved. On some other issues — the singleness of the religious relation,
the life-denying ethic, the supposed renunciation of the world and mankind
— he rejected Kierkegaard, while clarifying some features of his own
dialogic and social thought in the process. When he first encountered
Kierkegaard (German translations of his work were made available during
the first decade of the century) Buber had recently abandoned religious
mysticism for the simplicities of Hasidic Judaism, with its emphasis on the
santification of common experience. In Kierkegaard he encountered a religious thinker who also stressed the everyday character of the relation of
faith, and saw man's address to God as a function not of a ritualized religion,
but of an immediate existential encounter with an unconditioned Thou.
'Kierkegaard', he wrote in 'What Is Man ?', was 'the critic of modern
Christianity who grasped like no other thinker of our time the significance
of the person.'[35] Kierkegaard's impassioned denunciations of clerical
Christendom, which reached their peak in his last great polemic, *Attack upon
Christendom*, marked a striving for a realized faith such as the Hasidic
zaddikim had counselled also in their revolt against the formalized legalism
of rabbinic Judaism. He confirmed for Buber the unity of faith and life which
he had encountered in Hasidism, but which followed logically also from his
rejection of the idealist I for an anthropology in which man's relation to
reality (including the reality of the unconditioned) was not that of detached
observer, but of an I inextricably linked with otherness.Through his interest
in Kierkegaard Buber was able to develop also the purely human aspects of
his anthropology, though, in this instance, by way of a highly critical reaction
to the event which dominated all of Kierkegaard's philosophy, the severing
of his relationship with Regine Olsen. In this Buber observed a conscious
renunciation by Kierkegaard of the otherness of the world and of mankind
for a salvation he (apparently) believed could be attained only through an
unworldly, monadic relation to God. In the spirit of Hasidic Judaism Buber
advocated a relation to God which could, and should, be fulfilled through

man's encounter with all of God's creation i.e., with the otherness of the world and mankind. Later he wrote eloquently in *I and Thou* of the essential interdependence of the two modes of relation, the divine-human and the interhuman. Kierkegaard's position, he argued, was inconsistent even with the Christian faith he professed: 'Kierkegaard, the Christian concerned with contemporaneity with Jesus, here contradicts his master. "In order to come to love" says Kierkegaard about his renunciation of Regine Olsen, "I had to remove the object." That is sublimely to misunderstand God. Creation is not a hurdle on the road to God, it is the road itself . . . God wants us to come to him by means of the Regines he has created and not by renunciation of them'.[36]

A close examination of Kierkegaard's work suggests, however, that Buber had overemphasized, possibly misrepresented, his supposed renunciation of the world for a purely spiritual relationship with God. He concedes there are occasions when Kierkegaard appeared to refute himself: the *Journal* entry, 'Had I had faith I would have stayed with Regine',[37] as he says, is a much quoted instance of Kierkegaard's ambivalence on the issue. It is significant, however, that Buber makes no mention of *Works of Love*, the text in which Kierkegaard elucidates the Christian ideal of a purely altruistic love. In the sections entitled 'Thou Shalt Love' and 'Thou Shalt Love Thy Neighbour' there is a crucial distinction between the selfishness of a profane or earthly passion and the selflessness of genuine Christian love.[38] Kierkegaard sees the romantic emotion as ego-determined, partial, corruptible and ultimately despairing; Christian love, he says, is self-denying, unconditional in its giving, and for the believer a duty intrinsically bound up with the primary obligation to love God.

An important fact which is unmentioned also in Buber's essays is the involuntary nature of the solitude forced on Kierkegaard by the manic-depressive psychosis to which he refers many times in his writings,[39] and which has since been confirmed in several biographical and psychological studies of his life and work.[40] Even allowing for this, it is still possible to cite many instances of a personal experience by Kierkegaard of the interhuman I-Thou. One, for example, is the poignant *Journal* entry on his love for his deceased father and for Regine: 'I entirely understood myself in being a solitary man, without relationship to anybody, with a deep inward pain, with only one comfort, God who is love, only one friend whom I crave, the Lord Jesus Christ, with a yearning for a deceased father, being separated by worse than death from the only person now living whom I have loved in a decisive sense.'[41] Buber, it would appear, does less than justice both to the tragedy of Kierkegaard's isolation from the world and to the self-denying imperatives implicit in the Christian command, 'Thou shalt love the Lord thy God with all thy heart and all thy soul and all thy mind. But the second commandment is like unto it: Thou shalt love thy neighbour as thyself.'[42]

Some aspects of Buber's social philosophy were developed also as a response to Kierkegaard's thought. Kierkegaard's warnings on commerce with the crowd ('a dangerous rapport with finitude'), his assertion that 'the crowd *in its very concept* is an untruth',[43] are recalled by Buber as further instances of a retreat by Kierkegaard from the otherness of man and the world. On this issue Buber offered a distinction between private and public modes of relation. He described the first as the decisive encounter with individual man in which the one can identify wholly with the concrete presence of the other. The apparently unbridgeable, multiple otherness of the crowd might be seen, he says, as an obstacle to such an identification. But he writes of a possible transformation of a public into a *communal* mode of relation, and therefore, of the possibility also that the impersonal relations of the multitude attain the character of the interhuman: 'The man who is living with the body politic . . . is bound up in relation to it, betrothed to it, married to it, therefore suffering his destiny along with it . . . but not abandoning himself blindly to its movements, rather confronting each movement watchfully and carefully that it does not miss truth and loyalty'.[44] In this kind of transformation lies the germ of the community socialism developed at length by Buber in *Paths in Utopia* and his writings on inter-community relations in Palestine.

But it is not simply his rejection of the Kierkegaardian solitude which marks the general direction of Buber's social anthropology. The particular insistence of most of his writings on social and community relations is the individual's *responsibility* to relate authentically to the community or group, to *engage* in rapport with finitude. In 'The Question to the Single One' he describes both the dialogic and community relationships as lying between the extremes of Kierkegaardian individualism and Marxist collectivism. The extreme solitude of Kierkegaard's invididualism is seen as a flight from responsibility: responsibility to resist the drift towards a collectivism in which individual freedom and responsibility are suppressed. 'The human person belongs,' he says, 'whether he wants to acknowledge it or take it seriously or not, to the community in which he is born or which he has happened to get into.'[45] Acting from the standpoint of individual conscience, he shares, reaffirms, or challenges the decisions of his group, refuses to yield the responsibility which is his by individual right: 'My group cannot relieve me of this responsibility, I must not let it relieve me of it: if I do, I pervert my relation of faith, I cut out of God's realm of power the sphere of my group.'[46]

Paradoxically, Buber felt that Kierkegaard had weakened the inter-dependence of the ethical and the religious in the whole sphere of social responsibility, both through his renunciation of the crowd, and through his continued emphasis on redemption through faith: a redemption, according to Lutheran doctrine, which is already accomplished through the sacrifice of Christ on the cross.[47] In his ethical works[48] Buber writes of the diminished importance of ethical *action* in Pauline theology and of its centrality in Judaism. His commentary on Kierkegaard reiterates the religious character of ethically directed action: 'This arch command, for whose sake the Bible makes its God speak from the very time of creation, defines anew, when it is heard, the relation of the Single One to his community.'[49] On the individual, not the community, is devolved the responsibility for such a response: 'I do not consider the individual to be *either* the starting-point or the goal of the human world. But I consider the human person to be the irremovable central place of the struggle between the world's movement away from God and its movement towards God.'[50] Questions of freedom, potentiality and choice are closely linked also with Buber's theories of social responsibility. In common with Nietzsche he conceives of freedom as radical ('the crystallized potentiality of existence')[51] but, unlike Nietzsche, he sees the exercise of freedom as a function of ethical choice: 'Man is not good, man is not evil; he is, in a pre-eminent sense, good and evil together. . . . Good is the movement in the direction of home, evil is the aimless whirl of human potentialities without which nothing can be achieved,'[52] In place of Nietzsche's will to power, and his Superman master-slave morality, Buber follows Kierkegaard's orientation of freedom towards the 'Single One's' relation to God, while departing from Kierkegaard in extending that responsibility to include the individual's relation to the world, to mankind, to things, to the body-politic, the crowd.

Ultimately, Buber's discussion of Kierkegaard leads to a fundamental issue encompassing all other aspects of his anthropology: the radical questionableness of individual existence and truth. He spoke of the historical circumstances which have made individual existence especially problematic and tensed at the present time: the decline in family and community life, the collectivizing impact of technological and economic change, the politicization of truth, the subjugation of individual thought to social and ideological processes — one hears echoes of Marx's 'It is not man's consciousness that determines his being but his social being that determines his consciousness.'[53] At the end of Buber's long and detailed discussion of Kierkegaard two conclusions are affirmed: one, 'the person has become questionable through being collectivized'; two, 'the truth has become questionable through being politicized'.[54] Simultaneously, he reasserted the historic responsibility of the individual to authenticate existence and truth: 'That man may not be lost there is need of the person's responsibility to truth in his historical situation. . . . True community and true commonwealth will be realized only to the extent to which the Single Ones become real out of whose responsible life *the body politic is renewed.*'[55]

Through these close and intensely critical investigations of Kierkegaard's writings, Buber identified the rudiments of a philosophical anthropology. The primacy of relation on the level of the interhuman was already suggested to him by Feuerbach. It was clarified by way of a lengthy critical questioning of Kierkegaard's solitude, and then linked with the divine-human encounter which Kierkegaard in his whole life had embodied and confirmed. In a way, the corresponding and dependent relations of the intersubjective human and divine encounters described in *I and Thou* could be said to mark a synthesis by Buber of the human anthropology of Feuerbach and the religious anthropology of Kierkegaard. It was his lengthy discussion of Kierkegaard's self-imposed solitude which gave him the basis also of a social anthropology and the accompanying theories of freedom, responsibility and potentiality. Kierkegaard pointed, finally, to the problematic situation of man, the tension of his relation to the cosmos, the ambiguous, paradoxical character of truth, and the radical functions of question and doubt — issues which Buber considered further through his discussion of the philosophies of Heidegger and Sartre.

## 3  Heidegger and Sartre

Buber's commentary on Heidegger and Sartre seems, in many respects, merely to restate or confirm positions that were already defined in his writings on Kierkegaard, Nietzsche, Feuerbach and the idealists. It has the important function, however, of establishing the *contemporary* relevance of his own philosophy, and it facilitates comparisons which help to locate his work in the context of twentieth-century thought. For these reasons it is essential that the essays on Heidegger and Sartre be discussed. Buber, somewhat controversially, treats both as the inheritors of Nietzsche's 'God is dead' philosophy. In the case of Sartre he proceeds from a predictable rejection of his atheism to a similarly emphatic rejection of his theories on freedom, subjectivity and choice. His treatment of Heidegger is more detailed and more complex. Certain aspects of Heidegger's philosophy, such as the 'solicitude' and Mitsein themes, because of their closeness to his own dialogic philosophy, are considered more elaborately by Buber than the issues he raised in his discussion of Sartre.

It is important to indicate firstly the enthusiasm expressed by Buber for the Husserlian phenomenology on which both Heidegger and Sartre were eventually to base their own philosophical methodologies. While Buber himself developed a method quite distinct from the phenomenological (this will be discussed in the fourth section of this chapter) he showed, in his writings on Husserl, a remarkable sensitivity to the intricacies of phenomenological method, and considered it appropriate to the needs of a philosophical anthropology. Mankind, 'struggling for self-understanding', 'wrestling with its own problematics', was properly recognized, he said,[56] as the phenomenon meriting the centrality accorded it by Husserl. The vital shift in emphasis, from the idealist conception of the distinctively rational man to the expanded phenomenon of man as distinctively non-rational also, had been made by Kierkegaard and Nietzsche. Husserl, who follows them chronologically, provided a method appropriate to its description.

Beyond recognizing the advances made through the development of phenomenological method by Heidegger and Sartre, Buber was otherwise profoundly critical of their philosophies. His comments were directed primarily at the 'proclaimed' atheism of Sartre and the 'historical' atheism of Heidegger. On the positive side, he quoted Sartre approvingly on the dilemmas presented by a persisting religious need at a time when the transcendent that is craved is no longer seen to exist: 'The silence of the transcendent, combined with the perseverance of the religious need in modern man, that is the great concern to-day as yesterday. It is the problem which torments Nietzsche, Heidegger, Jaspers.'[57] While he agreed with the presentation of the dilemma, Buber differed fundamentally from Sartre in his insistence that the religious need is not merely a surviving phenomenon, but exists inherently in man and is fulfilled in the Thouness of the interhuman, through its extension into the infinite Thouness of God. He rejected particularly the Sartrean conception of God as 'the quintessence of otherness': on the grounds that the term 'quintessence' did not convey the infinitude of God as other, and that the Sartrean otherness — 'the other is he who makes me into an object as I make him'[58] — is radically *in conflict* with individual subjectivity, and therefore excludes the reciprocity which is the fundamental feature of the religious relationship. For this quintessential otherness of Sartre Buber substitutes a God who is the *absoluteness*. of the other. But the other, in this instance, is the infinite, ever-loving Thou. In place of a universe of free-flowing subjectivity he conceived one of reciprocity and dialogue, and affirmed its ontic primacy.

Not surprisingly, Buber found little to commend either in the Sartrean theory of creative freedom. In language strongly reminiscent of his commentary on the humanism of Feuerbach, he challenged the concept of man as recovering for himself the freedom traditionally ascribed to God, and thereby affirming himself as the being through whom the world exists: 'That ordering of known phenomena which we call the world is, indeed, the composite work of a thousand human generations, but it has come into being through the fact that manifold being, which is not our work, meets us, who are, likewise, together with our subjectivity, not our work. . . All that being is *established*, we are established, our meeting with it is established, and in this way the becoming of a world, which takes place through us, is established.'[59] On the specific question of the free invention of values he spoke of radical correspondences between the free-flowing, directionless subjectivity of Sartre — on which the choice and definition of values is based — and the defective faith of the Nietschean will-to-power. In both instances values are said to originate, not in established freedom, but in the spurious freedom of the self-directing ego. 'Sartre says literally, ''someone is needed to invent values'' (*pour inventer les valeurs*). . . . Life has no meaning *apriori* . . . it is up to you to give it a meaning, and value is nothing else than this meaning which you choose. That is almost exactly what Nietzsche said, and it has not become any truer since then.'[60] Throughout the essays of *Eclipse of God* Buber conceives of freedom as the possibility for a relation with the human or unconditioned Thou, and of value as the authentic choice presented by that relation. On this issue he clearly had little in common with Sartre.

And yet, there are intimations in Buber's discussion of Sartre that he would have welcomed a form of critical atheism which, if properly defined and formulated, would clear the way for a renewed religious meaning, freed from the rituals and theologies of the past. Such, of course, was not the intention of Sartre, though, from Buber's standpoint, any radical challenging of conventional theologies could add momentum to this process. There are some signs that this was one of his preoccupations also in his much lengthier analysis of Heidegger's philosophy. One of the attractions of Heidegger for Buber was that he had not decided positively or negatively on the religious question. His view that we live in an interim stage in time, between that 'of the gods who have fled and of the god who is coming' was consistent with the notion of 'God concealment' which Buber, rightly or wrongly,[61] inferred from Sartre. But the Heideggerian position, as Buber saw it, was flawed by the idea of a God revealed through the time-bound process of history. In place of the Nietschean dispensing with the absolute, Heidegger, he said, constructed a new ontology in which Being is the totally other, but attains its illumination through man. The possible reappearance of the divine, in new and unanticipated forms, would be a function of such a human illumination. The traditional God who *transcended* human thought, and revealed himself to man through the immanent, would therefore be replaced by one disclosed through thought.

Buber's second objection concerned the reduction of anthropological questions by Heidegger to the level of the purely ontological, i.e. to the problem of human existence in its relation to its own being. Such an ontology, he argued, was necessarily monological. Taking as examples two of Heidegger's foremost existential themes — the 'primal human guilt' and 'Being-towards-Death' — he perceived in the self-illumination they disclose a concentration on the existence of the self in relation to its own being, rather than something other than itself. What Heidegger had constructed, in his attempts to devise a fundamental ontology, was ultimately, an ontology of self- being, or, as Buber expressed it in the third section of 'What is Man?', something of an elaborate solipsism: 'Apparently nothing more remains now to the solitary man but to seek an intimate communication with himself. This is the basic situation from which Heidegger's philosophy arises. . . . There remains, however, one irrefragable fact, that one can stretch out one's hands to one's image or reflection in a mirror, but not to one's real self.'[62]

Thus far, it would seem that a clear-cut distinction can be drawn between Heidegger's monological primacy of self-illuminated being and Buber's primacy of dialogic being. A complication arises, however, with the Heideggerian idea of solicitude,[63] i.e., man's being-with-others, which appears to contradict the claim by Buber that the Heideggerian ontology is focussed ultimately on the primary reality of self-being. Self-being, by Heidegger's description, attains illumination through a knowing which is grounded in 'being-with'. This being-with-others, Buber says, is mere 'co-existence', a relation ontically less significant than his own primary dialogic. Despite the usage by Heidegger of such terms as 'primordial understanding' for the relation of solicitude, Buber restates his fundamental objection that the relation does not have primacy or essentiality: 'In an essential relation which includes solicitude, the essentiality', he writes, 'is derived from another realm which is lacking in Heidegger. An essential relation to individual men can only be a direct relation from life to life in which a man's reserve is resolved and the barriers of self-being are breached.'[64] In essential relation, he says, a new phenomenon appears: that of the ontic, primary relation which is the constitutive principle of man's existence. Man, by this description, reaches the full reality of his being through a living essential relation to man, God and world. Otherwise, he lives in partial unreality, on the level of the inessential.

The discussion of solicitude and the whole question of the inter-subjective leads back once again to the problem of 'historical' atheism, the problem with which Buber's analysis of Heidegger began. If Heidegger could not conceive of an essential bond between self and other he could not, obviously, conceive of the absoluteness of such a relation either. In 'What Is Man?' Buber made this comparison between Heidegger and Kierkegaard: 'Heidegger's philosophical secularization of Kierkegaard had to abandon the religious conception of a bond of the self with the Absolute, a bond in real mutual relation of person with person. . . . The Absolute has its place in Heidegger's philosophy only in the sphere to which the self penetrates in its relation to itself, that is, where the question about the entry into a *connexion* with it ceases to be asked.'[65] And yet, this may not represent the full complexity of Heidegger's position. A sense of the *mystery* of being, as Buber allows, is not lacking in Heidegger, and is especially apparent in those of his writings which were influenced by the poet, Holderlin,[66] but it does not expand into a meeting with essential otherness. Some commentators[67] have pointed to writings by Heidegger which appeared later than those covered by Buber's analysis as evidence of significant modifications of the monological ontology of *Being and Time*, but such revisions fall far short of the ontical dialogue of Buber's philosophy. Again certain scholars[68] have found in Heidegger a more intensive search for the divine than Buber's critique seems to allow. Ironically, Buber himself may have given support to such speculation by his reference to a possible attestation by Heidegger, in an isolated passage from a work of 1944,[69] to some form of relation between a human and a divine spontaneity. The passage reads: 'The gods can only enter the Word if they themselves address us and place their demand upon us. The Word that names the gods is always an answer to this demand.'[70] Much could be made of this statement were it not that its implications remain unelaborated by Heidegger himself, and, as Buber remarks, the issue is not raised in these terms again in his philosophy. At the very least, however, it suggests that Heidegger's intention was that the religious question would have to remain temporarily unresolved.

There appears to be general agreement that Heidegger did not construct a coherent social philosophy. Indeed, what he seems to contemplate in his treatment of the individual's relation to the multitude is an *escape* from a servitude of the impersonal,[71] rather than the possibility of some form of authentic relation. In his fear of a dispersion of the self through enforced anonymity or conformity he seems a good deal closer to Kierkegaard's 'rapport with finitude.'[72] than to Buber's ideal of community life. The one significant feature of Buber's reference to Heidegger in this context is his use of a terminology that is elaborated elsewhere in writings where he deals specifically with his social philosophy. In the section of 'What Is Man?' where he deals with Heidegger he introduces the phenomenon of essential We-ness. The basic structure of community is defined in this essay as the relation of an I to a human multiplicity which can be transformed through dialogue into an essential We: 'Only men who are truly capable of saying Thou to one another can truly say We to one another. . . A man is truly saved from the "one" not by separation (as in Heidegger and Kierkegaard) but only by being bound up in general communion.'[73] This is an important advance on the decentralized community of Buber's writings on Marxism and gives substantial philosophical support to the theories advanced in *Paths in Utopia*.

In his analysis of Heidegger and Sartre, therefore, Buber re-emphasized the essential principles of his emerging anthropology: the ontical primacy of dialogue, the interrelation of its human- divine and interhuman forms, the secondary significance of ontological questioning, the essential We-ness, and the possible transformation of the dialogic I-Thou into the structure of the community group. Together they constitute the principal elements in a coherent and unified, but non-systematized thought. Two main issues remain to be clarified before each of these points is examined in detail and their relation to education is established. It is necessary, first, to specify the methodology adoped by Buber for the description of his anthropological perspectives. Since he had chosen not to adopt or refashion to his purposes the phenomenological method of Husserl, his particular style of philosophizing needs to be defined. This will be attempted in the section which follows. Secondly, the major issue arising from the philosophical critique — embracing, as it does, so many questions of a fundamentally religious nature — is the interconnection of his philosophy and his inherited Jewish culture. This will be the subject of the following chapter.

### 4 The Anthropological Method

Methodologically, the main complication of Buber's anthropology is its interpretation of two spheres of thought normally designated the philosophical and the theological. His critique of philosophy from Kant to Sartre shows a progression towards a dialogic which encompasses man's address to the absolute and simultaneously to the world of men and things. In this conception there is clearly an advance from the sphere of the purely philosophical into that of the religious. Yet it would be wrong to describe Buber as, in any conventional sense, the creator of a theological system. His analysis of rationalist, idealist and materialist philosophies indicated inadequacies equally present in theological as in philosophical thought-systems. Traditional philosophies from the Greeks to Hegel could not, he said, encompass a rational ontology which of its nature is primarily and essentially intersubjective, other than through the radical contradiction of comprehending the intersubjective in terms of object. The 'logicized God'[74] of traditional theologies would involve a similar and ever cruder objectification: the reduction of the infinite Thouness of the dialogic relation to the realm of cognitive thought. Yet, the relation to the absolute, which is essentially religious, and the relation to man and the world, which ultimately comes within the scope of the religious also, are together the essential and inseparable features of his anthropology. It was necessary for him to devise a methodology which would embrace the two modes of relation without recourse to the abstraction and objectification of traditional philosophies and theologies.

The complementary relation of knowledge and faith in Buber's conception of the primary dialogic has a considerable bearing on his development of such a methodology. The dialogic relation, as he says in *Eclipse of God*, is itself the primary reality — what is decisive is that I relate myself to the divine as to Being which is over against me.'[75] Believing and knowing are two of the main relational modes through which this primary dialogic is attained. Faith is the relation to 'a believed in, unconditionally affirmed, absolute Being or God.'[76] Knowledge is similarly a function of essential meeting with otherness in its finite and absolute forms: 'Only he reaches the meaning who stands firm, without holding or reservation before the might of reality and answers it in a living way.'[77] Such a relation would have to be expressed purely in terms of meeting or betweenness, in the lived immediacy of its occurrence, in its existential concreteness as an encounter of faith whose meaning is known in the reciprocity of the relation itself. Yet it would be wrong to infer from Buber's identification of the intersubjective as the primary concern of the anthropologist that his methodology did not embrace the function of objectification also. The world of objective phenomena, as he saw it, is the concern principally of the I in its relation to the world of things (the world of It), and is particularly the domain of the scientist. In anthropological terms, however, the observation of the It-world has a limited relevance, though in *I and Thou* Buber spoke of the constitutive functions of I-It relationships as potential sources of the I-Thou.[78] But if the ultimacy and primacy of relation were to be expressed adequately this would require the kind of totalizing methodology which would encompass the whole being of man in all its possible modes of relation.

There are some important pointers as to how this was achieved by Buber in his writings on the religious philosophy of Franz Rosenzweig. By the time he came to write *I and Thou* he had encountered a developed methodology in Rosenzweig's *The Star of Redemption* which bore remarkable similarities to his own. Rosenzweig, his friend and collaborator on a translation of the Bible, had attacked Hegelian philosophy in *Understanding the Sick and the Healthy*[79] and had evolved a religious philosophy which had strong proto-existentialist tendencies. He sought in *The Star of Redemption*, as Buber did in *I and Thou*, to disengage religion from rationalistic philosophy. The word religion does not occur in *The Star*, but its primary concerns are relational in the non-theological, religious sense that Buber's are in *I and Thou*. The three relations specified by Rosenzweig are those between God and the world, between God and man, and between God, man and world i.e., the relations of creation, revelation and redemption. The threefold relation is seen as a reality which is primary, irreducibly given, and known only in the experience of its reciprocity. Buber, in a commemorative essay on Rosenzweig that reveals much of his own thinking on methodology, analysed the particular style of philosophizing exemplified in *The Star* and described by Rosenzweig himself in an appended supplement called 'The New Thinking'. Rosenzweig distinguished between the thinking which is directed towards externality and otherness and that which looks towards the concrete situation of the subject himself in his confrontation with otherness. It was a mode of thinking, Buber wrote, which 'availed itself of the philosopher's concrete existence.'[80] Rosenzweig did not rationalize, deduce or objectify, but through a method which Buber describes as 'narrative evocation'[81] sought to illuminate the livid, concrete reality of the subject in its relation to the otherness which it addressed. He speaks of a genuine alliance of interpretive and evocative method in *The Star*, of a *realized* truth which is not reducible to dogma, creed, proposition or logicized statement:

> The architectontic of *The Star* is of a purity and legitimacy of correspondences such as I have not found in any other writing of our time, and it is a dynamic one. As the three 'substances' of which it speaks — God, man, world — can only be understood in their relations — creation, revelation, redemption — so these must not be frozen into principles; they must remain in the 'entirely real' time, they must be *narrated*[82] (my italics).

Buber differed from Rosenzweig on issues such as the nature of ethical action, and Rosenzweig, for his part, though a fervent believer in Judaism, did not share Buber's passion for Hasidism. Otherwise, their links were remarkably close, especially on the methodology of philosophical and religious affirmation. The narrative-evocative method, the dynamic of correspondences, the fact of realization are strongly paralelled in the concepts of myth-creation, 'pointing to' and essential witnessing in Buber's reflections on method in his autobiographical writings. In his old age he wrote of his aversion to typological labelling, and insisted he merely created a philosophical framework for the decisive encounters of his life, all of which became present, he said, 'as one great experience of faith.'[83] He spoke of supralogical realities that would be expressed not through a systematized theology, but through a 'connected body of thought', 'resolved in itself', 'more transmittable'[84] than the theological. He described his philosophy as a 'witness to a meeting': to a dialogic that would not be transmitted conceptually, but, in a phrase he used frequently, 'pointed to': 'I have no teaching — I only point to something. I point to reality. I point to something in reality that had not or had too little been seen.'[85] On the possible charge of subjectivism he simply reaffirmed the everyday, observable character of the reality pointed to: "The experience for which I witnessed is naturally a limited one. But is is not to be understood as a "subjective" one. I have tested it through by appeal and test it ever anew. I say to him who listens to me: "It is your experience. Recollect it and what you cannot recollect, dare to attain it as experience".'[86] 'Metaphysical impressionism'[87] and 'radical empiricism'[88] are some of the terms that have been used to describe Buber's anthropology. Neither seems adequate to describe the relational immediacy of the dialogic, and the second term has connotations that conflict fundamentally with the definition of 'experience' in *I and Thou*. An important key to his method is given in a prose work, *Daniel*, which was written some years before *I and Thou* and anticipates several of its major themes. Of the five 'Dialogues on Realization' in *Daniel*, the fourth deals particularly with problems of structure and form. Having taken as his main theme in the work the distinction between an 'orienting' response to reality and the fulfilled relation of 'realized' truth, he writes of the inclusive character of myth, its unifying and embodying functions, and its formal expression of the truth realized in the relation of the knower to the known:

> As in myth, a significant event of nature or mankind, say the life of a hero, is not registered in a knowable connection, but is preserved as something precious and consecrated in itself, adorned with the pride of all the spheres and elevated as a meaningful constellation in the heaven of inward existence . . . so he who stands in the love of the world does not know a part of a continuity but an event which is fully complete and formed in itself as a symbol and seal which bears all meaning. This is meaning: *the mythical truth of the unconstrained knower*[89] (my italics).

Grete Schaeder, author of an important study of Buber and editor of his letters, sees the poetic as the element which brings the whole person into focus in *I and Thou:* 'The speech of poetry', she writes, 'remains indispensable to him. . . But he does not succumb to intoxication or confuse religious dedication with aesthetic enthusiasms. He opens himself to the whole of reality.'[90] A recently published biography of Buber [91] displays for the first time the range of his poetic output over a period of seventy years and fully vindicates the claims made for the refining presence of a poetic energy in his work. These diverse but interrelating styles — the narrative-evocative, the witnessing and pointing to, the poetic and the mythic — intimate something of the complexity of a methodology consciously devised to reach beyond the rational and the objectified and to embrace the rational dialogic in its primacy and immediacy. And yet, as Buber confirmed in one of his autobiographical essays,[92] he turned whenever necessary to the It-ness of analytic commentary. The closely reasoned logic of his writing on the German idealists, the materialists and existentialists, on which most of this chapter has focussed, is an instance of his capacity to engage the rational when he considered such a procedure was necessary. As he said, with characteristic succinctness: 'I had to make an It out of that which was experienced in I-Thou and as I- Thou.'[93] But the mythic proved to be a particularly enduring feature of his anthropological methodology, for in Hasidic Judaism he encountered a culture as full of mythic purity as the scriptures from which the zaddikim drew the inspiration for their legends and stories. In Hasidism the mythicizing function attained a perfection and consistency unknown in western philosophy; it was, as Buber intimated in this passage from his Introduction to *The Legend of the Baal Shem*, the unifying link between his philosophical anthropology and his Judaism:

> In myth there is no division of essential being. It knows multiplicity but not duality. Even the hero only stands on another rung than that of the god, not over against him: they are not the I and Thou. The hero has a mission but not a call. He ascends but he does not become transformed. The god of pure myth does not call, he begets; he sends forth the one whom he begets, the hero. The god of the legend calls forth the son of man — the prophet, the holy man. The legend is the myth of I and Thou, of the caller and the called, the finite which enters into the infinite and the infinite which has need of the finite.[94]

# III

# The Cultural Roots of Buber's Educational Thought

> The realer religion is, so much the more it means its own overcoming. It wills to cease to be the special domain 'Religion' and wills to become life.[1]
>
> In the last resort, religious life means concreteness itself, the whole concreteness of life without reduction, grasped dialogically, included in the dialogue.[2]
>
> I must confess that I don't like religion very much and I am very glad that in the Bible the word is not ever found. I even feel that nothing in the world is as apt to mask the face of God as religion if it means religion instead of knowing God.[3]

The relational I-Thou, in its interhuman and divine-human forms, lies at the centre of the search by Buber for a philosophical and a religious anthropology. I have endeavoured in the previous chapter to show that its reality is established in his purely anthropological writings through a methodology which embraces analytic, narrative-descriptive and mythic styles. Indeed, the precise character of the anthropology can be defined quite adequately on this basis alone, and its basic principles can be explained without reference to religious traditions.[4] But a more enriched understanding comes from those writings in which Buber examined the Jewish traditions which he inherited from his parents and grandparents, which he abandoned in adult life but re-embraced subsequently in a form that was quite distinct from the Judaism of his childhood. As the excerpts quoted above will confirm, he maintained a thoroughly unconventional relation to Judaism throughout the whole of his adult life; he did not, so far as we know, observe the rites of the Jewish faith and there are several instances in his writings of a distinction between genuine 'religiosity' and religious orthodoxy.[5] He drew heavily, nonetheless, on aspects of Judaism that strengthened and reinforced his dialogic thought. The specific tradition towards which he turned, and which he re-interpreted in a substantial body of writings, was the Hasidic Judaism of the East European Jewish communities amongst whom he spent his early youth. In several ways, this tradition of Judaism renewed and vitalized the religious insights of his anthropological writings. This chapter will attempt to show how this process occurred. It will be necessary, first, to examined the historical evolution of Hasidism from its beginnings in the

1770s to its eventual rapprochement with rabbinic Judaism in the face of the twin threats of secular Zionism and anti-semitic hostility in the late eighteenth and early nineteenth centuries. Buber's autobiographical recounting of his personal rediscovery of Hasidism will be discussed also, together with the major themes of his Hasidic writings and their impact on his dialogic philosophy. The relationship of the Jewish to the Christian faith and Buber's exegetic writings on Scripture will be considered briefly, and some discussion will follow on the contemporary relevance of Hasidism, and specifically, on its links with modern existentialist and phenomenological philosophies.

## 1  The Historical Evolution of Hasidic Judaism
It is essential to have some understanding of the social and cultural traditions of Polish Jewry before any attempt is made to explain the emergence of the Hasidic communities in the southern provinces of Poland in the 1770s.[6] Small numbers of Jews had come to Poland in the eleventh and twelfth centuries from the Crimea, Russia and the Middle East, but the first major migration occurred in the fifteenth century when several thousand Ashkenazic,[7] Yiddish-speaking communities arrived from Spain. By 1500 A.D. Polish Jews numbered 15,000;[8] by the end of the Thirty Years' War (1648) this number had grown to 150,000.[9] Members of the settled communities worked as managers of large estates, as merchants, craftsmen, fiscal agents, money-lenders and manufacturers of various agricultural products. Usually, they adopted the Ashkenazic system of self-government; the local kehillot elected a ruling committee to collect taxes and provide for educational and social needs. At the centre of the community structure was the Rabbinate, elected for its expertise in talmudic law, and entrusted with an almost absolute authority on most matters affecting the communities. Rabbis had a particular function in the organization of yeshivah or talmudic academies for the education of Jewish youth. Boys were trained in the techniques of textual exegesis, the subtleties of talmudic argument, and interpretation of the sacred books. The cohesion and self-sufficiency of these communities was a significant factor in their integration into Polish life.[10]

The first major threat to Polish Jews came at the end of the Thirty Years War when Cossacks of the Ukraine revolted against their landlords (many of them Polish noblemen) and marched into Poland, slaughtering large numbers of Poles and Jews. A Russian invasion of North-East Poland and a further invasion by the Swedes followed within a few years. By 1660 the country was almost totally in the control of Ukrainians, Russians and Swedes. The Jews, who were regarded as agents of the Polish nobility by the Russians and as allies of the Swedes by Polish partisans, died in great numbers. Massacres of entire Jewish communities occurred at Nemirov, Tulczyn,

Ostrog and Naval. Epidemic and famine increased the death-toll. It was estimated[11] that one-quarter of all Jews in Poland died in the fighting. As the political decline of Poland continued, constant intervention by foreign powers added to the insecurities of Jewish life. Further blood libels continued and yet another massacre of Jews took place at Uman in 1768. Shortly afterwards, in 1772, large sectors of Polish territory were annexed by Russia, Prussia and Austria. The second and third Partitions of Poland followed in 1793 and 1795.

Against this background of social and political turmoil, a split developed between the followers of rabbinic Judaism and the masses of Jews who were drawn by the teachings of the 'holy men' or 'Hasidim'. The Hasidim, who had revolted against the intellectuality of rabbinic Judaism, based their teaching on the Kabbala,[12] a series of Jewish mystical writings, of which the most prominent was the Zohar collection that appeared in Spain in 1250 and had become the main source-book for Kabbalist study by the seventeenth century. The Hasidim took the central concepts of their faith from the Kabbala, but transformed its gnostic and theosophical teachings into a simple everyday piety which held an immense appeal for the masses who had by then grown disillusioned with the elitist intellectualism of rabbinic Judaism. The Hasidic reforms did not, however, lead to a total substitution of pietistic spirtuality for the traditional orientation of Judaism towards the study of talmudic and Biblical texts. Hasidism, Buber says, united two traditions, 'without adding anything essentially different to them other than a new light and a new strength.'[13]

From the Polish provinces of Podolia and Wolhynia where Hasidism first appeared at the beginning of the eighteenth century the movement spread throughout most of southern Poland, parts of North-East Hungary, the Moldau valley and the Ukraine. The guiding figure in the movement in the early years was Israel ben Eleazer, the Baal-Shem Tov (Master of the Good Name), a teacher from Okop in Podolia who spent some years contemplating the mysteries of the Kabbala in the solitude of the Carpathian mountains, before returning to Podolia in the 1730s to minister to the spiritual needs of the local Jewish community. His gifts for story-telling and his reputation as a healer drew a large following of disciples who also preached a life of prayer, based on a hallowing of everyday experiences. The successor to the Baal-Sham Tov, the Maggid of Meseritch, Dov Baer, continued to emphasize the pietistic character of Hasidic Judaism, but defined a firmer foundation for it in traditional Jewish learning and the writings of earlier Jewish mystics. The Hasidim radically reinterpreted the role of the rabbi (or zaddik); he now became the spiritual leader of the masses rather than the mere 'teacher' of Jewish tradition. To their followers the zaddikim were intermediaries between God and man despite long-standing Jewish opposition to any concept of religious ministry; unlike the rabbis also, they provided guidance on everyday living and encouraged a comradeship such as rarely existed in the austere study-houses.

Opposition to the Hasidic reforms had been growing, however, in Lithuania where prosperous Jewish communities were vitalizing the more learned traditions of rabbinic Judaism under the leaderhip of Elijah ben Zalman, usually known as the Gaon of Vilna. The Gaon, a learned commentator on the sacred texts of Judaism, strongly advocated asceticism and the pursuit of learning as the traditional pathways to ultimate union with God. He denounced the Hasidic reforms for their trivialization of learning and ritual, and for their elevation of the zaddik to the status of minister or spiritual intermediary. Hostilities between the two sides increased as the Hasidim charged their opponents (the Mithnagdim) with indifference to the needs of the masses. Hasidic writings were burned publicly in the rabbinic strongholds of Lithuania and Northern Poland, while the mithnagdim suffered persecution in the southern provinces and other centres of Hasidic teaching. Both sides became deeply entrenched in their own communities until a common enemy, the Haskalah[14] (Jewish Enlightenment) caused them to suppress their differences and unite against the threat of secular Zionism.

At the time of Buber's discovery of Hasidism, the Mithnagedic and Hasidic leaders had already formed the Agudat Israel (League of Israel) to combat the spread of secular ideologies amongst all Jewish communities. By the 1920s the Agudat had become an important political and social movement throughout Central and Eastern Europe and maintained an extensive network of schools where traditional Jewish teaching was promoted. Many philosophers opposed to positivism and marxism were attracted by the non-rationalistic, semi-mystical character of Hasidism. Apart from Buber, whose interest in the movement will be discussed presently, two modern Jewish writers, Hillel Zeitlin[15] and Abraham Joshua Heschel,[16] developed philosophies that drew heavily on Hasidic teaching. Zeitlin, a Warsaw Jew who died in 1942 on his way to the extermination camp at Treblinka, discovered in Hasidism an orientation towards everyday sanctification that coincided closely with his own somewhat unorthodox Jewish beliefs. Heschel, also a Warsaw Jew, who in the post-war years worked mainly in the U.S.A., developed a synthesis of phenomenology and Hasidic piety that has some parallels with the existentialist/Hasidic synthesis of Buber's thought.

## 2   Buber's Rediscovery of Hasidism
It was largely through Buber's retelling of its legends, and his coherent interpretations of Hasidic teaching, that it claimed the attention of scholars such as Zeitlin and Heschel. Buber himself has described his 'rediscovery'

of Hasidism in several of his autobiographical writings.[17] A passage from
*Between Man and Man* tells of his progress from German mysticism — to
which he had turned for a fulfilment of the spiritual needs that remained
unsatisfied by the Zionist nationalism in which he was involved since his
student years at Vienna and Leipzig — to the non-ascetical, life-affirming
mysticism of the Polish Hasidim: 'Since 1900 I had first been under the
influence of German mysticism from Meister Eckhart to Angelus Silesius,
according to which the primal ground of being, the nameless, impersonal
godhead, comes to birth in the human soul; then I had been under the
influence of the later Kabbala and of Hasidism, according to which man has
the power to unite the God who is over the world with his *shekinah* dwelling
in the world.'[18] Buber had been introduced in early childhood to Hasidic
prayer practices by his grandfather, Solomon Buber, with whom he lived for
some time after his parents' divorce. Solomon Buber, though himself a
well-known Midrashic scholar, went on occasions to pray with the Hasidim
and took his grandson to the prayer-meetings. Buber in 'My Way to
Hasidism' recalls childhood impressions of his grandfather's simplicity and
great devotion to learning — 'The spiritual passion which manifested itself
in his incessant work was combined with the untouchable, imperturbable
childlikeness of a pure human nature and an elementary Jewish being'[19] —
as well as the companionship and unsophisticated holiness of the Hasidic
communities they visited:

> This I realized at that time, as a child, in the dirty village of Sadagora from
> the "dark" Hasidic crowd that I watched . . . that the world needs the
> perfected man and that the perfected man is none other than the true helper.
> . . . At that time there arose in me a presentiment of the fact that common
> reverence and common joy of soul are the foundations of genuine human
> community.[20]

This childhood passion for the religious was soon to decline, however, and
it was some years again before Buber recovered his enthusiasm for Hasidic
Judaism. His temporary abandonment of Judaism coincided with a
developing interest in Nietzsche and Kant.[21] Seized by the 'fermenting
intellectuality'[22] of idealism and existentialism, he turned also to another
German tradition — that of the seventeenth century mystics, Boehme and
Eckhart. An essay on Boehme[23] which appears in 1901 suggests a reluctant
approval by Buber of the solitude and asceticism of German mysticism, but
the publication in 1906 of an edition of the writings of Meister Eckhart by
his close friend, Gustav Landauer,[24] prompted a much more enthusiastic
assessment: 'All genuine creation rests in the most radical negation, all pure
world-affirmation proceeds from the most ultimate despair philosophers and
mystics of all ages have intimated; but none has won this insight for our

immediate life feeling and made it as fruitful as he (Landauer) had.'[25] Shortly before this Buber had been awarded a doctorate for his dissertation on the mysticism of Nicholas of Cusa and Jacob Boehme. In *Ecstatic Confessions* (1909) he assembled personal descriptions of mystical ecstacy from various sources, though the works cited were mainly by West European Catholic and Protestant mystics. He described this work as 'a document of the greatest importance for the soul of humanity.'[26] By the following year, however, he had radically changed his perceptions of western mysticism. His dialogue, 'With a Monist',[27] focusses on themes which entered subsequently into his Hasidic writings, such as fulfilment through unification and wholeness of being. In this work he clearly disavows the life-denying mysticism of Boehme and Eckhart. The passage where he responds to the monist's description of him as a mystic strongly anticipates the 'livid concrete' existential relation of the Hasidic mystical encounter:

> 'No,' I answered, and looked at him in a friendly way, 'for I still grant to reason a claim that the mystic must deny to it. Beyond this, I lack the mystic's negation. I can negate convictions but never the slightest actual thing. The mystic manages, truly or apparently, to annihilate the entire world, or what he so names — all that his senses present to him in perception and in memory — in order, with new disembodied senses or a wholly supersensory power, to press forward to his God. But I am enormously concerned with just this world, this painful and precious fullness of all that I see, hear, taste. I cannot wish away any part of its reality. I can only wish that I might heighten this reality.[28]

It would appear from this that Buber's interest in ascetical mysticism was short-lived, and was confined mainly to the writings of Meister Eckhart. Even then his admiration for Eckhart was closely bound up with his great personal attachment to Gustav Landauer. In response to a letter from his biographer, Maurice Friedman, Buber confirmed that he himself never practised mystical meditation.[29] Certain elements of German mysticism remained in his Hasidic writings — the themes of presentness and union, the conception of God as the incomprehensible and ineffable — but its life-denying, world-rejecting philosophy was incompatible with the radical dialogic of Hasidic Judaism to which he returned in his twenties for a religious fulfilment and for a restatement of the relational truth already emerging in his anthropological writings. In 'To a Monist' he points to the Hebrew meaning of the verb 'to know' as 'to embrace lovingly.'[30] On several occasions, in his purely philosophical writings, he asserted that true knowledge could not be reached through reason alone.[31] Of his reawakened interest in Judaism he writes: 'I professed Judaism before I really knew it. So this became, after some blind groping, my second step: wanting to know it. To know — by this I do not mean a storing up of anthropological, historical, sociological knowledge, as important as these are; I mean the immediate knowing, the eye-to-eye knowing of the people in its creative primal hours. On this way I came to Hasidism.'[32] This re-encounter with Hasidism as a world-affirming mysticism decisively determined Buber's religious development. Significantly, in his retrospective commentary, he gives particular emphasis to its 'human religiousness':

> The primarily Jewish opened to me, flowering to newly conscious expression in the darkness of exile: man's being created in the image of God I grasped as deed, as becoming, as task. And this primally Jewish reality was a primal human reality, the content of human religiousness. Judaism as religiousness, as piety, as *Hasidut* opened to me there. The image out of my childhood, the memory of the zaddik and his community, rose upward and illuminated me. I recognized the idea of the perfected man. At the same time I became aware of the summons to proclaim it to the world.[33]

His decision to withdraw from his Zionist activities and to devote himself solely to study for several years is a measure of Buber's dedication to the Hasidic way of life. For an intensely active involvement in cultural and nationalistic Zionism he substituted a life of solitude, study and prayer, but emerged from it with unshakeable convictions. He set about reworking Hasidic stories which, in many instances, had been written down verbatim from oral tradition and had not yet acquired a literary structure or form. 'My aim', he wrote in a letter to his colleague, Samuel Horodetzky, 'is not to accumulate new facts but simply to give a new interpretation of the interconnections, a new synthetic presentation of Jewish mysticism and its creations and to make these creations known to the European public in as artistically pure a form as possible.'[34] From this came the various collections of legends[35] and allegorical tales which now constitute the authentic Hasidic tradition. In a letter to a friend after the pogrom against the Jews at Bialystok in 1906 Buber described the excitement of this work and its importance for the revivification of Judaism: 'I am writing now a story which is my answer to Bialystok . . . I have a new answer to give to everything. Now only have I found the form for my answer. I have grown inward into my heaven — my life begins. I experience nameless suffering and nameless grace.'[36] He spoke of the translator's task as one requiring genuine dialogue with the legends and their authors, a sense of faithfulness in the rendering, and, as he expressed it graphically in his introduction to *The Legend of the Baal Shem*, an intimacy based on heredity, rootedness, 'blood':

> I have received it from folk-books, from note-books and pamphlets, at times also from a living mouth, from the mouths of people still living who even in their lifetime heard this stammer. I have received it and have told it anew.

I have not transcribed it like some piece of literature; I have not elaborated it like some fabulous material. I have told it anew as one who was born later. I bear in me the blood and the spirit of those who created it, and out of my blood and spirit it has become new. I stand in the chain of narrators, a link between links; I tell once again the old stories, and if they sound new, it is because the new already lay dormant in them when they were told for the first time.[37]

The germ of the I-Thou dialogic can be traced in Buber's versions of the Hasidic legends to a collection that was published as early as 1907[38] — some sixteen years before the appearance of *I and Thou*. Two stories from the collection, 'The Return' and 'From Strength to Strength', vividly exemplify the reality of comradeship and love in terms of encounter at the level of interhuman and divine-human dialogue. Some years later, introducing a further collection, *The Great Maggid and his Followers*, Buber spoke of man's love for his fellowmen as the means by which he comes to know and love God. It is a theme whic pervades all the Hasidic legends and the one which identifies the spirit of Hasidism as a world-affirming celebration of the immanent presence of God and his accessibility to man through the world which He created:

> In other teachings the God-soul, sent or released by heaven to earth, could be called home or freed to return home by heaven; creation and redemption take place in the same direction, from 'above' to 'below'. But this is not so in a teaching which, like the Jewish, is so wholly based upon the double-directional relation to the human I and the divine Thou, on the reality of reciprocity, on the *meeting*. Here man, this miserable man, is, by the very meaning of his creation, the helper of God. . . . God waits for him. From him, from 'below' the impulse toward redemption must proceed. Grace is God's *answer*.[39]

## 3  *The Major Themes of Buber's Hasidic Writings*

Buber's versions of the legends and his exegetic commentaries reveal the centrality of the dialogic relation in the whole Hasidic way of life. The core of Hasidism, he said, is man's entering into dialogue with God through his address to God's creation: 'Man cannot reach the divine by reaching *beyond* the human; he can approach him through becoming human. To become human is what he, this individual man, has been created for. . . . You cannot really love God if you do not love men, and you cannot really love men if you do not love God.'[40] The religious element is here no longer separated from the common, existential situation of man in his relation to the world and to his fellow-man. As a religion, Hasidism strives for the renewal of the person on the level of everyday life and through this seeks the fulfilment of his relation to God. Buber writes of God's participation in the destiny of his creation through his unification of two spheres frequently separated by religion, the heavenly and the human: 'Above and below — the decisive importance is ascribed to the "below". Here on the outermost margin of having become, the fate of the aeons is decided. The human world is the world of authentication.'[41]

Since it aims at the sanctification of all life, of every thought, purpose and deed, Hasidism strongly supports the ideal of authentication developed by Buber in his philosophical and ethical writings.[42] To the Hasid there was no radical distinction between the sacred and the profane: the profane was merely a preliminary stage of the holy; it was the not-yet hallowed. The separation, therefore, of religion from everyday life, its existence as a ritual remote from the world of common activity, the application of faith within the province only of the separate sphere of the religious, the restriction of activities claimed for hallowing or sanctifying — these and other symptoms of the modern disillusionment with religion discussed by Buber in *Eclipse of God* are healed in the Hasidic teaching that life can be regenerated constantly at the level of common experience. Buber's elucidation of the teaching conveys its fundamental simplicity:

> Basically the holy in our world is nothing other than what is open to transcendence, as the profane is nothing other than what at first is closed off from it, and hallowing is the event of opening out. . . . They (the teachings of the Hasidim) can be summed up in a single sentence: God can be beheld in each thing and reached through each pure deed.[43]

The virtues of service, presentness and prayer are the particular manifestations of man's willingness to engage in dialogue. In Hasidic terminology *avoda*[44] is man's acknowledgement of his willingness to serve God through the spiritual service of study and prayer and the corporeal service of hallowed activity. It is the means to *devekut*:[45] man's unceasing attestation of God's presence, his active searching for reciprocity, his presentness to God and to the world in which this reciprocity is manifested. Hasidic mysticism is essentially, therefore, an attachment to the world. Unlike the world-denying mysticism of Eckhart and other Christian writers, it advocates a striving towards union with God through a union also with the world of God's creation. 'It is a mysticism', Buber says, 'that may be called such because it preserves the immediacy of the relation, guards the concreteness of the absolute and demands the involvement of the whole being.'[46]

This conscious and intentioned quest for the divine finds expression particularly in the act of prayer, an important and habitual feature of the Hasidic way of life. In *The Origin and Meaning of Hasidism* and in his Hasidic novel, *For the Sake of Heaven*, Buber illustrates the fervour of

Hasidic prayer. In the first work he cites the advice given by the Kabbalist scholar, Isaac Luria,[47] to disciples who had complained of a loss of vitality in their praying: 'You have put all your strength and all your striving for the goal of your thoughts into the *kavanot*[48] of the holy names and the intertwined letters and have fallen away from what is essential: to make the heart whole and to unite it to God — therefore you have lost the life and feeling of holiness.'[49] *For the Sake of Heaven* describes the Yehudi's habit of delaying his prayer until the moment of genuine fervour has come. In this passage he is replying to the remonstrations of his friend at his apparent *neglect* of prayer:

> The word, that it may be a living word, needs *us*. True, it has appointed times and seasons. But those who neglect them and wait do not do so in order to have an easier time. They tarry till they can enter wholly into the spirit of the praying and thus prepare in their aloneness the rebirth of the congregation. When I stand alone before the Lord , I stand there, not as a single soul before its Maker, but as the community of Israel before its God.[50]

Buber's description of the Hasidic dialogue as a mystical union between man and God needs to be clarified, in view of his use of the term, with significantly different connotations, in his writings on Boehme and Eckhart. He stresses the active character of the Hasidic *yihud*,[51] describing it not as a 'subjective' but a 'subjective-objective' event — an 'event of meeting' in which the identities of the self and the other are maintained. Following Kabbalist teaching he writes of an essential unity between God and his creation, and of man's quest for union as a dynamic striving for this. Secondly, he distinguishes the *yihud* union from the magical. The latter is defined as the influence exerted by a subject on a power greater than himself, but which he compels into action through the exercise of magical power. *Yihud*, however, is a joining anew of spheres temporarily apart, a response by man to God's intention towards unity in his creation: '*Yihud* signifies not the influence of a subject upon an object but the working out of the objective in a subjectivity and through it, of existing being in and through what is becoming.'[52] The hallowing of the worldly is the means to the achievement of *yihud*: its source is the non-magical practice of prayer associated with the Lurian[53] tradition of Kabbalism.

An implicit distinction between Hasidic and Christian mysticism occurs in the sixth section of *The Origin and Meaning of Hasidism*. Buber cites Plotinus in support of a phenomenon common to all varieties of Christian mysticism: 'What is decisive is that the act of contemplating is obliterated in the contemplator; not the dissolution of the phenomenal multiplicity, but that of the constructive duality, the duality of experiencing I and experienced object.'[54] What is commonly known as the ecstasy of mystical experience is the temporary suppression of the duality of the I and its subject (God) in the rare moments of total union between the two. The Christian mystic strives, therefore, for a union with a Godhead of pure being, above and *before* creation, transcending the duality of God and world. The Hasidic mystics, however, followed an old Jewish distinction between this Godhead of pure being (*YHVH*)[55] and God who became Person or *Elohim*[56] through the becoming of creation and who extends his love to man and the world and invites its reciprocity. The mystic's love, in this instance, is an entering into *reciprocity*, an acceptance of its duality, its concrete immediacy, its hallowed time-bound reality:

> He is the great lover who has set man in the world in order to be able to love him — but there is no perfect love without reciprocity, and He, the original God, accordingly longs that man should love Him. Everything follows from this, all teaching, all 'morality', for in the innermost core nothing is wanted and nothing is demanded from above but love of God. Everything follows from this; for man cannot love God in truth without loving the world in which He has set His strength and over which his Shekina rests. People who love each other in holy love bring each other toward the love with which God loves His world. In Hasidism — and in it alone, so far as I can see, in the history of the human spirit — mysticism has become *ethos*. Here the primal mystical unity in which the soul wants to be merged is no other form of God than the demander of the demand. Here the mystical soul cannot become real if it is not one with the moral.[57]

## 4  The Way of the Hasidim

The close relationship of Hasidism to existentialism will be apparent from the foregoing discussion of the centrality of the dialogic relation in Buber's Hasidic writings, just as previously the existentialist character of the dialogic was established in his philosophical anthropology. Their interrelation may be further demonstrated through a consideration of the values, ideals and virtues peculiar to the Hasidic way of life. The Hasidic emphasis on the uniqueness of the religious relationship might be said, in some respects, even to anticipate the phenomenalist personalism of Kierkegaard's *Christian Discourses*, despite significant differences between Kierkegaard and the Hasidim on the question of ascetic renunciation and withdrawal from the world. There are many examples given of the highly particularized character of Hasidic religiousness in Buber's expository studies and in his versions of the legends. In *Hasidism and Modern Man*, for example, he cites the response of Rabbi Baer of Redoshitz to the Seer of Lublin who had asked him to indicate a 'general way' to the service of God. The Rabbi replied: 'It is impossible to tell men what way they should take. For one way to serve God is through learning, another through prayer, another through fasting and still another through eating. Everyone should carefully observe what way his heart draws him to, and then choose this way with all his strength.'[58]

This individualized relationship to God is strongly reinforced in the Hasidic ideal of *hitlahavut*, defined literally by Buber as 'the inflaming of the moment'.[59] In Hasidic teaching *hitlahavut* grows from the sanctification of all deeds and events in the moment of their occurrence.

Buber writes of a commutation of past and future in the existent moment, an ecstacy in time attained through the consecration of present action: 'Time shrinks, the line between the eternities disappears, only the moment lives and the moment is eternity.'[60] In this, however, there exists a paradox that runs through all of Buber's dialogic writings, both philosophical and religious. It was shown earlier that the interpersonal dialogue expands naturally into the social, communal relationship:[61] that the I-Thou finds fulfilment ultimately in the I-We-ness of community life. Similarly, the uniqueness of the Hasidic relation between man and God, and the existential uniqueness of the sanctifying action of *hitlahavut*, find completion not in an individualized solitude, but in the closeness of Hasidic brotherhood.

Hasidism, therefore, strongly confirms the interrelating dialogic and social philosophies of Buber's anthropological commentaries. The very essence of its faith is the striving for santification through brotherhood. He writes enthusiastically of the 'democratic' society created by the Hasidim to replace the aristocratic hierarchies of rabbinic Judaism. The unenlightened Polish and Lithuanian Jewry brought forth a phenomenon he describes as unique in the history of the spirit — a 'society that lives by its faith'[62] A passage in *The Origin and Meaning of Hasidism* describes how the Hasidic movement, through the simplification of its mythic teaching, did not dilute the original Jewish traditions, but rendered them accessible to the Jewish populace and created a spirit of brotherhood where none had previously existed:

> Its spiritual structure was founded upon the handing on of the kernel of the teaching from teacher to disciple, but not as if something not accessible to everyone, was transmitted to him, but because in the atmosphere of the master, in the spontaneous working of his being, the inexpressible How descended swinging and creating. The very same teaching, only blended and less condensed, was communicated in the word of counsel and instruction, and was developed in the customs and brotherly life of the community. This absence of ranks in the sphere of its teaching, this anti-hierarchical position insured Hasidism its popular power. As it did not abolish from without the precedence of possession, but removed its value from within through uniting rich and poor as equal members, before God and the zaddik, of a community of reciprocal outer and inner help, a community of love; so it overcame, in its highest moments fully, the far stronger, in Judaism elementally strong, precedence of learning, the

> Talmudic but also the Kabbalistic. The "spiritual" man, the man who works
> with his brains, is by his nature no closer to the divine, indeed, so long as
> he has not gathered the multiplicity and ambiguity of his life into unity, so
> long as he has not subdued the violence of his pains to composure, he is
> farther from the divine than the simple man who, with the simple trust of
> the peasant, leaves his cause to heaven.[63]

The individualized quest for the divine, the doctrine that salvation is
attained through brotherhood, and the ideal of the santification of all action
in the existent moment of its occurrence, leads to a concept of redemption
which differs radically from the Christian teaching that man is redeemed
through Christ's sacrifice on the cross.[64] Buber distinguishes the 'saviour'
religions (Christianity and Buddhism) from Judaism on the basis of their
conflicting approaches to this. To the 'saviour' religions redemption is an
*historical* fact, one transcending history yet localized within it, while in
Judaism it is an ever-recurring prospect.[65] In Christianity the decisive act of
redemption has taken place and is renewed in man's union with Christ; in
Hasidic Judaism it occurs in the here and now, in man's constant, intentioned
striving for sanctification.[66] It is an everyday, existential experience, a
constant exercise by man of the freedom granted him by God, a response to
God's indwelling in his creation. The radically existentialist character of the
concept is conveyed in this definition of the messianic function:

> The Hasidic message of redemption stands in opposition to the Messianic
> self-differentiation of one man from other men, of one time from other
> times, of one act from other actions. All mankind is accorded the co-working
> power, all time is directly redemptive, all action for the sake of God may
> be Messianic action.[67]

Two metaphors particularly favoured by Buber express the precarious
nature of this existential quest for the redemptive. The first is what he
described as the state of 'holy insecurity:'[68] man's sense of the impotence of
knowledge, of the incongruence of 'possessed truth' — his lack of certainty
in the face of the divine. Amongst his criticisms of the Kabbala one was the
'inner certitude' underlying its highly systematized doctrinal content: a
certitude, he observes in *The Origin and Meaning of Hasidism*, which was
significantly modified by the zaddikim.[69] The second metaphor is closely
linked with this and, while it was developed mainly by Buber in his
philosophical writings, it originates in Hasidic legend. This is the image of
the 'narrow ridge' which was first used in an early version of *The Legend of
the Baal Shem*. Buber's biographer, Maurice Friedman, has translated the
passage from the story in which the image first occurs:

> The angel of the Lord seized me in the night, and I stood in the void. . .

There was a circle between two abysses, a narrow round ridge. And within this circle was a red abyss like a sea of blood, and outside of it stretched a black abyss like a sea of night. And I saw: a man walked on the ridge like a blindman, with staggering feet, and his two weak hands rested on the abysses to the right and to the left, and his breast was of glass, and I saw his heart flutter like sick leaves in the wind, and on his forehead was the sign of ice. . . . And already he was near the end of the circle which is its beginning. . . and the man suddenly looked up and saw to the right and to the left, and he stumbled and out of the abysses arms rose to catch him. . .Then the man raised his wings, and no weakness and no numbness was in him any longer, and the ridge disappeared underneath his feet, and God's fountains of water swallowed the abyss of blood, and the abyss of the night disappeared into God's light, and the city of the Lord lay there, open in all directions.[70]

Buber himself in 'What Is Man?' indicates how aptly this image conveys the existential problematic of man's pursuit of the redemptive : 'I wanted by this to express that I did not rest on the broad upland of a system that includes a series of sure statements about the absolute, but on a narrow rocky ridge between the gulfs where there is no sureness of expressible knowledge but the certainty of meeting that remains undisclosed.[71]

This discussion of Buber's interpretations of Hasidic tradition would be seriously incomplete if no mention were made of the controversies they have provoked amongst a number of Jewish scholars. Seltzer in his monumental *Jewish People, Jewish Thought* points to a tendency by Buber to read his own existentialist predilections into Hasidism,[72] though his comments suggest an excessive emphasis by Buber on those aspects of Hasidism that confirmed his anthropological insights, rather than radical misinterpretations of Hasidic teaching. A Hebrew scholar, Rivkah Schatz-Uffenheimer, in a lengthy analysis,[73] suggests that Buber overemphasized the relation to the concrete as a means to *devekut*: that the concrete has a secondary importance in Hasidic teaching, and that *devekut* ultimately involves a relinquishing of the secular world and all sensory phenomena.[74] He writes of a latent gnosticism[75] in Hasidic doctrine that Buber overlooked in his repeated insistence that evil is merely the not-yet hallowed. The following passage gives a fair indication of the main substance of this critique:

I think that Buber's excessive concentration on the element of the encounter of man and God within the world gives rise to a disproportion in his rendering of the Hasidic world image: he purchases the redemption of the moment at the price of that which was the declared goal of Hasidism. He wishes to see the goal in the 'moment' itself; he abhors the pretensions to greatness, the Messianic phrases 'I have come in order to. . .'; he has no love for the banners proclaiming the goal by its name. The goal must remain hidden, undefined, for otherwise it is doomed to burst apart. Buber is indeed correct in his feeling that in this respect Hasidism was more moderate than the movement that preceded it, Sabbatianism; but it by no means stands for an atomistic ideology in which every moment and every action is of equal worth and equally endowed with 'sacramental possibility.'[76]

Louis Jacobs reiterates the view that Buber misrepresents Hasidic teaching on the ultimate annihilation of the self in a union with God which is reached through God's creation, but is divested finally of all links with the phenomenal world.[77]

Buber in 'Replies to my Critics' responded that he had not aimed at 'a historically or hermeneutically comprehensive presentation of Hasidism.'[78] His intention, he wrote, was to 'act as a filter'[79] for some of its most remarkable insights and achievements. In a consciously selective inter- pretation, which clearly shows the influence of existentialism, he declared that he had sought to convey its 'proper truth' — the fervour of its faith, its non-ascetic emphasis, its central dialogic, its authenticating ethic, its vital embracing of the everyday, its hallowing of lived life, its inherent simplicity, its fundamental extension of the interpersonal into the sphere of the social. On the issue of gnosticism he cites the authority of Gershom Scholem, author of *Major Trends in Jewish Mysticism*,[80] in support of his view that the Hasidim retained a *dialectic* of hallowing and radical spiritualization which existed in a more extreme form in Kabbalism, but which was refined by the zaddikim with a greater emphasis on the hallowing of the world. This, he explains at some length in the essay, is the paradox which is missed or oversimplified by his critics. The particular attention he gave to redemption was prompted by a concern to demonstrate the immediacy of the Hasidic relation between man and God and its particular relevance for the present age.

Before we consider the question of the present relevance of Hasidic teaching, it is necessary first to clarify an important issue which has not so far been mentioned. Comment on the Biblical roots of Hasidism has been avoided lest the relation of Buber's religious anthropology to Judaic Revelation should be excessively emphasized and the universal relevance he claimed for his religious thought should thereby be diminished. The validity of his religious writings can be established purely on the basis of the anthropological dialogic, as the opening chapter has attempted to show. Yet the anthropology itself is enriched immeasurably by the ancient, mythic- historical representations of these same dialogics from Biblical and Hasidic sources. Biblical Revelation has a fundamental, though by no means essential, bearing on his religious thought. It is important that it be related to the philosophical and religious traditions so far described.

## 5 The Two Types of Faith: Judaism and Christianity

Existentialism, as McQuarrie[81] and others have shown in their studies of the interpenetrations of modern philosophical and religious thought, has profoundly influenced approaches to scripture exegesis. Kierkegaard, in works such as *Christian Discourses* and *Works of Love*, prepared the way for twentieth-century exegetes such as Bultmann,[82] Ebeling[83] and Ricoeur[84] who, together with Buber, have found striking affinities between the scriptural and the existentialist understanding of the nature and destiny of man. To these writers, the Hebrew prophets of the fifth century B.C. (Amos, Hosea, Isaiah, Jeremiah) and their contemporaries, the pre-Socratic philosophers, together with the authors of Job, Ecclesiastes and the Psalms, are the real forerunners of modern existentialism. And existentialism, in turn, has provided them with an appropriate and highly adaptable hermeneutic for their interpretations of the scriptures.

Buber's involvement in Biblical scholarship began when he undertook a full translation of the Hebrew Bible into German with his friend, Franz Rosenzweig, in 1925. In addition to the actual work of translation, Buber and Rosenzweig prepared an explanatory volume[85] on the methods they had used to maintain fidelity to the original Hebrew text. Following Rosenzweig's death in 1929, Buber himself continued the work of translation for more than thirty years. He added four substantial commentaries to the collaborative study with Rosenzweig: *The Kingship of God, The Prophetic Faith, Moses* and *The Two Types of Faith*. These books, together with several complementary papers, deal with a vast range of problems in exegetic methodology, and give elaborate interpretations of Biblical texts which Buber considered relevant to his Hasidic and anthropological interests. Nahum Glatzer,[86] author of studies on Buber and Rosenzweig, indicates Buber's concern for the primacy of the spoken word and his efforts to retain the rhythmic structures of the Hebrew in the German text:

> Buber's translation of the Bible has freed the ancient text of the layers upon layers of overgrowth. The most often quoted passages especially had lost their original freshness and immediacy of impact. Primeval speech forfeited its power before the mighty array of theological, historical, psychological, and literary ideas. A language of concepts abstracted from reality replaced a language of living words. Moreover, the primary intention of the word-historically important translations, the Septuagint, the Vulgate, Luther's, was not preservation of the original character of the Bible, but establishment of a valid testimonial writ for their respective communities: the Jewish diaspora, the early Christian oikumene, the church of the Reformation. In such historically determined situations the need to accentuate certain facets of biblical teaching far outweighed concern for the structure of the text, the primal meaning of the word, and the correlation between content and form.[87]

One basic theme unifies all of Buber's writings on the Bible: from Genesis to the New Testament the narrative is essentially a record of the encounter between the Israelite people and God. The various books of the Bible elucidate different facets of the dialogic which is the primary focus of his interpretations. To illustrate the Hasidic theme of realization, for example, he quotes the Book of Amos, where God announces his plans to man and invites him to join in the fulfilment.[88] Amos is cited also on the multiple character of this encounter: the Lord's address to the people of Israel is interpreted by Buber as an expression of the dialogic I-Thou on the level of the communal as well as the interhuman.[89] The penitential dialogue is witnessed, he says, in the stories of Cain and David: each has killed and transgressed, but one finds salvation in the dialogue which the other rejects.[90] The Psalms celebrating the wonder of nature[91] attest an unending dialogue between God and the world. The world responds by glorifying his presence. The love songs[92] similarly celebrate the love of man for womankind. In this love is the seed of the infinite love manifested in the encounter between man and God. These and many other instances can be given to illustrate the application by Buber of the existentialist dialogic to the scripture narrative.

Particular attention is given by Buber to the *historical* character of the encounter which the Bible describes. The concept of 'scripture as history' is discussed in some detail in *The Prophetic Faith* and several essays. In the ancient Orient legend and song were the 'natural forms of the popular oral presentation of historical events,' he writes: 'they represent a vital kind of history memorizing as it happens.'[93] The Bible, he explains, does not necessarily depict actual events in history: its descriptions and stories are 'the organic, legitimate ways of giving an account of what existed and what happened.'[94] Its narratives are shaped by the formative, myth-creating, oral memory which produced them. But the encounters recorded represent the individualized or communal responses of the Israelite people in specific historical situations. Of these the responses of the prophets express with particular intensity the convenantal relationship between God and the Israelite people. The prophet is individual man engaged in dialogue with God: he represents individual man in the full exercise of his freedom to fulfil or to reject the divine will. On this prophetic dialogue is based an interpretation of history which Buber considered to be directly at variance with the apocalyptic theory that he identified with the Pauline view of history as the fulfilment of the divine plan for redemption, with Hegel's dialectic of universal reason, and ultimately with marxist determinism which he treated as a secularized apocalyptic. He stressed the radical character of the distinction between a freely entered into dialogue by which man influences the process of meta-historical decision, and the pre-ordained depersonalized determinism which excludes or limits the force of individual action.

The distinction between the prophetic and apocalyptic theories of history is at the centre of Buber's comparison of Christianity and Judaism: a comparison which is supported by detailed interpretations of scripture in *The Two Types of Faith*. Two basic forms of belief[95] are defined in this book: the first is defined as a spontaneous trust which includes, but does not depend upon, the process of rational thought; the second is defined as an 'acknowledgement' of truth on the evidence of logic or reasoned proof. The relationship of trust, he says, is one which engages the whole being, while the second relationship depends primarily on a rational acceptance of what is acknowledged to be true. In the first, man 'finds himself' in the relation of faith; in the second he is 'converted' to it. Buber places Christ in the company of the Hebrew prophets whose faith was based on trust and the totality of a personal dialogue with God. To this he attributes his own lifelong, personal affinity with Christ:

> For nearly fifty years the New Testament has been a main concern in my studies, and I think I am a good reader who listens impartially to what is said. From my youth onwards I have found in Jesus my great brother. That Christianity has regarded and does regard him as God and Saviour has always appeared to me a fact of the highest importance which, for his sake and my own, I must endeavour to understand. . . . My own fraternally open relationship to him has grown ever stronger and clearer, and to-day I see him more strongly and clearly than ever before. I am more than ever certain that a great place belongs to him in Israel's history of faith and that his place cannot be described in any of the usual categories.[96]

In contrasting the Christian and Jewish traditions, therefore, he has in mind not the New Testament faith of Christ — which still embodied the essential dialogic of Judaism — but the 'Hellenized' faith he associates with the teaching of Paul and the theology of the medieval and scholastic writers. The Hellenistic influence he traces in Paul has two main forms: It is, first, the knowledge-related faith of the Epistles to the Romans, Hebrews and Galatians; and secondly, it is the Pauline 'justification by faith' which diminishes the individual responsibility for the redemptive characterized in the Hebrew dialogic. In both instances the non-Jewish influence — the gnosticism of knowledge-related faith, and the gnostic concept of man as inherently disposed towards evil but already redeemed through Christ — is attributed by Buber to Greek influences from the post-Socratic period.[97] He distinguishes *devotio* from *gnosis* in the section of *The Origin and Meaning of Hasidism* where he deals with Christianity and Judaism. *Devotio* is defined as 'unreduced service to the divine made present' and *gnosis* as a 'knowing relationship to the divine' — an inner certainty 'that all is knowable.'[98] The *Two Types of Faith* gives several instances from scripture of the *devotio* of pure faith and the *gnosis* of rationalized belief. To illustrate his meaning of *devotio*, for example, he recalls Christ's 'All things are possible to him who believeth'[99] (to the boy possessed by a demon), and his rebuke to Thomas, 'Blessed are they who have not seen and yet believe.'[100] He mentions, by way of comparison, Paul's concept of faith as *elenchos*[101] i.e., rationalized conviction; he condemns Paul's misinterpretations of Abraham's simple trusting faith,[102] and his mediated, unspontaneous concept of prayer[103] which is contrasted with the prayer advocated by Christ in the Sermon on the Mount.[104]

The doctrine of justification, in Buber's view, further dilutes or even denies the Jewish teaching on individual man's existential responsibility for redemption. He speaks of the 'plain, concrete, situation-bound dialogicism' of the 'original man' of the Bible who found salvation not in the realm of supra-temporal spirit but in the depth of the actual moment.[105] He stresses the Old Testament religiosity of the *deed:* its insistence that every activity be oriented towards the divine.[106] This same striving towards deed is attested, he says, in Christ's Sermon on the Mount: in the various injunctions to action in the beatitudes, in Christ's assurance to his disciples that he had come 'not to abolish the law and the prophets but to fulfil them',[107] in his paraphrase of Leviticus, 'You shall be perfect as your heavenly Father is perfect.'[108] As a Jew, he declares, he can identify spontaneously with this teaching: 'We Jews knew him (Christ) from within, in the impulses and strivings of his Jewish being, in a way that remains inaccessible to the peoples submissive to him.'[109] But early Christianity, he argues, was diverted from all this by the syncretist elements introduced to it by Paul and his followers from Hellenist sources. In this new, misdirected, radically non-Jewish Christianity, faith assumed the primary place, to the exclusion virtually of the Jewish doctrine of sanctification through deed.[110] The Jewish 'reaching towards realization' was supplanted by a teaching according to which man himself was powerless and was saved only through the grace of 'him who knew no sin.'[111] To this Pauline reconception of Christian faith Buber traces the dualism of historical Christianity, which, with its emphasis on the intrinsic evil of the material and the worldly, its sense of human impotence and the unavailing force of human deed, culminates in the modern characterization of man as the 'radically unredeemed':

> He transmitted Jesus' teaching, transformed by this ideology, to the nations, handing them the sweet poison of faith, a faith that was to distain works, exempt the faithful from realization, and establish dualism in the world. It is the Pauline era whose death agonies we to-day are watching with transfixed eyes.[112]

Despite his declared intention to establish the relevance of the religious for the modern age, Buber on several occasions explicitly disassociated his religious writings from orthodox or conventional influences. The quotations given at the outset[113] will indicate something of his distrust of institutionalized faith. Referring in *Eclipse of God*[114] to his lifelong dedication to Biblical exegesis, he stressed that 'it was not mixed up with any orthodoxy'. While his preoccupations with Hasidism were entirely serious and profound, he confessed in an autobiographical memoir that he had carefully avoided practice of its rituals and formal observances: 'It would have been an unpermissible masquerading had I taken on the Hasidic manner of life — I who had a wholly other relation to Jewish tradition.'[115]

There was nothing formal or didactic in his relation either to scripture or to Hasidism; each had assumed for him the character of an historical or mythic reality with which he could enter into meaningful dialogue. It is on this informal, non-doctrinal basis also that he addresses the question: what is the reality of religion for man, and on what conditions can a living reality be ascribed to its historical revelation, at a time when a variety of factors conspire to render it impotent or meaningless.

I have referred to the two main causes advanced by Buber in his Biblical studies for the decline of the religious spirit. The first is the gnostic power-lessness of man he associated mainly with the Paulinist doctrine of re-demption through faith. The second is the gnostic intellectualism, and the resultant weakening of the *relation* of faith, which he attributed also to Hellenist influences in Paulinist theology. Several of the essays in *Eclipse of God, On Judaism, The Two Types of Faith* and *Israel and the World* examine the contemporary evidence for this twofold gnosticism. One of its chief manifestations, he says, is the prevailing sense of individual powerlessness in a universe irreparably in the grip of destructive forces — a modern 'demonocracy of the world', to adopt the Paulinist terminology.[116] Kafka's stranger squandering his life before the castle gateway where he begs vainly for admission is an image of man tragically unaware of the existential sources of the redemptive. His despair, however complex and elaborate its presentation in the imagery of Kafka's fiction,[117] is rooted ultimately in tendencies which Buber traces to the Paulinist corruption of the Judaeo-Christian spirit:

> Man is called into this world, he is appointed in it, but wherever he turns to fulfil his calling he comes up against the thick vapours of a mist of absurdity. This world is handed over to a maze of intermediate beings — it is a Pauline world, except that God is removed into the impenetrable darkness and that there is no place for a mediator.[118]

The contemporary alienation of man from religion is attributed in large part by Buber to the persistence of this gnosticism of the 'powerless' and the 'unredeemed'. Its accompanying gnosticism of the rational and the sceptical gains widespread acceptance also as exalted claims are made for the revelations of philosophy and science at the expense of the dialogic of faith. Taking as an example the psychology of Jung,[119] Buber questions the attempted explanation of the religious on the basis of science alone. In Jung's, as in all attempts to philosophize on the religious, he finds an untenable reductionism: the reduction of the unconditionally I-Thou to a conditional It-ness and objectivity. More specifically, as is claimed in this passage from 'The Power of the Spirit', this modern glorification of intellect involves a disjunction of the unity in being from which the relational powers of knowledge, love and faith themselves must spring:

> The relation of the spirit to the elemental forces and urges must not be interpreted from the view of pure thought. An attempt at interpretation must consider the influence of the spirit upon life. But — regardless of what it may call itself or be called at any given moment — the spirit which is not content in the area of thought and expresses itself in all of life becomes manifest as the power of *faith*. In the domain of the human soul, it appears as faithful courage and faithful love.... These constitute its power and may well govern the elemental forces because it has known them from the earliest times, and knows what is their due. Though in one historical era after another the spirit may seem dethroned and exiled, it does not lose its power. Again and again, unexpectedly and unpredictably, it causes what is intrinsic in the course of history through its agents, faithful courage and faithful love.[120]

It is significant, from the standpoint of the educationalist, that much of Buber's comment on this issue is addressed directly to the young, or to those concerned with their upbringing and care. Intellectualization — 'the hypertrophy of intellect that has broken out of the context of organic life and become parasitic'[121] — has brought a 'depressing loneliness' to modern youth, he writes. It is a loneliness of internal division, such as he describes in the passage above from 'The Power of the Spirit', but is also the separation from, and yearning for, the bonds of a religiously creative I-Thou and genuine community life.[122] In this excerpt from an address to a convention of Jewish youth representatives at Antwerp in 1932 he castigates the 'intellectuals' for denying generations of youth the happiness of 'believing in the spirit':

> It is not only the intellectuals, who are now finding a suspicious reception for their disquisitions, who must suffer for this treason. What is worse is that their audience, above all the entire younger generation of our time, is deprived of the noblest happiness of youth: the happiness of believing in

the spirit. It is easily understood that many of them now see nothing but
"ideologies" in intellectual patterns, nothing but pompous robes for very
obvious group interests; that they are no longer willing to believe there is a
truth over and above parties, above those who wield and are greedy for
power. They tell us, tell one another, and tell themselves, that they are tired
of being fed on lofty illusions, that they want to go back to a "natural"
foundation, to unconcealed instincts, that the life of the individual as well
as that of every people must be built up on simple self-assertion.[123]

The character of modern atheism, he writes, has been largely determined
by this inherited gnosticism. Atheism itself is seen by Buber as a passing
phenomenon: it is a temporary darkening or 'eclipsing' of God's presence,
an interruption in the historical divine-human dialogue. In *Eclipse of God* he
deals with three of its existential manifestations in the present age. The first
is man's apparent incapacity to apprehend a reality wholly and absolutely
separate from the self: by virture of his 'not- hearing', his failure to respond
to the dialogue addressed to him by God, man himself contributes to the
modern eclipse of the divine. His not-hearing is explained by Buber as a
consequence of rationalist reductionism i.e., the reduction of the reality of
God to the level of Idea, with a resultant weakening of his reality as Thou.
From this has come the disjunction of religious dialogue which now culminates in *atheos*.[124] This, as we have seen earlier, is the conclusion drawn
ultimately by Buber also in the anthropological critique. In this instance, the
argument is reinforced by the evidence presented for a further disjunction:
that between twentieth century man and the reciprocity of *historical* dialogue.
This is the second of the existential manifestations of *atheos*.

In 'The Man of Today and the Jewish Bible' Buber explains the con
temporary indifference to scripture as an evasion of meaningful relation with
the past, which, in turn, is based on an illusory concept of the future as
post-historical time: the illusion by which man rationalizes his rejection of
the religious:

> The man of today knows of no beginning. As far as he is concerned, history
> ripples towards him from some prehistorical cosmic age. He knows of no
> end; history sweeps him on into a posthistorical cosmic age. What a violent
> and foolish episode this time between the pre-historical and the post-
> historical has become! Man no longer recognizes an origin or a goal because
> he no longer wants to recognize the midpoint. Creation and redemption are
> true only on the premise that revelation is a present experience. Man of today
> resists the Scriptures because he cannot endure revelation. To endure
> revelation is to endure this moment full of possible decisions, to respond to
> and to be responsible for every moment. Man of today resists the Scriptures
> because he does not want any longer to accept responsibility. He thinks he

is venturing a great deal, yet he industriously evades the one real venture, that of responsibility.[125]

The evidence of moral decline of which Buber writes in essays such as 'Religion and Ethics', 'Religion and Modern Thinking' and 'On the Suspension of the Ethical'[126] is the third of the modern manifestations of *atheos*. The essential dependence of the ethical on the religious is explained at length in these essays. The ethical, he writes, exists in its purity only where man authentically reassesses his thoughts, actions and purposes according to the informed, dialogic criteria of conscience. Since the authentic is bound inextricably to the everyday reality of relation, and the religious dialogue is the absolute form of this relation, the decline of the religious involves a separation of the ethical also from the absoluteness of the authentic. To quote from *Eclipse of God*: 'Only out of a personal relationship to the absolute can the absoluteness of the ethical co-ordinates arise without which there is no complete awareness of self.'[127] The alternative to the religious ethic is a relativizing of all values, a dissolution of the absoluteness of ethical co-ordinates, ultimately a self created morality, a degenerate scepticism or even nihilism. Discussing the contemporary evidence of such a decline, Buber advocates a rediscovery or restatement of the *relational* basis of the ethical. The terms on which such a rediscovery might be conceived are those of the undogmatic, non-orthodox conception of relation as ultimatley religious which pervades his own religious and ethical thought:

> There is no escape from it until the new conscience of men has arisen that will summon them to guard with the innermost power of their souls against the confusion of the relative with the Absolute, that will enable them to see through illusion and to recognize this confusion for what it is. To penetrate again and again into the false absolute with an incorruptible probing glance until one has discovered its limits, its limitedness — there is to-day perhaps no other way to reawaken the power of the pupil to glimpse the never-vanishing appearance of the Absolute.[128]

We have seen earlier that Buber in his anthropological studies addressed himself to the contemporary problematic of the *relevance* of the religious. The solution advanced was a religious dialogic, conceived independently of traditional ideologies. A similar claim is made for the contemporary meaningfulness of Hasidic teaching. Hasidism, he maintains, can accommodate the spiritual needs identified in his discussion of *atheos*: firstly, because of its inherently non-ideological character; secondly, because of its integration of the religious into everyday life; thirdly, because of its unifying of all spheres of human experience in a 'religiosity' which parallels, and intertwines with, the anthropological dialogic. Describing his own encounter with

Hasidism in the face of approaching catastrophe in World War I, he recalls the attractions of its non-systematized teachings, its freedom from didactic emphasis, and, as this passage indicates, its contemporaneity with the present age:

> But I became more and more aware of a fact that has become of utmost significance for me: that the kernel of this life is capable of working on men even today, when most of the powers of the Hasidic community itself have been given over to decay or destruction, and it is just on the present-day West that it is capable of working in an especial manner. After the rise and decline of that life in the Polish, Ukrainian, Lithuanian ghettos, this kernel has entered into a contemporaneity, which is still, to be sure, only reminiscent, only an indication in the spirit, but even so can accomplish something in this manifestation that was basically foreign to the reality of that time. From here comes an answer to the crisis of Western man that has become fully manifest in our age. It is a partial answer only, not an ideological one, however, but one stemming directly out of reality and permeated by it.[129]

A deficiency noted by Buber in messianic religious movements was their separation of the sacred from the reality of the everyday.[130] The sacred, in instances where religion is mainly a matter of ritualized observance, becomes a self- constituted holiness remote from the profanity of worldly life. The great importance of Hasidism is that it overcomes the gap between sacred and profane; to the 'salvational confusion'[131] of ritual it opposes its hallowing of the everyday in which the demonic is overcome through being transformed. Buber rejects the purely secularist and scientific explanations of psychic disunity in modern life; he mentions, as examples, the socio-economic alienation described by Marx and the neuro-psychotic disorders described by Freud.[132] While agreeing with the latter that the primary modern disorder is a corrosion of the 'power to meet', he traces its origins to a deeper disjunction in the comprehensive dialogic of man in all his relations: with the world, with his fellowman and with the absolute Thou. He sees the modern separation of the profane from the holy as a symptom of this disjunction, and the alienation of the psychic disturbances identified by Marx and Freud as further symptoms of the same basic disorder. The holy, he explains, is merely that which is open to transcendence; the profane is merely that which is at first closed off from transcendence.[133] Because Hasidism facilitates an entering into dialogue at the level of everyday life, and this dialogue involves the whole being of man in all its possible spheres of relation, its healing of the divisions described in secular terms by Marx and Freud has a comprehensiveness which secular philosophies cannot provide. In 'Jewish Religiosity' Buber reiterates the distinctly non-ideological connotation of his use of the terms 'holy' and 'religious'. Those who wish to proclaim the dissolution of orthodoxies, and those who strive for their renewal, both seek a new beginning: a new unity in being fulfilled in what he describes as an undogmatic, non-formal 'religiosity'. The term aptly describes the unconventional but inclusive dialogic of Hasidism. Since the concept itself has a crucial importance in Buber's thought, the passage in which he distinguishes it from the traditional connotations of the religious is worth quoting in full:

> I say and mean: religiosity. I do not say and do not mean: religion. Religiosity is man's sense of wonder and adoration, an ever anew becoming, and ever anew articulation and formulation of his feeling that, transcending his conditioned being yet bursting from its very core, there is something that is unconditioned. Religiosity is his longing to establish a living communion with the unconditioned, his will to realize the unconditioned through his action, transposing it into the world of man. Religion is the sum total of the customs and teachings articulated and formulated by the religiosity of a certain epoch in a people's life; its prescriptions and dogmas are rigidly determined and handed down as unalterably binding to all future generations, without regard for their newly developed religiosity, which seeks new forms. Religion is true so long as it is creative; but it is creative only so long as religiosity, accepting the yoke of the laws and doctrines, is able to imbue them with new and incandescent meaning, so that they will seem to have been revealed to every generation anew, revealed today, thus answering men's very own needs, needs alien to their fathers. But once religious rites and dogmas have become so rigid that religiosity cannot move them or no longer wants to comply with them, religion becomes uncreative and therefore untrue. Thus religiosity is the creative, religion the organizing, principle. Religiosity starts anew with every young person, shaken to his very core by the mystery; religion wants to force him into a system stablilized for all time. Religiosity means activity — the elemental entering-into-relation with the absolute; religion means passivity — an acceptance of the handed-down command. Religiosity has only one goal; religion several. Religiosity induces sons, who want to find their own God, to rebel against their fathers; religion induces fathers to reject their sons, who will not let their father's God be forced upon them. Religion means preservation; religiosity, renewal.[134]

Hasidism, according to Buber's interpretation of its validity for twentieth-century man, is the living, creative, dialogic religiosity described in this passage. Its defining characteristic is its unifying of all life in a single, unfragmented response to otherness, whether this be interpreted as the otherness of the world and humankind or the infinite otherness of the divine. In various respects it confirmed and reinforced the religious anthropology developed by Buber from purely philosophical sources: its central dialogic of the interhuman, the divine-human, the communal and the historical, its anti-rationalist ethos, its doctrine of redemption in the moment, its ethic of authentication — in these and other respects it clarified, strengthened and enriched the anthropological conception of the nature and destiny of man. In both instances, the anthropological and the Hasidic/Biblical, an alternative way of being is proposed to the rejected options of *atheos* and a religion detached from life. The religiosity which is the proposed alternative strives for unity and fulfilment where the evidence of disorder — emotional, social, intellectual, moral and spiritual — compels redefinition of the purposes which religion originally purported to serve.

# IV
# Teaching, Learning and Knowing

## 1 *Sculptor or Gardener?*

There are two basic approaches to education and the task of the educator. According to the first, 'to educate' means to draw out of the child that which is in him; not to bring the child anything from the outside, but merely to overcome the disturbing influences, to set aside the obstacles which hinder his free development — to allow the child to 'become himself'.

According to the second approach, education means shaping the child into a form which the educator must first visualize, so that it may serve as a directive for his work. He does not rely on the child's natural endowment but sets up an opposing pattern which determines how such endowment is to be handled.

The first approach may be compared to that of the gardener who fertilizes and waters the soil, prunes and props the young plants, and removes the rank weeds from around it. But after he has done all this, if the weather is propitious, he trusts to the natural growth of that which is inherent in the seed.

The second approach is that of the sculptor. Like Michelangelo, he sometimes sees the shape hidden in the crude marble, but it is the image which exists in his soul which guides him in working on the block, and which he wishes to realize in the material at his disposal.

In the first case, education indicates the care given to a soul in the making, in order that the natural process of growth may reach its culmination; in the second, it means influencing a soul to develop in accordance with what the educator who exerts the influence considers to be right. Whoever employs the gardener's method is apt to believe that — fundamentally — man is good, but also that the individual is predetermined by his innate endowment. The educator with the sculptor's outlook tends to regard man as a creature, with diverse potentialities, but plastic and educable, and, therefore, not rigidly bound inside a pale of possibilities. The first kind of education is more humble, but also more passive; the second shows greater initiative, but carries with it graver responsibilities. The dangers of the first are laissez eller and excessive indulgence, those of the second, restraint and compulsion. The gardener educator has not enough confidence; the sculptor has too much.

One might think that both these forms of education are individualistic, that the first gives full scope to the individualism of the pupils, in that it does not set a common ideal against their personal differences, while the second gives free rein to the individualism of the educator, whose theory apparently empowers him to shape everyone in his own image. But this second supposition, at any rate, does not correspond to the truth. If every teacher could confront his pupils with a particular pattern he wished them to strive toward, the result would be anarchy rather than individualism.[1]

I am quoting this important passage from Buber's essay, 'On National Education,' at some length because it succinctly represents his evaluation of two major traditions in educational thought. These could be identified broadly, perhaps, as the classical-realist and the 'progressive' tradition (I am using these terms in the sense in which they are used by writers such as Peters, Bantock, Hirst and Maritain),[2] though Buber's own practice in such matters was to make simple distinctions such as the one he offers in *Between Man and Man* between 'the old theory of education which was characterized by the habit of authority' and the 'modern theory which is characterized by tendencies to freedom'.[3] While ultimately he rejected all ideological formulations of educational theory (for reasons which will be examined later in this chapter) he considered both of these traditions closely just the same and, as is evident from the passage quoted, rejected much of what each represented. While the main concern of this chapter will be Buber's dialogic philosophy of teaching and learning, his evaluations of these two traditions will be considered initially so that his conception of the teacher/learner relationship can be located in the context of the broader issues informing his philosophy.

On three issues Buber particularly challenged the 'progressive' or 'modern' approach to education. These were, firstly, the nature of individual potentiality, secondly, the nature and purpose of individual freedom, and thirdly, the nature of authority and its place in the educational process. In his address to the Heidelberg Conference of 1923 — the theme of which was 'The Development of the Creative Powers of the Child' — he condemned the reductionist practice common amongst certain modern educators of identifying creative potentialities in terms of specific energies and abilities, and of characterizing creativity as essentially an expression of individual selfhood. The originative instinct, he argued, is grounded in the wholeness of human consciousness, in its inwardness, and is nurtured, not by the free expression of individual selfhood, but by the relational experience through which human potentiality is ultimately fulfilled.

It is important to recognise that the instinct of origination is autonomous and not derivatory. Modern psychologists are inclined to derive the multiform human soul from a single primal element — the 'libido', the 'will to power', and the like. But this is really only the generalization of certain degenerate states in which a single instinct not merely dominates but also spreads parasitically through the others. . . . In opposition to these doctrines and methods, which impoverish the soul, we must continually point out that human inwardness is in origin a polyphony in which no voice can be 'reduced' to another, and in which the unity cannot be grasped analytically, but only heard in the present harmony. One of the leading voices is the instinct of origination.

This instinct is therefore bound to be significant for the work of education as well. Here is an instinct which, no matter to what power it is raised, never becomes greed, because it is not directed to 'having' but only to doing; which alone among the instincts can grow only to passion not to lust; which alone among the instincts cannot lead its subject away to invade the realm of other lives. Here is pure gesture which does not snatch the world to itself, but expresses itself to the world. Should not the person's growth into form, so often dreamed of and lost, at last succeed from this starting point?[4]

Individual growth, he insisted, is enlivened, deepened and fulfilled by the various relationships (interpersonal, aesthetic and social, the relationship of learning and knowing, etc.) which constitute human existence. The nurturing of relational capacities, rather than the provision of opportunities for self-expression and growth, becomes therefore the main function of education. Development, conceived independently of its relational contexts, would lead ultimately, he warned, to a solitariness as damaging and abhorrent as that resulting from the repressive authoritarianism which progressive educators had themselves condemned:

> Yes: as an originator man is solitary. He stands wholly without bonds in the echoing hall of his deeds. Nor can it help him to leave his solitariness that his achievement is received enthusiastically by the many. He does not know if it is accepted, if his sacrifice is accepted by the anonymous receiver. Only if someone grasps his hand not as a 'creator' but as a fellow- creature lost in the world, to be his comrade or friend or lover beyond the arts, does he have an awareness and a share of mutuality. An education based only on the training of the instinct of origination would prepare a new human solitariness which would be the most painful of all.[5]

The ideas of potentiality and inwardness, therefore, are firmly rooted in Buber's anthropological view of man as intrinsically a relating, loving, reciprocating, rather than self-fulfilling, individually creative, or merely socially oriented being. This position is emphasized further in the second of his criticisms of the progressive or 'modern' approach to educational theory. In this instance, he challenges the 'progressive' concept of individual freedom: the notion on which the 'child centred' ideals are mainly founded. In fashioning their alternatives to the old repressive authoritarianism, the new educators, he said, conceived of freedom as a mere negation, i.e. a 'freedom from' rather than a means to an end beyond itself. Buber attributes a great many of the ills of modern society, and specifically of modern education, to this negatively defined freedom. He distinguished two basic orders of freedom: the first being the individual's freedom of decision or choice, the second being his freedom for self-development and growth. The fundamental flaw of progressive education, he claimed, was its confusion of these two functions, to the extent that the first order of responsible, morally directed freedom was subsumed in the second order of uninhibited growth. He challenged this false presentation of the nature and purpose of individual freedom and affirmed his concept of freedom as affording the possibility for personal i.e. relational, fulfilment. Freedom, by this definition, is not itself an end but a means towards a higher end: the attainment of the ultimate goal of existence which is fulfilment through communion and love:

> The release of powers can be only a presupposition of education, nothing more. Put more generally, it is the nature of freedom to provide the place, but not the foundation as well on which true life is raised.
>     There is a tendency to understand the freedom, which may be termed evolutionary freedom, as at the opposite pole from compulsion, from being under a compulsion. But at the opposite pole from compulsion there stands not freedom but communion. Compulsion is a negative reality, communion is the positive reality; freedom is a possibility, possibility regained. . . . Freedom in education is the possiblity of communion; it cannot be dispensed with and it cannot be made use of in itself; without it nothing succeeds, but neither does anything succeed by means of it: it is the run before the jump, the tuning of the violin, the confirmation of that primal and mighty potentiality which it cannot even begin to actualize.[6]

On a third issue, that of authority and discipline, Buber differed radically also from 'progressive' educators. His views on this issue are closely bound up with the ascetic/erotic dichotomy discussed in his essay on creativity. While the term 'ascetic' is used by Buber with its ordinary connotations of self-discipline, self-control or self-restraint, his use of the term 'erotic' in this context requries some clarification. Generally, he follows the Platonist distinction between a 'soul directed' Eros which signifies a regenerating dynamism in the world of material existence and the profane Eros which signifies earthly desire and sensual gratification.[7] Applying the distinction to education, he strongly emphasizes the need for a dynamic life-affirming outlook in the teacher, while rejecting the sentimentalized, child-indulging tendencies associated with some progressive conceptions of teaching. He calls, therefore, for a synthesis in education of the ascetic principles of authority and discipline and the life-informing, hope-affirming principles associated with the soul-directed Eros. While rejecting both the excesses of the old repressive authoritarianism and the sentimentality and inefficacy of the progressive model of teaching, he insists nonetheless on a formative, disciplinary and highly purposeful role for the teacher:

> In education, then, there is a lofty asceticism: an asceticism which rejoices in the world, for the sake of the responsiblity for a realm of life which is entrusted to us for our influence but not our interference — either by the will to power or by Eros. The spirit's service of life can be truly carried out only in the system of a reliable counterpoint — regulated by the laws of the different forms of relation — of giving and withholding oneself, intimacy and distance, which of course must not be controlled by reflection but must arise from the living tact of the natural and spiritual man.
>
> Yet the master remains the model for the teacher. For if the educator of our day has to act consciously he must nevertheless do it 'as though he did not'. That raising of the finger, that questioning glance, are his genuine doing. Through him the selection of the effective world reaches the pupil. He fails the recipient when he presents this selection to him with a gesture of interference. It must be concentrated in him; and doing out of concentration has the appearance of rest. Interference divides the soul in his care into an obedient part and a rebellious part. But a hidden influence proceeding from his integrity has an integrating force.[8]  *117*   *122*

Buber's analysis of classical theory is a great deal less complex than his assessment of progressive positions. Indeed, his comments on the dualistic character of teaching and learning, together with his characterization of the teacher as 'master', suggests a certain approval of classical viewpoints. There is no denying his profound distaste, however, for the authoritarianism of the 'old educator'. In his essay, 'Education,' he condemns the 'will-to-power' tendencies of authoritarian teachers in the same way that he condemned progressive teachers for their 'degenerate eroticism'.[9] Each in a different way was seen to deny his pupils the openness to relation that Buber considered an essential condition of a fruitful teaching/learning encounter. Significantly, however, he refrained from outright condemnation of the classical approach, maintaining that its excessive authoritarianism was essentially a debasement of traditions which otherwise he esteemed highly:

> It is usual to contrast the principle of the 'new' education as 'Eros' with that of the 'old' education as the 'will to power'.
>
> In fact the one is as little a principle of education as the other. A principle of education, in a sense still to be clarified, can only be a basic relation which is fulfilled in education.
>
> This situation of the old type of education is, however, easily used, or misused, by the individual's will to power, for this will is inflated by the authority of history. The will to power becomes convulsive and passes into fury, when the authority begins to decay, that is, when the magical validity

of tradition disappears. Then the moment comes near when the teacher no longer faces the pupil as an ambassador but only as an individual, as a static atom to the whirling atom.[10] /20 - 12/

Buber objected further to the classical justification of authority on the basis of criteria that are external both to the teacher and the student. In common with existentialist educators generally, he rejected the notion of an objectivist theory of knowledge and, in his own epistemological writings, such as the essays in *The Knowledge of Man*, developed a theory of knowledge which is grounded in the primary reality of relation. He writes of truths that are disclosed through the knowing, loving, believing and other relationships of everyday life, i.e. truths that are disclosed thorugh relational rather than objectivist criteria. The moral authority, which classical philosophers would justify on the basis of the objective validity of the truths imparted through teaching, is justified by Buber on the basis of criteria that are neither objectively nor subjectively determined. It is grounded in the integrity and truth of the relation in which the teacher is reciprocally engaged with his pupils and by the various forms of relational truth towards which he can guide them by his word and example.

Yet another criticism of Buber's is directed at the impersonal, formalistic and highly didactic strategies employed by classical educators. In *Between Man and Man* he contrasts the respective teaching styles of classical and progressive educators through an illustration drawn from classroom practice. Taking the example of a drawing lesson, he sees the teacher of the 'compulsory school' as working prescriptively from models and rules, while the teacher of the 'free school' encourages a spontaneous expression of individual tendencies and interests. While rejecting the latter approach for its aimless individualism, he condemns the former for its stultification of personal freedom, its denial of possibilities for reciprocal encounter and for the proper nurturing of originating capacities.[11]

The same polarization is further represented by Buber in three vivid metaphors that are used at various points in his writings. The first is the funnel/pump analogy which he used on the occasion of the Heidelberg Conference.[12] According to this comparison, the classical educator sees learning as a passive assimilation by the child of ideas that are poured through the funnel of his consciousness, while the progressive educator sees learning as a drawing forth or 'pumping out' of powers that are latent in the child's consciousness. A second analogy, suggesting a similar dichotomy, is used in the same essay when the two types of educator are compared to the different proponents of evolution theory in the seventeenth and eighteenth centuries: the animaculists who believed the whole germ was present in the spermatozoon, and the ovists who believed it was wholly present in the ovum.[13] A third, more familiar, comparison is based on the sculptor/gardener analogy which was cited at the beginning of this chapter. The progressive teacher, in this instance, is compared to a gardener. He releases potentialities that are latent in the child's nature in the same way that a gardener fertilizes and waters the soil while trusting to the natural powers of growth which are inherent in the seed. The traditionalist teacher, however, seeks to influence his pupils' development in accordance with certain preconceived ideals. He is likened, therefore, to the sculptor who shapes and refines the crude marble to his own image and design.[14]

Despite the criticisms directed by Buber at progressive and classical educators, and despite the extreme nature of the polarities implied in these three metaphors, it would be wrong to describe him as having totally rejected the positions represented by either. While denouncing progressive theorists for their misconceptions of childhood potentiality, their negative concept of freedom, and their diminished sense of the teacher's status and authority, he nevertheless recognized that they had liberated school classrooms from the repressive authoritarianism of the older system. A similar assimilation may be seen in his treatment of classical positions. While rejecting the 'will to power' excesses, the objectivist epistemology and the impersonal teaching strategies associated with traditionalist approaches to education, he spoke enthusiastically of their effective transmission of the spiritual/cultural heritage and their provision for a genuine historical self-understanding in the child. The 'old educator', he declared, was 'the bearer of assured values which were strong in tradition'. He was 'the ambassador of history'; he carried within him 'the magic of the spiritual forces of history'. He reduced the great cosmos of history to the level of personal encounter.

## 2   Teaching as dialogue

Buber did not attempt therefore to resolve the conflicting viewpoints of classical and progressive educators. Apart from the specific criticisms mentioned above, he objected fundamentally to the ideological orientation of these philosophies, regarding them as expressions of values, norms and ideals peculiar to certain societies at particular stages in history. He spoke, for instance, of the dominance of classical ideals in European society virtually from Greek antiquity up to the French Revolution and of the emergence and popularity of utilitarian and empirically oriented educational theories from the seventeenth century to the present time. Rejecting both on the grounds of their ideological constrictions, he challenged the validity of prescriptive approaches to the definition of educational aims in the context of present circumstances and needs. 'The question which is always being brought forward — to where, to what, must we educate — misunderstands the situation. Only times which know a figure of general validity — the Christian, the gentleman, the citizen — know an answer to that question.'[15] He called for a redefinition of the essential realities of the educational process: a redefinition, particularly, of the relation of teacher and learner which he considered the most fundamental of these realities and the one least subject to the exigencies of cultural and ideological change:

> The education of men by men means the selection of the effective world by a person and in him. The educator gathers in the constructive forces of the world. He distinguishes, rejects, and confirms in himself, in his self which is filled with the world. The constructive forces are eternally the same: they are the world bound up in community, turned to God. The educator educates himself to be their vehicle.
>
> Then is this the 'principle' of education, its normal and fixed maxim? No, it is only the principium of its reality, the beginning of its reality — wherever it begins.
>
> There is not and never has been a norm and fixed maxim of education. What is called so was always only the norm of a culture, of a society, a church, an epoch, to which education too, like all stirring and action of the spirit, was submissive, and which education translated into its language.
>
> In a formed age there is in truth no autonomy of education, but only in an age which is losing form. Only in it, in the disintegration of traditional bonds, in the spinning whirl of freedom, does personal responsibility arise which in the end can no longer lean with its burden of decision on any church or society or culture, but is lonely in face of Present Being.[16]

This chapter will attempt to identify the elements constituting the teacher/learner relationship as it is conceived in Buber's educational writings. It will be shown that it is located firmly within the framework of his dialogic philosophy as a whole: that is the characterized, firstly, by a trusting reciprocation, albeit one limited by the different reciprocating capacities of teacher and student, secondly, by the exemplary integrity of the teacher, thirdly, by the counselling/healing nature of the teacher's role, forthly, by the process of confirming potentiality which is central to that role, and fitthly, by the effectiveness with which the teacher promotes the disciplined, critical, reflective methods of enquiry which Buber considers necessary for authentic leaning and knowing. Two images are used recurrently by Buber to convey the precise nature of all these functions and to emphasize their interdependence and complexity. The first is the metaphor of generation or birth-giving which is used in *I and Thou* to signify the spontaneous reciprocation of dialogic inclusion, and which is applied subsequently in his educational writings to the specific form of dialogic inclusion occurring between teacher and learner. It is interesting and profoundly ironic, in the context of its application to education, to find that Buber himself attributed his discovery of the notion of dialogue to his own childhood awareness of its absence, when his parents decided to separate, and he was effectively orphaned, at the age of four. To this childhood experience of 'mismeeting' he attributed his lifelong interest in the nature of human mutuality. It will be recalled that in the passage from his autobiography in which he describes this episode that he used the image of maternal/filial reciprocation to intimate the immediacy of dialogic inclusion.[17]

In *I and Thou* the image of dialogue as birth-giving occurs again in a seminal passage where he compares the experience of mutual inclusion to the involuntary bodily reciprocity of the mother and the unborn foetus: 'The prenatal life of the child is a pure natural association, a flowing towards each other, a bodily reciprocity and the life horizon of the developing being appears uniquely inscribed, and yet also not inscribed, in that of the being that carries it; for the womb in which it dwells is not solely that of the human mother.'[18] The image is applied explicitly by Buber to the teacher/learner relationship. In 'Teaching and Deed,' for instance, he cites orthodox Jewish support for the comparison of teaching with birth-giving: 'He who teaches the tradition to his fellowmen,' he writes in a passage paraphrasing the Talmud, 'is regarded as though he has formed him and made him and brought him into the world.'[19] The essential characteristic of the relationship is the trust which should be developed between teacher and student, a trust which he suggests in this passage from his address to the Heidelberg Conference on Creativity, is comparable to the spontaneous reciprocation and love we associate with parenthood.

> The relation in education is one of pure dialogue. I have referred to the child, lying with half-closed eyes waiting for his mother to speak to him. But many children do not need to wait, for they know that they are unceasingly addressed in a dialogue which never breaks off. In face of the lonely night which threatens to invade, they lie preserved and guarded, invulnerable, clad in the silver mail of trust.
>
> Trust, trust in the world, because this human being exists — that is the most inward achievement of the relation in education. Because this human being exists, meaninglessness, however hard pressed you are by it, cannot be the real truth. Because this human being exists, in the darkness the light lies hidden, in fear salvation, and in the callousness of one's fellow men the great love.
>
> Because this human being exists; therefore he must be really there, really facing the child, not merely there in spirit. He may not let himself be represented by a phantom; the death of the phantom would be a catastrophe for the child's pristine soul. He need possess none of the perfections which the child may dream he possesses, but he must be really there. In order to be and to remain truly present to the child he must have gathered the child's presence into his own store, as one of the bearers of his communion with the world, one of the focusses of his responsibilities for the world. Of course,

he cannot be continually concerned with the child, either in thought or in deed, nor ought he to be. But if he has really gathered the child into his life then that subterranean dialogic, that steady potential presence of the one to the other is established and endures. Then there is reality between them, there is mutuality.[20]

The second image conveying the special nature of the teacher/learner relationship is one derived from Buber's interest in Hasidic culture. This is the traditional Jewish image of the zaddik, a figure celebrated in Hasidic legend as a teacher and healer of souls and one who occupied a central place in the lives of the Hasidic communities. The zaddik is the historical embodiment of all the qualities Buber valued most highly in the teacher. There are vivid descriptions of individually named zaddikim in several of the legends he translated, and a detailed description of their lifestyle is provided in *The Origin and Meaning of Hasidism*. In this work Buber traces the historical evolution of the zaddik from the saintly paragon of Kabbalistic tradition — 'a man united in a special way with God, not only beholding his mystery but also acting as his representative' — to the simple healer and teacher of later years whose entire life was a living attestation of the reality of dialogic trust.[21]

Unlike their rabbinic forebears who were seen by their subordinates as hierarchical, erudite figures, the zaddikim stood for a simple personal witness to truth, in their lives exemplifying their active and loving concern for their followers and their wholehearted communion with them. While learning was important to them — many were notable Talmudists — it occupied a secondary place to the personal integrity they exemplified. Their influence was ascribed not to their superior learning but to the way they lived. They 'did not proceed from a teaching but to a teaching'; their pastoral concern embraced the entire lives of their followers, 'from their concern about bread to the concern about the purification of the soul.' The zaddik was the 'true human being, the rightful subject of the act in which wants to be known, loved, wanted.' He sought in all his actions to promote the same interpersonal relations with each.[22] Two striking passages from *The Origin and Meaning of Hasidism* describe the role of the zaddikim and particularly emphasize the degree to which their lives attested to the ideals of reciprocation and care they sought to promote amongst their followers.

The zaddik has to help his Hasidim. But in order to help them, in order to bring them to God with their whole lives — not merely something of them, their thought, their feelings, but their whole lives — he must embrace their whole lives, from their concern about bread to their concern about the purification of the soul. He does not have to do something for them, but everything. And because he shall do all, he must be capable of all. 'Why,' it is jestingly asked. 'is the zaddik called 'the good Jew'?' If one wished to say that he prays well, then one would have to call him a 'good prayer'; if one wished to say that he learns well, a 'good learner'. A 'good Jew' thinks well;and drinks well and eats well and works well and means well and does everything well.'

The zaddik is not a priest or a man who renews in himself an already accomplished work of salvation or transmits it to his generation, but the man who is more concentratedly devoted than other men to the task of salvation that is for all men and all ages, the man whose forces purified and united, are directed towards the one duty. He is, according to the conception of man, the man in whom transcendental responsibility has grown from an event of consciousness into organic existence. He is the true human being, the rightful subject of the act in which God wants to be known, loved, wanted. In him the 'lower' earthly man realises his archetype, the cosmic primordial man who embraces the sphere.[23]

The pastoral concerns which Buber emphasizes in these portraits of the zaddikim embrace functions that would nowadays be served mainly by school counsellors and therapists. The clear implication of Buber's work, however, is that the teaching and counselling functions should be integrated. It is significant that he frequently treated the roles of teacher and therapist as interchangeable; several commentators have remarked on the closeness of his thinking on psychotherapy and his thinking on education.[24] Clearly he intended that the figure of the zaddik-teacher should embody the unity of both functions and his ideal teacher was one who would personally exemplify that unity. It is important, however, to indicate his precise conception of the counselling/healing role of the zaddik-teacher. The healing powers he attributed to the zaddikim were concerned primarily with the restoration of faith and self-meaning to those whose hopes and beliefs had been shattered by hardship and misfortune. He describes, for instance, what the zaddikim achieved for the Polish Jews whose faith had been destroyed by the great social and political upheavals of the eighteenth century and by the endemic persecutions to which they had been subjected.

> Stirred in his innermost core by the Sabbatian revolution, shaken to his foundations by its outcome, the Polish Jew longed passionately for leadership, for a man who would would take him under his wing, give certainty to his bewildered soul, give order and shape to his chaotic existence, who would make it possible for him both to believe and to live. The Hasidic movement educated such leaders. Rabbis who only bestowed advice as to how the prescriptions of the law should be applied could no longer satisfy the new longing, but sermons on the meaning of the teaching also did not help. In a world in which one could no longer muster the strength for reflection and decision, a man was needed to show one how to believe and to say what was to be done.[25]

The need for a similar form of healing is strongly suggested in a modern context in 'The Prejudices of Youth,' where the problems he describes — moral uncertainty, social alienation, the decline of faith, the diminished status of cultural traditions — call for the same meaning-giving capacities in the teacher as were exemplified by the zaddikim.[26] A particularly significant feature of the counselling process in this context is the act of 'confirming' which was explained by Buber in the course of a moderated discussion with the psychotherapist, Carl Rogers. The notion of 'confirming the other' is directly relevant both to the practice of psychotherapy and of teaching; in the latter instance it helps particularly to identify the nature of the impact exerted by the teacher over his students and the manner in which he influences the growth and development of their potentialities.

To understand the full meaning of the idea of 'confirming' it is necessary to turn to Buber's essay, 'Elements of the Interhuman,' and to the distinction made there between 'being' and 'seeming'. The essential problematic of the sphere of mutuality, he says, arises from the duality of 'being' and 'seeming' in human experience. The person whose experience is dominated by 'being' projects himself freely and spontaneoulsy to the other, regardless of the image he calls forth. But the person whose experience is dominated by 'seeming' is concerned to call forth an appropriate image of himself in the eyes of the other and, to this end, is ever prepared to project himself falsely so as to be affirmed by the other — a tendency which is highly destructive of the authenticity of the relationship between them. Buber suggests that, if the tendency towards seeming can be penetrated, one can reach the potentiality for real becoming and ultimately the potentiality for good which is present in all men. In a passage which is profoundly indicative of the potential influencing power of the educator he points to the capacity for goodness, or the latent redeemability, which is inherent in man's nature.

> The widespread tendency to live from the recurrent impression one makes instead of from the steadiness of one's being is not a 'nature'. It originates, in fact, on the other side of interhuman life itself, in men's dependence upon one another. It is no light thing to be confirmed in one's being by others, and seeming deceptively offers itself as a help in this. To yield to seeming is man's essential cowardice, to resist it, is his essential courage. But this is not an inexorable state of affairs which is as it is and must so remain. One can struggle to come to oneself — that is, to come to confidence in being. One struggles, now more successfully now less, but never in vain, even when one thinks he is defeated. One must at times pay dearly for life lived from the being; but it is never too dear. Yet is there not bad being, do weeds not grow everywhere? I have never known a young person who seemed to be irretrievably bad. Later indeed it becomes more and more difficult to penetrate the increasingly tough layer which has settled down on a man's

being. Thus there arises the false perspective of the seemingly fixed 'nature' which cannot be overcome. It is false; the foreground is deceitful; man as man can be redeemed.[27]

Mutual confirmation is essential, therefore, for the realization of individual potentiality. The act of confirming involves the 'personally making present to the other', confirming what he wishes, thinks or feels. It means being able to perceive every reality from the standpoint of the other. It is distinguished by Buber from 'acceptance' of the other though ultimately the act of confirming includes acceptance as well. While the latter is mainly an affirmation of the other's reality, the act of confirming requires that the educator or therapist be prepared to struggle with the other, to wrestle with him against himself. It particularly means being prepared to resist the 'seeming' tendencies in the other. It is concerned, therefore, with stimulating the process of growth in the other and can embrace the entire polarity of authentic and inauthentic tendencies present in him. It is founded on a deep regard for the other's worth and potentiality, on a willingness to discover what he can become and to assist towards its fulfilment. The notion is fully explained in this passage from the Buber/Rogers debate:

> MARTIN BUBER: I would say every true existential relationship between two persons begins with acceptance. By acceptance, I mean being able to tell, or rather not to tell, but only to make it felt to the other person, that I accept him just as he is. I take you just as you are. . . I would say there is not as we generally think in the soul of a man good and evil opposed. There is again and again in different manners a polarity, and the poles are not good and evil, but rather yes and no, rather acceptance and refusal. And we can strengthen, or we can help him.
>
> Well, so, but it is not yet what I mean by confirming the other. Because accepting, this is just accepting how he ever is in this moment, in this actuality of his. Confirming means first of all, accepting the whole potentiality of the other and making even a decisive difference in his potentiality, and of course we can be mistaken again and again in this, but it's just a chance between human beings. I can recogize in him, know in him, more or less, the person he has been (I can say it only in this word) created to become. In the simple factual language, we do not find the term for it because we don't find in it the term, the concept of being meant to become. This is what we must, as far as we can, grasp; if not in the first moment, then after this. And now I not only accept the other as he is, but I confirm him, in myself, and then in him, in relation to this potentiality that is meant by him and it can now be developed, it can evolve, it can answer the reality of life. He can do more or less to this scope but I can, too, do something. And this is with goals even deeper than acceptance. Let's take, for example, man and a woman, man and wife. He says, not expressly, but just by his whole relation to her: 'I accept you as you are.' But this does not

mean, 'I don't want you to change'. Rather it says, 'Just by my accepting love, I discover in you what you are meant to become.' This is, of course, not anything to be expressed in massive terms. But it may be that it grows and grows with the years in common life.[28]

The notion of 'confirming' will be raised again later in the context of moral and religious education. In the general context of teaching it points to the formative role that Buber envisaged what he declared his belief in the 'mastering' model for the teacher and spoke regretfully of its decline. The terminology he used — 'the influencing of the lives of others with one's own life becomes here a function and a law'[29] — indicates the high degree of influence that he envisaged. The influencing he describes, however, is one which remains rooted in the trust, the personal exemplification of integrity and the pastoral-counselling concern that have been identified as the essential characteristics of the teacher. Yet, ultimately, Buber concedes on the grounds of realism — the limited experience of the learner, his inability to see wholly from the standpoint of the other — that the dialogic reciprocation between teacher and student is likely to be a limited and partially unfulfilled mutuality. While in no way diluting the trusting, caring quality of the relationship, he acknowledges the existential limitations imposed on the degree of inclusion that is likely to be attained:

> But however intense the mutuality of giving and taking with which he is bound to his pupil, inclusion cannot be mutual in this case. He experiences the pupil's being educated, but the pupil cannot experience the educating of the educator. The educator stands at both ends of the common situation, the pupil only at one end. In the moment when the pupil is able to throw himself across and experience from over there, the educative relation would be burst asunder, or change into friendship.[30]

## 3   Critical Meaning Making

Thus far, four characteristics of the teacher/learner relationship have been identified. They are: the presence between teacher and learner of a trusting and mutually affirming reciprocation; the personal exemplification by the teacher of the integrity of potentialities he seeks to call forth in the student; the teacher's active promotion of a pastoral/healing concern for the personal well being of the student; and his confirmation of the student's potentiality for self-fulfilment and personhood. While recognizing that the relationship between teacher and learner is limited in its scope for dialogic inclusion by the differences that exist between them — and the relationship, therefore, is essentially one which *aspires* towards the condition of dialogue — Buber insists, nonetheless, that the teacher's influence over the lives of his pupils is both active and decisive. 'Through him,' he says, 'the selection of the effective world reaches his pupil.'[31] This influence is particularly decisive in the sphere of learning and knowing where some further characteristics of the relationship can now be identified.

Buber's treatment of the learning-knowing process embraces five closely related concepts. (The term 'learn' is generally used in his work to connote the 'becoming' character of the act of knowing.) Firstly, he represents both as activities of critical meaning-making in which teacher and student engage collaboratively. Secondly, he sees both these activities as being dependent, in turn, on the existence of authentic and mutually illuminating modes of communication between teacher and learner. Thirdly, he stresses the tentative and freely oriented character of both activities. Fourthly, he sees each as involving a radical process of conversion by which objectified, impersonal meaning is converted into the realm of the personal, or the I-Thou. And fifthly, he insists that both activities are inescapably informed by tradition and must be developed, therefore, in the context of their historical relationships.

As was indicated in the previous section, Buber saw the teacher as having a crucial role to play in the process of confirming his pupils' potentiality and growth towards personhood. The search for meaning is seen as a vital part of this whole process. The child's encounter with the world, he says, is essentially his attempt to deal critically with its reality; that is, to engage in that fundamental activity of selection, of determining the personal significance for himself of all the realities he encounters. It is this act of selection which particularly characterizes the processes of learning and knowing. It is represented by Buber as essentially an activity of critical reflection, a deepening of self-awareness and self-consciousness through the processes of disciplined enquiry and understanding which characterize the act of relating dialogically to the world:

> The dispositions which would be discovered in the soul of a new-born child — if the soul could in fact be analysed — are nothing but capacities to receive and imagine the world. The world engenders the person in the individual. The world, that is the whole environment, nature and society, 'educates' the human being: it draws out his powers and makes him grasp and penetrate its objections. What we term education, conscious and willed, means a selection by man of the effective world. It means to give decisive effective power to a selection of the world which is concentrated and manifested in the educator. The relation in education is lifted out of the purposelessly streaming education by all things, and is marked off as purpose. In this way, through the educator, the world for the first time becomes the true subject of its effect.[32]

Significantly, Buber points in this passage to the active role of the educator in assisting his pupils towards that encounter with meaning or effective selection of the world that he characterizes as essential features of the activity of knowing. By his confirmation and example, the teacher enables his pupil to develop those habits of critical enquiry, intellectual discipline and individual sense-making which are part of the whole process of learning to know. He confirms that vital potentiality to know — not alone through his care and concern, his integrity and his example, but through his pedagogic efficiency and his decisive intervention in the learning process. In this image of the teacher as 'rabbi' or 'master', therefore, Buber insists on the formative nature of teaching and the impact the teacher exerts on the course and direction of his pupil's learning:

> Yet the master remains the model for the teacher. For if the educator of our day has to act consciously, he must nevertheless do it 'as though he did not.' That raising of the finger, that questioning glance, are his genuine doing. Through him the selection of the effective world reaches the pupil. He fails the recipient when he presents that selection to him with a gesture of interference. It must be concentrated in him, and doing out of concentration has the appearance of rest. Interference divides the soul in his care into an obedient part and a rebellious part. But a hidden influence proceeding from his integrity has an integrating force.[33]

The mode of communication occurring between teacher and learner is central to all these activities. In essays such as 'The Word that is Spoken' and 'What is Common to All' Buber develops a dialogic theory of communication which parallels the various modes of dialogic discourse set forth in his essays on education. His entire dialogic theory of language will be considered fully in later chapters on aesthetics and community education where its implications can be more fully explored. For the present purpose it will be sufficient to point to his view that a genuine speaking and listening is essential for all true communication, for truly effective learning and ultimately for the entire pursuit of truth. In 'The Word that is Spoken' he stresses the importance of being present through language, whether as speaker or listener, to the reality of the other and thereby enabling a genuinely dialogic and effective relation of teaching and learning to occur:

> The importance of the spoken word, I think, is grounded in the fact that it does not want to remain with the speaker. It reaches out toward a hearer, it lays hold of him, it even makes the hearer into a speaker, if perhaps only a soundless one. But this must not be understood as if the place of the occurrence of language is the sum of the two partners in dialogue, or, in the terminology of Jakob Grimm, of the two 'fellows in speech'; as though the occurrence of language were to be understood through the psychophysical comprehension of two individual unities in a given period of time. The word

that is spoken is found rather in the oscillating sphere between the persons, the sphere that I call 'the between' and that we can never allow to be contained without a remainder in the two participants.[34]

Dialogic knowing, however, presumes an openness in the search for meaning and truth which must also be fully accommodated by the teacher, however decisive his influence on his pupil's learning. The search for meaning originates in the consciousness of the individual person, and his knowing is ultimately concerned with the appropriation of all meaning in terms of its personal significance for him. His 'selection of the world' is based on a free choosing of its reality, a free venturing into the unknown and the undisclosed. Ultimately, therefore, the individual is responsible for his own knowing. But his innate disposition to appropriate meaning freely can be fostered by the teacher. While he contributes actively and decisively to his pupil's learning — by virtue of his mature knowledge and experience and his pedagogic efficiency — he is equally required to promote that openness and freedom in his pupil's learning which is a crucial condition of authentic meaning-making. In this unusually self- revealing passage from *Israel and the World* Buber writes of the importance of maintaining this spirit of intellectual openness:

> The one thing which has become clearer and clearer to me in the course of my life is that keeping an open mind is of the utmost importance. The right kind of openness is the most precious human possession. I said, the right kind of openness. One can take a certain stand and hold to it passionately but one must remain open to the whole world, see what there is to see, experience what experience offers, and include all of experience in the effectuation of whatever cause one has decided for. Though constantly changing our stand will yet remain true to itself, but deepened by an insight which grows more and more true to reality. We need to take a firm stand, but we also need to feel that we have not thus put our feet in shackles. Wherever we stand, we should stand free and unbiased and grow aware of the world.[35]

The dialogic character of knowing is expressed ultimately by Buber in terms of the conversion of impersonal into personal meaning-making. In 'Distance and Relation' and 'Elements of the Interhuman' — the two most explicit presentations of his epistemology — he explores the difference between knowledge which is subjectively and objectively significant — knowledge belonging in the spheres of the I-Thou or I-It — and suggests that each holds the possiblity of being changed into the other. Just as knowledge in the sphere of the I-It (objective knowledge) may be transformed into the sphere of the I-Thou (subjective and personally significant knowledge), so the latter can degenerate into the realm of the objective and impersonal. He

suggests that the goal of teaching must be to seek in every way possible —
especially through the confirming action of the teacher — to bring about the
process of conversion by which objectified knowledge is transformed into
the realm of the I-Thou — the sphere where it becomes personally
meaningful. In 'Distance and Relation' Buber represents this process as an
activity of 'synthesizing apperception' through which the tensions and
contradictions between objectivity and subjectivity — between personal and
impersonal meaning — can be bridged:

> We may characterize the act and the work of entering into relation with the
> world as such — and, therefore, not with parts of it, and not with the sum
> of its parts, but with it as the world — as synthesizing apperception, by
> which we establish that this pregnant use of the concept involves the
> function of unity: by synthesizing apperception I mean the apperception of
> a being as a whole and as a unity. Such a view is won, and won again and
> again, only by looking upon the world as a world. The conception of
> wholeness and unity is in its origin identical with the conception of the world
> to which man is turned. He who turns to the realm which he has removed
> from himself, and which has been completed and transformed into a world
> — he who turns to the world and looking upon it steps into relation with it,
> becomes aware of wholeness and unity in such a way that from then on he
> is able to grasp being as a wholeness and a unity; the single being has
> received the character of wholeness and the unity which are perceived in
> the world. But a man does not obtain this view simply from the 'setting at
> a distance' and 'making independent'. These would offer him the world
> only as an object, as which it is only an aggregate of qualities that can be
> added to at will, not a genuine wholeness and unity. Only the view of what
> is over against me in the world in its full presence, with which I have set
> myself, present in my whole person, in relation — only this view gives me
> the world truly as whole and one. For only in such an opposition are the
> realm of man and what completes it in spirit, finally one. So it has always
> been, and so it is in this hour.[36]

Implicit in all this is a clear rejection of the kind of epistemic relativism
which would represent the activities of learning and knowing as self-
justifying and self-fulfilling processes of individual growth. Buber, on
numerous occasions, reiterated his view that all knowing is directed
ultimately towards an absolute truth: the truth of the unconditioned infinity
of Thouness towards which all reality and meaning are pointed, and towards
which all values and truths are referrable. In this passage from 'The
Prejudices of Youth' he warns, therefore, against the dangers of a relativist
theory of truth:

> The prejudice against truth follows on the heels of the prejudice against
> spirit. It is connected with a theory which won more and more converts in

the course of the last quarter of a century, the theory that truth is relative. Applied to everyday life, this theory implies that there is no definitive truth for mankind, but only a special something for every individual which he regards as the truth, but which is wholly determined by his own psychic constitution and by the social environment in which he grew up. According to this theory, a man is conditioned by various external and internal circumstances, and these conditionally enter into his concept of the truth, and what he terms true. This theory is both right and wrong. It would be quite absurd to regard the individual as a vessel which is to hold one general truth. The individual can most certainly think, and know, and express himself only on the basis of his own particular being.

But what is the real situation? Is there a truth we can possess? Can we appropriate it? There certainly is none we can pick up and put in our pocket. But the individual can have an honest and uncompromising attitude toward the truth; he can have a legitimate relationship to truth and hold and uphold it all his life. A man may serve Truth for seven years and yet another seven and still not win her, but his relationship has become more genuine and true, more and more truth itself. He cannot achieve this relationship to truth without breaking through his conditionality. He cannot shed it altogether; that is never within his power, but he can, at least, sense something of unconditionality— he can breathe its air. From that time on, this 'something of' will quicken his relationship to the truth. Human truth becomes real when one tries to translate one's relationship to truth into the reality of one's life. And human truth can be communicated only if one throws one's self into the process and answers for it with one's self.[37]

## 4   Tradition and Rebirth

Young people like to assume that the world begins with them. 'What the old folks have done is nothing but patchwork. We'll do it differently.' There is something fine and fruitful about this point of view. In order to accomplish anything youth must have faith in itself. But the very same prejudice can become a dangerous stumbling block to a generation which in consequence of this prejudice rejects the effects of past history, and the forces that have produced this generation. This prejudice prevents the living stream of tradition from entering their souls. When this occurs they are diverted from the eternal values they were to represent and incarnate in this era in their own particular way. Their urge to realization is severed from the primal reality of being itself. True, every new generation is a link in the great chain, and every new ring must be white-hot in the passion of its new existence before it can be welded to the chain as a new link. But both, the passion for a new beginning and the ability to join as a link in the chain, must go together. Youth must have the essential knowledge that the generations which produced them are within them, and that whatever new thing they accomplish draws its real significance from that fact.[38]

In this essay from *Israel and the World* Buber sees the tendency to disclaim the past as an inherent characteristic of the youthful outlook on the world. The passage raises an issue which is central to the process of curriculum planning and design: how to accommodate the tensions of inherited and contemporaneous knowledge and demonstrate the continuing relevance of the cultural heritage. The whole matter is given a good deal of attention by Buber in the course of his evaluations of progressive and traditionalist philosophies of education and is closely bound up with his attempt to offer an alternative to the positions represented by each. While rejecting the diminished emphasis on tradition in the progressive approach[39] he simultaneously affirms the need for an organic relation to tradition, characterizing the whole process once again in terms of dialogic encounter, and ultimately suggesting a much more dynamic traditionalism than what he rejected in the works of classical educationalists.[40] He writes of the need for a dialogic response to history, seeing the individual's engagement with the past as simultaneously a rebirth and a process of self- understanding achieved through a deepened historical consciousness.

Earlier I referred to Buber's prophetic theory of history. In two essays from *Pointing the Way* he rejects the Hegelian view of the historical order as one determined by the universal laws of reason and the divine action for redemption, on the grounds that it denies, or diminishes, the freedom of individual response to specific historical situations.[41] In place of the Hegelian theory — which he characterized as monologic and apocalyptic — he proposed a dialogic view of history based on free reciprocation between man and God. In 'The Demand of the Spirit and Historical Reality' he considers the implications of this for the activity of knowing. Once again, he reiterates his view that for a genuine knowing the individual 'exists only as a person open to the subject of thought.'[42] But he asks whether this free activity of knowing can occur independently of the social and historical realities impinging on individual consciousness. The knowing subject, he writes, is in the paradoxical situation of freely entering into the activity of knowing, while bringing to that activity the remembered experience his consciousness presents him with. He speaks of the 'problematic of the historical hour' with its indwelling possibilities of two complementary/contradictory attitudes — one rooted in the memory, the other pointed towards present and future time.[43]

The problematic of history embraces one of the fundamental paradoxes of all human existence: that it is simultaneously grounded in necessity and freedom. The individual exists in a necessary relation to his past, but this relation may be chosen and conducted with the same degree of freedom, and the same degree of dialogic reciprocity, as the various other relations informing his existence. It is interesting in this regard to compare Buber's conception of the historical dialogic with the notion of 'historical orthodoxy' put forward by T.S. Eliot in *After Strange Gods*.[44] Eliot and Buber both distrusted the excessive emphasis on contemporaneity in modern educational theory, and both argued vehemently that education should foster dispositions appropriate to the furtherance of historical awareness and the sense of cultural continuity. Eliot, like Buber, stresses the ambiguities and tensions inherent in this task. He writes of an historical awareness which is not merely an inert conservatism, or a petrefaction of traditions detached from present concerns, but one dynamically informing these concerns and conversely being informed by them. In *After Strange Gods* he puts forward the notion of orthodoxy: 'Tradition by itself is not enough,' he writes, 'it must be perpetually criticized and brought up to date under the supervision of what I call orthodoxy.'[45] Tradition, therefore, does not merely influence present concerns, but is itself refined and revitalized by those concerns. Buber represents the historical dialogic in similar terms in the essays from his collection, *On Judaism*. He writes of the paradox of historical awareness. 'Tradition,' he says, 'constitutes the noblest freedom for a generation that lives it meaningfully but is the most miserable slavery for the inheritors who merely accept it, tenaciously and complacently.'[46] He calls for an organic relation with the past, an integration of remembered and immediate consciousness:

> In those stillest of hours when we sense the ineffable, we become aware of a deep schism in our existence. This schism will seem insuperable to us so long as the insight that our blood is the creative force in our life has not yet become a living, integral part of us. To attain unity out of division we must become aware of the significance of this blood within us, for in the hustle of our days we are conscious only of the world around us, and of its effects. Let the vision of those stillest hours penetrate even more deeply; let us behold, let us comprehend, ourselves. Let us get hold of ourselves; let us draw our life into our hands, as a pail out of a well; let us gather it into our hands, as one gathers scattered corn. We must come to a decision, must establish a balance of powers within us.[47]

'Blood' is a familiar and recurrent metaphor employed by Buber in all these essays on history. He writes of the conflicting tendencies between which the individual person is torn: those of 'environment' and 'blood', those of 'the memory of lifespan' and the 'memory of millennia', those of 'the world about him and the world within him'.[48] The individual cannot evade his past, cannot shed his inherited culture; it is a force assimilated in the innermost resources of his consciousness. He thinks not merely in terms of present subjectivity but in terms of the resources of his 'blood" — in terms of race, community and his cultural inheritance. It is this awareness of heritage which makes his present meaningful by placing it in the continuum of historical time. Buber speaks, therefore, of the need for a unified consciousness; for a meaningful linking of present, past and expected or hoped for experience. He expresses the synthesis with particular force in the context of his own Jewish 'blood' consciousness:

> The forces that carve man's life are his inwardness and his environment; his disposition to assimilate impressions, and the matter creating these impressions. But the innermost stratum of man's disposition, which yields his type, the basic structure of his personality, is that which I have called blood: that something which is implanted within us by the chain of fathers and mothers, by their nature and by their fate, by their deeds and by their sufferings; it is time's great heritage that we bring with us into the world. We Jews need to know that our being and our character have been formed not solely by the nature of our fathers but also by their fate, and by their pain, their misery and their humiliation. We must feel this as well as know it, just as we must feel and know that within us dwells the element of the prophets, the psalmists, and the kings of Judah.[49]

The notion of communal race memory is used also by Buber to convey the organic nature of man's relation to the past. The chief factor in the survival of the Jewish people in the Diaspora, he says, was the expanding nature of racial memory that gained in power and scope as the heritage was transmitted from each generation to the next. With the new emotional and cultural life which was constantly informing the racial memory, it was able to sustain the Jewish people through the trials of history and especially against the threat of cultural assimilation endangering the survival of a dispersed race. This awareness of history found expression, not as a sentimental nostalgia, but as a force for the renewal of their traditions through the vitalizing memories of successive generations:

> We Jews are a community based on memory. A common memory has kept us together and enabled us to survive. This does not mean that we based our life on any one particular past; even on the loftiest of pasts; it simply means that one generation passed on to the next a memory which gained in scope — for new destiny and new emotional life were constantly accruing to it — and which realized itself in a way we can call organic. This expanding memory was more than a spiritual motif; it was a power which sustained, fed and quickened Jewish existence itself. I might even say that these memories realized themselves biologically, for in their strength the Jewish substance was renewed.[50]

A third image representing the process of historical awareness as an organic renewal of tradition and heritage is a more elaborate form of the familiar metaphor of birth giving. The use of that image in the context of

Buber's characterization of the teacher will be recalled: 'The influence of the teacher upon the pupil,' he wrote, 'is not merely compared to, but even set on a par with divine works which are linked with the human maternal act of giving birth.'[51] But he insists that the teacher's influence consists essentially in bringing about a *rebirth* in the minds of his pupils — 'The educator who brings the precious ore in the soul of his pupil to light and frees it from dross affords him a second birth, birth into a loftier life.'[52] Applying this simile to the transmission of the heritage, he stresses the dynamic, changing nature of the tradition handed down. It is handed down, not as a finished, inflexible product of history, but as something that requires newness in the act of transmission. It is no more an exact reproduction of the past than a child is an exact reproduction of his parents:

> A child does not represent the sum total of his parents; it is something that has never been before, something quite unpredictable. Similarly, a generation can only receive the teachings in the sense that it renews them. We do not take unless we also give. In the living tradition it is not possible to draw a line between preserving and producing. The work of embodiment takes place spontaneously; and that person is honest and faithful who utters words he has never heard as though they had come to him; for it is thus — and not as if he had 'created' them — that such words live within him. Everyone is convinced that he is doing no more than further advancing that which has advanced him to this point, and he may, nonetheless, be the originator of a new movement.[53]

There are two clear implications — the one concerning matters of pedagogy, the other the selection and design of school curricula — present throughout all these considerations of the nature of historical awareness. The historical dialogic is represented by Buber in the same terms as the more inclusive interpersonal dialogic informing his entire conception of human relation. What he describes is essentially a critical-reflective encounter with history, a meaning-making engagement with all those traditions constituting the spiritual-cultural heritage. The teacher is obliged to develop and confirm the potential for such an engagement in his pupil. This, in turn, implies that a curriculum faithfully representing the heritage is made available to the teacher and the pupil. In his critique of contemporary educational ideologies Buber was deeply critical of the tendency amongst certain educationalists to devalue the culture of the past. 'All true education,' he declared, 'must be linked to the origin, to the ''whence'', must be bound up with history and tradition.'[54] He calls, therefore, for the reinstatement of the heritage at the centre of contemporary school curriculum:

> Today what was once matter of course — our language, the Scriptures, our history — must become curriculum of the most crucial importance. The

passion to hand down can be replaced only by the passion to study, the passion of the fathers only by that of the sons, who must work unremittingly to regain the approach to the ancestral treasure and thus reestablish the bond of memory that joins the community together. Whether there are many such sons or few, they constitute a beginning.[55]

Earlier I referred to Buber's conception of the teacher as one who gives decisive effect to his pupil's learning. That obligation is greatly strengthened by Buber's identification of the educational process with the active conservation of historical values and truths. 'We have already indicated that in our case teaching is inseparably bound up with doing,' he declares, in his essay 'Teaching and Deed'.[56] The teachings of the past must not simply be made known, he says; they must enter fully into the lives of the teacher and his pupils. Contrasting the Biblical concept of *hokmah* with the Greek concept of *sophia*[57] — the first connotes the human thought of everyday life, the second a sphere of thought detached from life — he advocates the active conjunction of thought and action as the dynamic which ultimately must inform the whole dialogic encounter embracing the activities of teaching, learning and knowing. The practical nature of the dialogue is particularly emphasized by Buber in the specific instance of the renewal of tradition:

> Either the teachings live in the life of a responsible human being or they are not alive at all. The teachings do not center in themselves; they do not exist for their own sake. They refer to, they are directed toward, the deed. In this connection the concept of 'deed' does not of course connote 'activism', but life that realizes the teaching in the changing potentialities of every hour. . . . . Again and again, from the Sayings of the Fathers down to the definitive formulation of hasidism, the simple man who acts is given preference over the scholar whose knowledge is not expressed in deeds. 'He whose deeds exceed his wisdom, his wisdom shall endure; but he whose wisdom exceeds his deed, his wisdom shall not endure.' And in the same vein: 'He whose wisdom exceeds his deeds — what does he resemble? A tree with many boughs and few roots. A wind, springing up, uproots it and overturns it. But he whose deeds exceed his wisdom — what does he resemble? A tree with few boughs but many roots. Though all the winds in the world come and blow at it, it cannot be budged.' What counts is not the extent of spiritual possessions, nor the thoroughness of knowledge, nor the keenness of thought, but to know what one knows and to believe what one believes so directly that it can be translated into the life one lives.[58]

## 5  Buber's Pedagogic Influence

There are significant indications that Buber's characterization of the teacher, with its emphasis on authentic reciprocation, integrity, care, and a decisive intervention in the learning process, together with his theory of knowing as a critical, reflective, freely oriented, but historically informed activity, is profoundly influencing contemporary conceptions of teaching and learning. The works of some other theorists particularly indebted to Buber may be cited briefly to indicate the extent of his influence. Bernard Curtis, in a work entitled 'Soul Contact' has considered the dialogic approach to teaching from the standpoint of the phenomenologist.[59] He describes the teaching/learning relationship as one which essentially aspires towards the integrity of 'loving encounter'. He cites a remarkable passage from Bertrand Russell's autobiography to illustrate his meaning of 'loving encounter' or 'soul contact': 'The loneliness of the human soul is unendurable; nothing can penetrate it except the highest intensity of the sort of love that religious teachers have preached; whatever does not spring from this motive is harmful or at best useless.'[60] Curtis argues for a consciously and voluntarily chosen relationship, in a manner strongly suggestive of Buber's description of teaching as dialogic inclusion:

> If we regard teaching as a matter of somehow helping and encouraging the child to share our conventions, standards, norms, institutions etc., then teaching seems to be a special case of relating to another as himself: a centre of caring. Using the word 'soul' to bring to mind this idea of a person as a centre of (effort-laden) caring, it will be accepted here (apparently in agreement with Mill and Russell) that good teaching of a child depends upon contacting his soul and, moreover, contacting it in a loving way.[61]

Echoing Buber's thoughts on the importance of acceptance, confirmation and trust, Curtis provides a detailed exposition of the efforts that must be taken to maintain that trust. His idea of 'care' includes attention, vigilance, concern, endeavour, perseverance and concentration. He also identifies the barriers to trust. He mentions indifference, insensitivity and selective attention as attitudes likely to obliterate all hope of 'fruitful contact' between teacher and pupil. He suggests that strong links exist, both of a positive and a negative character, between pupils' attitudes towards teachers and their attitudes towards the subject they teach, thus emphasizing the highly personalised nature of the knowing relationship. Significantly, he reiterates Buber's idea of teaching as 'mastering' (the term he employs is 'directional' to stress the decisive nature of the teacher's influence), though he warns of the possible degeneration in the relationship that is likely to follow from excessively formal or arbitrary methods of teaching:

> In spite of the lack of awareness on both sides of what is happening, the teacher's unconscious unpleasantness and its effect on the children may, however, be such that we have to refer to the conscious and reasoned expectations of both parties in describing it. People can be unconsciously unpleasant in ways that the weather cannot. To fill out our example a little,

let us suppose that the teacher's behaviour includes the following unconscious postures, gestures and mannerisms; an habitual, apparently
threatening sweep of the arm and glint in the eye; frequent occasions when
his voice, never very warm or gentle, rises and rasps; a tendency to interrupt
children when they are answering and to correct their mistakes scornfully;
a preference for difficult questions; a way of neglecting or ignoring a
particular child who is a bit slower than the rest at catching on; a general
insensitivity towards the difficulty the children have in understanding and
towards their consequent tensions and apprehensions. We think these things
are affecting the children in ways we feel entitled to call unpleasant or
aggressive. . . . That is, we are calling the teacher's behaviour unpleasant
because of the unwanted and avoidable effects it is having on the children,
and these effects are modifications of the child's will, as we shall call them.
We call them so because the effect is to make it more difficult for the child
to make certain choices and to acquire certain habits of feeling, thought and
action, and perhaps they make it easier for him to make other choices and
acquire other habits.[62]

David Holbrook has applied Buber's dialogic philosophy to the complex
processes involved in the formation and growth of symbolic experience. He
has looked to existentialist and phenomenological philosophers for alternatives to the positivistic, highly functionalised theories dominating contemporary approaches to language education. In *English for Meaning* he calls
for a rejection of the empiricist/objectivist paradigm of learning emanating
from behaviour theory and the communications sciences, and argues for a
refocussing of classroom methdologies on the indivisible unity of individual
consciousness, and on learning as an expression of that unity. In place of the
fragmentation of functionalist theory he advocates a focussing on consciousness and intentionality (i.e. the capacity to confer meaning) as the true
dynamic of learning, and for greater attention by teachers to the processes
by which the dynamism is released in the child. In the specific instance of
first language learning he sees a particular need to maintain the radical unity
and wholeness of intentional meaning-making:

So English is a discipline of thought; and it has to do with language as the
expression of the 'whole' experience — that is, all our existential reality. It
deals not only with ideas that can be taken and abstracted from our minds,
but our bodily feelings, and emotions, our dreams, our unconscious fan-
tasies, our creative powers, and our hopes for tomorrow. So it is a
phenomenological discipline concerned with the phenomena of consciousness. Thus it is inadequate to regard English, as linguisticians and the
'language men' do, merely as a discipline of 'language use'. We have only
to utter a word, or even make a silent sign, such as a wink or a pointed finger,
to point beyond the word or sign, and express a meaning which involves the
self and the other, our own body and the world, the individual dynamic

psyche and a tradition of culture: the whole being-in-the-world, in time. Any symbol involves many tacit elements deep within us, even feelings in our body life, and our pretensions — that is, expectancies in the flux of time, towards ever opening possibilities and goals towards which we are drawn. English has to do with meanings, and 'meaning is an intention of the mind' (Husserl).[63]

Holbrook echoes Buber's description of teaching as essentially a re-plication of the original inclusion existing between mother and child. 'I believe,' he writes, 'all teaching is a version of the processes which go on between mother and infant in the formative beginnings and depends upon tacit dynamics of the same kind.'[64] In language strongly reminiscent of *I and Thou* he describes how the child discovers his own reality and the reality of the surrounding universe through his ability to form meaningful relation-ships. Since all such relationships are the product of the original mother/child relationship, the learning process, he argues, must be seen as an extension of that first encounter into more complex forms of encounter. Consciousness, and its capacities to internalize meaning, are themselves grounded in those formative encounters and are developed through successive encounters and the possibilities they afford for meaning-making through dialogue. 'Man,' he writes, 'lives in a mansion of consciousness and this is created by interaction with the other.'[65] *Liebende Wirheit* (loving communion), he declares, is the primary reality of existence; the basis of its freedom and the source and ground of the understanding consciousness. It begins in the spontaneous dialogue between mother and child and can be renewed con-tinuously through teaching encounters conceived in the same spirit as the first involuntary dialogue:

> There are two great mysteries with which we live and which we take for granted — and yet we are often annoyed if anyone tries to inquire into them. One is our consciousness, asserting its intentionality and autonomy, as we have seen. The other is the origin of these powers in the baby and very small infant; with the concomitant residue, in each one of us, of aspects of this period of psychic gestation. As a number of thinkers have pointed out, there are considerable resistances to the exploration of these origins in adult human life; we will look everywhere but at our beginnings. And the reason is our fear of the infant within each of us, who is not fully grown and whose existence threatens us because of his vulnerability and unsatisfied needs.
>
> However, if we dare to contemplate infancy and the amazing processes by which we become ourselves, we may find insights which will help us in our work of teaching — which, after all, is an encounter with childhood. Our capacities to see and know the world, and other people, and to deal with these effectively, are bound up with our earliest relationships. One may even go back before anything that may be called 'relationship'. . . . These

processes are bound up with problems of self and other, self and world, and thus with the deepest poetic and philosophical problems. They are thus bound up from the beginning with meaning, and they are worked on by imagination, play and symbolism. In a number of works I have tried to show what happens if these processes go 'wrong' as they have for the schizoid individual: his struggles to complete them often generate the most remarkable art. Thus a study of these processes is essential for anyone concerned to see what English as a subject has to do with the discovery of the 'other', of the world; of the self; 'reparation' and love.[66]

(This whole matter is discussed in detail in Chapter 6 where some important differences between Holbrook and Buber are examined also.)

In a work called *Learning through Writing* Bernard Harrison further explores the nature of teacher/learner relationships in the same context of the development of symbolic and linguistic experience. Like Buber, he rejects the hierarchical, cognitionally dominated model of learning, and argues that truly effective and personally significant learning is primarily the product of meaningful encounter between teacher and student. The search for meaning, he writes, demands the whole-hearted personal involvement of the learner, if it is to be truly fruitful; equally, it needs the active support and encouragement and the formative discipline that a teacher can provide. In this passage from *Learning through Writing* he asserts the fundamental principle informing the work: that the efficacy of all learning depends ultimately on the presence of a loving mutuality in the relations between teacher and student:

> If we are to gain new forms of knowing, we have to move forward; we are required, even at great cost, to renounce old forms, old cliches, worn-out patterns of knowledge in seeking renewal. It is harder to learn as we grow older, since by then we have more of our old selves to lose — though it is not impossible, so long as we choose to live rather than merely survive. As in personal relations, the quality of learning depends on the spirit in which it is enacted — that is, on the quality of love. This guiding principle has long been known, if only recently formulated as a 'scientific' proposition. The principle is embedded in Shakespeare's metaphor of the c(h)ords of love with which Cordelia freely ties herself again to her father. Cordelia's act of renewed commitment as an adult to her father was made possible by her earlier choice against his possessive claims on her. In exercising her volition, her capacity for choice, she discovers the strength of her own identity. It is such acts of volition that need to be rehearsed in the learning 'play' of the young adults in our classrooms, so that their capacity to confront life's difficulties with resilience and skill can grow.
> In good teaching and learning, the play will motivate the discipline; and

the discipline will serve, shape and justify the play. In the realms of language play, this will become an essentially poetic activity of creative interplay between individual and world, aimed at the shaping and revealing of meaning. For it is the natural task of learners to discover and express their being through their inherited language(s); and it is the teacher's task to give space and provision for this process, allowing — and even, when needed, coercing — the learners to take full responsibility for their own experience.[67]

In the latter part of the passage the principle of dialogic learning is applied to the sphere of symbol-making and specifically to linguistic symbol making. Citing Cassirer in support of his view that all symbolic experience originates in pre-verbal, non-rational states of feeling, and depends for its regeneration therefore on the constant nurturing of the life of feeling, Harrison writes of the centrality of affectional encounter or dialogue in the growth of linguistic potentialities — the potentialities on which all other forms of learning depend. The full implications of this will be considered in detail in a later chapter which will attempt to locate the processes of linguistic and symbolic learning in the broader context of aesthetic development and the cultivation and growth of the creative imagination.

# V

# Religious and Moral Education

## 1   Towards a Meaning-giving Faith: Defining the Aims of Religious Education

Of the various causes identified by Buber for a contemporary decline in religious faith (see Chapter 2, Section 6) three are given particular attention in his writings on education. He spoke, firstly, of the rigidifying effect of the institutions and conventions of religion on the free and spontaneous growth of the genuine religious spirit. He particularly complained of their relegation of religious practice to a special sphere of life and their consequent separation of religion from much of the reality of everyday existence. Secondly, he spoke of the further stultification of the spirit of religious faith resulting from the abstract intellectualization of religious thought which he associated particularly with the traditions of rationalist theology. Thirdly, he spoke of the diminishing relevance of religious symbology for the needs of the present time, and the diminished meaningfulness especially of the anthropomorphic imagery of Jewish and Christian traditions. He wrote optimistically, none-theless, of the possibilities of achieving a renewal of the religious spirit — especially amongst the young — and foresaw an important role for educators in bringing such a renewal to fulfilment.

His conception of the aims of religious education is determined largely by his understanding of the ways in which the decline of faith could be arrested. Since he concerned himself particularly with the above mentioned explanations for this decline, it is necessary to inquire more closely into all three so that his proposals for a renewal of religious faith can be properly understood. In his essay, 'The Prejudices of Youth', he sees the decline in faith as the inevitable consequence of the distorted spirituality frequently propagated in the name of religion. 'For during the past decades the race of man has not, by and large, fared well at the hands of the spirit,' he writes. 'For the spirit was not simply silent; it spoke falsely at junctures when it should have had an important voice in history.'[1] 'The spirit,' he says, 'had sacrificed the very factor which makes it legitimate': its 'readiness to expose itself to reality, to prove and express itself, in reality.'[2] For the separation of the spiritual from the wholeness of reality he particularly blames the institutional churches:

. . . the religious institutions and procedures which are supposed to be objective expressions of the reality of faith are so often and in so many different ways contrary to true faith and to the truth of faith. They have become stumbling blocks in the path of the true believer; they have placed themselves in opposition to his humble life, and on the side of whatever happens to be powerful and accepted as valid in the world. This error, which is in the foreground of our time, has affected the souls of the generations which grew up in a time of crisis; it has invalidated their faith. Here again, the right has been abandoned along with the wrong. Real faith does not mean professing what we hold true in a ready-made formula. On the contrary: it means holding ourselves open to the unconditional mystery which we encounter in every sphere of our life and which cannot be comprised in any formula. It means that , from the very roots of our being, we should always be prepared to live with this mystery as one being lives with another. Real faith means the ability to endure life in the face of this mystery.[3]

A further cause put forward by Buber for the decline of religious faith is the reduction of religious truth to the abstract categories of rationalist theology. In Chapter 2 this was represented as a modern survival of the gnosticism which he ultimately attributed to the Hellenist influences in Judaism and 'Paulinist' Christianity. To this gnostic influence he attributed a general weakening of the *relation* of faith and the resultant corruption of the religious spirit. Modern atheism, he states, is largely the product of this inherited gnosticism. In his essay, 'Herut: On Youth and Religion', he sees it as having a particularly baleful impact on modern youth. Its main consequence is the destruction of the interpersonal and social dialogue in which the spirit of faith is ultimately rooted:

Intellectualization, in the making for centuries and accomplished within recent generations, has brought a depressing loneliness to the youth of present-day Europe. By intellectualization I mean the hypertrophy of intellect that has broken out of the context of organic life and become parasitic, in contradistinction to organic spirituality, into which life's totality is translated. Because the bridge of immediate community, whether its name be love, friendship, companionship, or fellowship, connects only man with man, and hence spirit with spirit, but not thinking apparatus with thinking apparatus, this intellectualization begets loneliness. Not the exultant loneliness of the summit experienced by the first climbers who are waiting, with silent hearts, for their companions who have fallen behind, but the negative loneliness of the abyss experienced by the lost and the forlorn. Out of the anxiety and depression of such a state of mind, modern Europe's youth longs for community, longs for it so powerfully that it is ready to surrender to any phantom of community, as we have so abundantly experienced.[4]

Religious thought systems are seen in the same essay as destroying the capacity for the personal appropriation of religious meaning which Buber identified as the creative principle in religion in his essay, 'Jewish Religiosity'. 'Religion,' he declared, 'is true as long as it is creative, but it is creative only so long as religiosity, accepting the yoke of the laws and doctrines, is able to imbue them with new and incandescent meaning, so that they will seem to have been revealed by every generation anew.'[5] (The editor of *On Judaism* instances the following movements as exemplifying the spirit of religiosity: the Essenes, the early Christian brotherhood, the Talmudic Aggadah, medieval mysticism, and eighteenth century Hasidism.)[6] Buber sees the originators of abstract religious theories as being especially responsible for the depersonalisation of religious meaning and for the consequent disillusion with which religion is regarded by the young:

> The originators of such theories overlook the fact that religious truth is not a conceptual abstraction but has existential relevance; that is, that words can only point the way, and that religious truth can be made adequately manifest only in the individual's or the community's life of religious actualization (Bewahrung). Indeed, they overlook the fact that a master's teachings lose their religious character as soon as they are taken out of the context of his own life and the life of his followers and transformed into a wholly non-personal, autonomous maxim, recognizable and acknowledgeable as such. Frozen into a declaration of what is or into a precept of what ought to be, the words of religious teaching represent a more inspirited, but also a more primitive, variation of the metaphysical or ethical ideology. But viewed as part of the utterances of a great life to which conceptualization cannot do justice, they are beyond the sphere of all ideologies, and not subject to their criteria; they are truth *sui generis*, contingent upon no other: religious truth. Here, not the words themselves are truth, but life as it has been, and will be, lived, and the words are truth only by virtue of this life.[7]

The third cause put forward by Buber for the decline of religious faith is the inadequacy of the symbology of religion to encompass the reality of the unconditioned, the intemporal and the infinite. 'What we call gods are nothing but images of God and must suffer the fate of such images,' he declares. 'What we really mean when we say that a God is dead,' he writes, 'is that the images of God vanish and that therefore an image which up to now was regarded and worshipped as God can no longer be so regarded and so worshipped.'[8] He sees the iconoclastic process, therefore, as inevitable; the images of God are certain to be discarded, but, he adds in a crucial caveat, the need for such images persists:

> For the iconoclast is the soul of man which rebels against having an image that can no longer be belived in, elevated above the heads of man as a thing that demands to be worshipped. In their longing for a god, men try again

and again to set up a greater, a more genuine and more just image, which is intended to be more glorious than the last and only proves the more unsatisfactory. The commandment, 'Thou shalt not make unto thee an image,' means at the same time, 'Thou canst not make an image.' This does not, of course, refer merely to sculptured or painted images, but to our fantasy, to all the power of our imagination as well. But man is forced time and again to make images, and forced to destroy them when he realizes that he has not succeeded.

The images topple, but the voice is never silenced, 'Ye heard the voice of words but ye saw no form' (Deut 4:12). The voice speaks in the guise of everything that happens, in the guise of all world events; it speaks to the men of all generations, makes demands upon them, and summons them to accept their responsibility. I have pointed out that it is of the utmost importance not to lose one's openness. But to be open means not to shut out the voice — call it what you will. It does not matter what you call it. All that matters is that you hear it.[9]

Recognizing the need for iconoclasm as a feature of the renewal of the religious spirit, Buber spoke approvingly of some aspects of the 'critical atheism' of Martin Heidegger. Heidegger, he wrote, recognised the phenomenon of 'God concealment' and correspondingly the persistence of the religious need. His expectation that the divine would re-enter human history 'in unanticipated forms' gave grounds for a profound optimism on the survival of religious faith. (I am quoting the relevant passage from *Eclipse of God* at some length because it has crucial implications for religious education which will be addressed presently).

It has been possible for Heidegger to erect this new position despite the 'death of God' because being for him is bound to and attains its illumination through the destiny and history of man, without its becoming thereby a function of human subjectivity. But by this it is already indicated that, to use an image that Heidegger himself avoids, God can rise from the dead. This means that the unfolding of the new ontological thought can prepare for a turning point in which the divine, or as Heidegger, in agreement with the poet Holderlin, prefers to say, the holy, will appear in new and still unanticipated forms. This thinking is consequently, as Heidegger repeatedly emphasizes, not atheism, for it 'decides neither positively nor negatively about the possibility of God's existing'. Rather 'through its adequate conception of existence' it makes it possible for the first time legitimately to ask 'what is the ontological state of the relation of existence to the divine.'

Heidegger not only protests against our regarding this view as atheism but also against our regarding it as an indifferentism which must deteriorate into nihilism. He by no means wants to teach an indifference toward the religious question. The single need of this hour is, to him, much more the thinking through of the basic religious concepts, the cognitive clarification of the meaning of words such as God or the Holy. 'Must we not first be able,' he asks, 'to understand and hear these words with the greatest care if we, as men, that is as existing beings, are to experience a relation of God to man?' But this in his opinion would belong to a new thinking of being through man. According to Heidegger's conception, to be sure, it is not for man to decide whether and how the divine will reappear. Such an appearance, he explains, will take place only through the fate of being itself. Since, however, he has stated as the presupposition for this appearance that 'beforehand and in long preparation being itself is clarified and is experienced in its truth', there can be no doubt as to what part is to be ascribed here to human thought about truth in the determination of 'whether and how the day of the holy will dawn.' It is indeed precisely in human thought about truth that being becomes illuminated. Heidegger usually conceives of this still uncertain sunrise of the holy as the clear background before which 'an appearance of God and the gods can begin anew.'[10]

Religious renewal is concerned simultaneously, it would appear, with the revivification of both the spirit of faith and the symbolic language through which the subject of man's faith is made manifest and known. In 'Herut: On Youth and Religion' Buber reasserts this point with a feeling of hopefulness similar to that which is evident in his essay on Heidegger:

Man's mind thus experiences the unconditional as that great something that is counterposed against it, as the Thou as such. By creating symbols the mind comprehends what is in itself incomprehensible, thus, in symbol and adage, the illimitable God reveals Himself to the human mind, which gathers the flowing universal currents into the receptacle of an affirmation that declares the Lord reigns in this and in no other way. Or man's mind captures a flash of the original source of light in the mirror of some rule that declares the Lord must be served in this and in no other way. But neither symbol nor adage makes man unworthy or untrue; they are rather forms the unconditional itself creates within man's mind, which, at this particular time, has not yet developed into a more effective tool. In mankind's great ages, the Divine, in invisible becoming, outgrows old symbolisms and blossoms forth in new ones.[11]

Ultimately, his hopefulness springs from his belief in the openness of mankind, and especially of the young, to the reality of the unconditioned and intemporal, despite the widespread prevalence of the prejudices that have been mentioned. That openness, he argued, is founded on man's innate capacity for wonder; it is a capacity, he said, which is particularly manifested in the imaginative vitality of the youthful outlook on life, which itself is deeply conducive to the nurturing of the religious spirit. Religiosity, the creative principle in religion, is identified by Buber with this openness to the unknown and undisclosed — it is 'man's sense of wonder and adoration,' he wrote, 'an ever anew articulation and formulation of his feeling that, transcending his conditioned being yet bursting from its very core, there is something that is unconditioned.'[12] And he further asserted that 'religiosity starts anew with every young person, shaken to his very core by the mystery.'[13] Youth is the time when the spirit of wonder and creative questioning are at their most potent and these are essential conditions for the growth of genuine religiosity:

> Youth is the time of total openness. With totally open senses, it absorbs the world's variegated abundance; with a totally open will, it gives itself to life's boundlessness. It has not yet sworn allegiance to any one truth for whose sake it would have to close its eyes to all other perspectives, has not yet obligated itself to abide by any one norm that would silence all its other aspirations. Its quest for knowledge knows no limits other than those set by its own experience, its vitality no responsibility other than the one to the totality of its own life.[14]

He restates his conviction that an awareness of the unconditioned, however dormant, is present in all men. While it may be suppressed or evaded, there are occasions throughout life when all men are confronted with its reality. This awareness is at its strongest in the time of youth but, for the reasons already mentioned, it is subsequently diminished in impact, neglected or ignored:

> At some time or other, be it ever so fleeting and dim, every man is affected by the power of the unconditional. The time of life when this happens to all we call youth. At that time every man experiences the hour in which the infinite beckons him, testing whether, sustained by the power of his vision and the creation of symbols, by his dedication and response, he can unflinchingly confront it. In this most inward sense, every man is destined to be religious. Indeed, what the total openness of youth signifies is that its mind is open not merely to all, but to the All. But most men fail to fulfil their destiny. Whether they remain close to their ancestral religion or become alienated from it, whether they continue to believe in and to practice this religion and its symbolism or refuse to adhere to its command, they are unable to withstand the impact of the unconditional and therefore evade it. They do not approach it with the power of their vision and their work, with their dedicated and responsive deed; they turn away from it, and toward the conditional.[15]

For the religious educator the crucial question emerging from all this is how the spirit of religiosity can be nurtured or renewed. Four main approaches to the problem are proposed by Buber. He argues, firstly, for a fostering of the questioning spirit amongst the young and suggests that their prejudices, like the critical atheism he approved in Heidegger, may be highly conducive to the personal clarification of spiritual and religious truths. He rejects the notion of religious teaching as the transmission of abstract knowledge: 'Its leading proponents', he said, 'sublimate the many-faceted and vital fullness of religion into a system of abstract concepts.'[16] That process of definitive systematisation would be profoundly in conflict with the spirit of openness, self questioning and wonder he considered to be essential ingredients for the nurturing of religiosity. He would encourage this spirit of openness therefore — even if it were to involve approving their prejudices — as an appropriate feature of the education of the young:

> The one thing which has become clearer and clearer to me in the course of my life is that keeping an open mind is of the utmost importance. The right kind of openness is the most precious human possession. I said, the right kind of openness. One can take a certain stand and hold to it passionately but one must remain open to the whole world, see what there is to see, experience what experience offers, and include all of experience in the effectuation of whatever cause one has decided for. Though constantly changing, our stand will yet remain true to itself, but deepened by an insight which grows more and more true to reality. We need to take a firm stand, but we also need to feel that we have not thus put our feet in shackles. Wherever we stand, we should stand free and unbiased and grow aware of the world.[17]

Maintaining the same opposition to abstract formulations of religious meaning, he argues, secondly, that the individual person's awareness of the unconditioned must always be a *relational* awareness since his access to the unconditional — the eternal Thou — is by way of the main relational potencies of human existence. These are the potencies of loving, believing, knowing and creating. All such relationships, he declares in *I and Thou*, extend into the reality of unconditional Thouness. 'Extended the lines of relationships intersect in the eternal You,' he writes. 'Every single You is a glimpse of that. Through every single You the basic word addresses the eternal You.'[18] One of the most poetic passages in *I and Thou* expresses it like this:

> In every sphere, in every relational act, through everything that becomes present to us we gaze toward the train of the eternal You; in each we perceive a breath of it; in every You we address the eternal You, in every sphere according to its manner. All spheres are included in it while it is included in none.
>
> Through all of them shines the one presence.
>
> But we can take each out of the presence.
>
> Out of life with nature we can take the 'physical' world, that of consistency, out of life with men, the 'psychical' world that of affectability; out of life with spiritual beings, the 'poetic' world, that of validity. Now they

have been deprived of their transparency and thus of sense; each has become usable and murky, and remains murky even if we endow it with shining names: cosmos, eros, logos. For in truth there is a cosmos for man only when the universe becomes a home for him with a holy hearth where he sacrifices; and there is eros for him only when beings become for him images of the eternal, and community with them becomes revelation; and there is logos for him only when he addresses the mystery with works and service of the spirit.

The demanding silence of forms, the loving speech of human beings, the eloquent muteness of creatures — all of these are gateways into the presence of the word.[19]

Since man's access to the intemporal and unconditioned is by way of the main relational potencies of his existence, it follows that the spirit of genuine religiosity is fostered mainly through his everyday relationships. Lived authentically, they disclose the possibility of the unconditioned, the perfection of relation itself. The mystery of the infinite and eternal is discovered in the simplicity of everyday existence:

The forms in which the mystery approaches us are nothing but our personal experiences. At times it is very difficult to live with the mystery, and to be constant to it in the midst of these ever new, unforeseen, surprising, precipitating and overpowering experiences. But there is something which can help us and there are helpers. There is the living transmission of those who have really lived with the mystery, and above all those who are of our kind and who had our tidings. They help us through the pure strength with which they experienced the mystery, faced it, and engaged their lives to it. For to believe means to engage oneself.[20]

Both passages echo the words of Father Zossima in *The Brothers Karamazov* to the woman who has sought his advice on how she might recover her lost faith: 'Love your neighbour actively and indefatigably,' he says. 'In so far as you grow in active love you shall grow surer of the reality of God and the immortality of your soul. If you attain to perfect self-forgetfulness in the love of your neightbour then you will believe without doubt, and no doubt can possibly enter your soul.'[21]

It is important, in this context, to clarify Buber's position on the notion of religious knowledge and its place in education. Clearly he rejects those approaches in which religious education was focussed principally on a system of ideas and values that were thought to constitute the knowledge content of faith. He rejected them on the grounds that they insufficiently nurture the relational capacities which disclose the potentiality of faith. But he does include the knowing relationship amongst his main relational potencies, signifying by this a personally appropriated understanding of religious meaning, rather than the abstract formulations traditionally constituting religious knoweldge. In 'Religion and Philosophy' he spoke of systems of thought as 'manifestations of genuine thought relations made possible through abstraction',[22] but he considered such knowledge was necessarily confined to the sphere of the It and was therefore of limited significance in the appropriation of religious truth. Underlying both his disenchantment with abstraction and his affirmation of the relational awareness of religious truth is his belief ultimately in an organic spirituality in which all spheres of human life and activity are integrated through the unifying power of religious faith. Thus, when he considers how religion is to be made manifest to the young, he calls for a process of 'religious actualisation' through which religious faith can penetrate the reality of their lives. Contrasting theoretical formulations of religious truth with the existential witness of its lived reality, he declares:

> The originators of such theories overlook the fact that religious truth is not a conceptual abstraction but has existential relevance, that is, that words can only point the way and that religious truth can be made adequately manifest only in the individual's or the community's life of religious actualization (Bewahrung). Indeed, they overlook the fact that a master's teachings lose their religious character as soon as they are taken out of the context of his own life and the life of his followers and transformed into a wholly non-personal, autonomous maxim, recognizable and acknowledgeable as such. Frozen into a declaration of what is or into a precept of what ought to be, the words of religious teaching represent a more inspirited, but also a more primitive, variation of a metaphysical or ethical ideology. But viewed as part of the utterances of a great life to which conceptualization cannot do justice, they are beyond the sphere of all ideologies, and not subject to their criteria: they are truth *sui generis*, contingent upon no other: religious truth. Here, not the words themselves are truth, but life as it has been and will be lived; and the words are truth only by virtue of this life.[23]

Religious truth, he writes, 'in contradistinction to philosophical truth, is not a maxim but a way, not a thesis but a process'. Religious formation, he argues, is a process of self-integration in which all aspects of existence are brought within the all-encompassing impact of the spiritual. It is a search for an organic integration, the elements of which are to be found within nature itself:

> Spirit is not a late bloom on the tree Man, but what constitutes man. The fact that man is a unit of substance which cannot be grasped if we regard it merely as a phenomenon of nature, the fact that there is a category of existence called Man, is based on the particular human consciousness. Spirit, then, is not just one human faculty among others. It is man's totality that has become consciousness, the totality which comprises and integrates

all his capacities, powers, qualities and urges. When a man thinks, he thinks with his entire body; spiritual man thinks even with his fingertips. Spiritual life is nothing but the existence of man, insofar as he possesses that true human conscious totality, which is not the result of development; it goes back to the origin of mankind, though it may unfold differently in different individuals. Nowadays the word spirit is used in a very different sense by persons who forget or scorn its great past in both the East and the West, and designate by it that part of human thinking which essentially regards all totality as something alien and hateful; the severed intellect. Severed from totality, yet greedy to govern all of man, for a number of centuries the intellect has been growing greedier and more independent and is attempting to reign from on high, but without the ability to flow freely into all organic vitality as the spirit it has dethroned can and does. The revolt of the 'tellurian powers' is not directed against the spirit, the master from time immemorial, but toward the imposter, the spirit turned into a homunculus. Not this usurper. but only the human spirit in its totality can overcome elemental force and elemental urges when occasion demands. They cannot be tamed like beasts of prey; they must be mastered as the artist masters and shapes the stuff he works with. Only the spirit in its totality can order and give true shape to the life of the individual and that of the species.[24]

It is the attainment of this organic spirituality, therefore, which is the chief aim of religious education. Through education the individual is assisted to discover the synthesising resources of the spirit within his own nature. It seeks to bring forth that holiness which is latent in all being — in the yet-unhallowed — and is brought to fulfilment through authentic relation. Most emphatically, the holy, in Buber's conception of what the term signifies, is not a separate sphere of existence. 'The spirit', he writes, 'does not embrace a holy world, rejoicing in its holiness, nor does it float above an unholy world, clutching all holiness to itself: it produces holiness and the world is made holy.'[25] While expressing itself in every facet of human existence, the spirit ultimately becomes manifest in the unifying phenomenon of faith: 'Based on the power of faith, the spirit exerts its influence upon the world through its agents, courage and love. These constitute its power which may well govern the elemental forces because it has known them from the earliest times, and knows what is their due. Though in one historical era after another the spirit may seem dethroned and exiled, it does not lose its power. Again and again, unexpectedly and unpredictably, it causes what is intrinsic in the course of history through its agents, faithful courage and faithful love.'[26]

## 2   Symbol, History and Myth: Education and the Traditions of Faith
Thus far, three main approaches to religious education have been identified. They are, firstly, the fostering of the questioning spirit and the sense of

wonder and openness which Buber considered especially conducive to the nurturing of creative religiosity; secondly, a focussing on faith as a relational phenomenon, and the development of the relational potencies of loving, believing, creating and knowing as the means through which the reality of the unconditioned, infinite and intemporal are disclosed; and thirdly, the fostering of an organic spirituality through which religious faith can penetrate and inform every facet of the individual person's life. A fourth approach which will be examined now concerns the symbolism of faith and the place of tradition in the whole process of religious education.

Some reference has already been made to Buber's concern that traditional religious symbols had become increasingly irrelevant to contemporary society. In the third section of *I and Thou* he places the whole matter in perspective in a passage where he writes of the names and images by which men have traditionally addressed God:

> Men have addressed their eternal You by many names. When they sang of what they had thus named, they still meant You; the first myths were hymns of praise. Then the names entered into the It-language; men felt impelled more and more to think of and to talk about their eternal You as an It. But all names of God remain hallowed — because they have been used not only to speak of God but also to speak to him.
>
> Some would deny any legitimate use of the word God because it has been misused so much. Certainly it is the most burdened of all human words. Precisely for that reason it is the most imperishable and unavoidable. And how much weight has all erroneous talk about God's nature and works (although there never has been nor can be any such talk that is not erroneous) compared with the one truth that all men who have addressed God really meant him? For whoever pronounces the word God and really means You, addresses, no matter what his delusion, the true You of his life that cannot be restricted by any other and to whom he stands in a relationship that includes all others.
>
> But whoever abhors the name and fancies that he is godless — when he addresses with his whole-devoted being the You of his life that cannot be restricted by any other, he addresses God.[21]

Here Buber offers a particular explanation for the diminished relevance of the symbols of religious faith — their objectification and relegation to the sphere of the It — but he insists, nonetheless, that the need to symbolize the relation of faith persists in man, by virtue of his inherent need to identify the infinity of the Thouness he addresses in the depth of his own participation in the interpersonal. He points, therefore, even to the atheist's awareness of this need, despite his rejection of religious traditions and his disavowal of the conventions and symbols of religious faith. The matter is further explained in 'The Man of Today and the Jewish Bible' where Buber sees a radical link between the decline of faith and the diminished historical awareness of modern man. The latter is attributed largely to the reduction of historical explanation to the level of the empirical and the scientifically verifiable:

> The man of today has two approaches to history. He may comtemplate it as a freethinker, and participate in and accept the shifting events, the varying success of the struggles for power, as a promiscuous agglomeration of happenings. To him history will seem a medley of the actions and deaths of peoples, of grasping and losing, triumph and misery, a meaningless hodge-podge to which the mind of man, time and again, gives an unreliable and unsubstantial semblance of meaning. Or he may view history dogmatically, derive laws from past sequences of events and calculate future sequences, as though the 'main lines' were already traced on some roll which need merely unroll; as though history were not the vital living, growing, of time, constantly moving from decision to decision, of time into which my time and my decisions stream full force. He regards history as a stark, ever-present, inescapable space.
>
> Both these approaches are a misinterpretation of historic destiny, which is neither chance nor fatality. According to the biblical insight historic destiny is the secret correlation inhering in the current moment. When we are aware of origin and goal, there is no meaningless drift; we are carried along by a meaning we could never think up for ourselves, a meaning we are to live — not to formulate.
>
> The man of today knows of no beginning. As far as he is concerned, history ripples towards him from some prehistorical cosmic age. He knows of no end; history sweeps him on into a posthistorical cosmic age.[28]

In 'The Prejudices of Youth' the same points are taken up, this time in the context of the youthful outlook on life. 'Young people like to assume that the world begins with them,' he writes. 'This prejudice prevents the living stream of tradition from entering their souls. When this occurs they are divided from the eternal values they were to represent and incarnate in this era in their own particular way.'[29] It is no more possible, he suggests, utterly to ignore scripture than it is to ignore the historical inheritance as a whole. Scripture, as the expression of the organic, racial memory of man, is part of his historical consciousness: it is a record of what happened but was experienced by man as wisdom revealed by God. In 'The Man of Today and the Jewish Bible' where he argues that the historical cannot be disentangled from the biblical, Buber rejects two notions of scripture: one, that it is merely metaphoric narrative, and two, that it is essentially a report of supernatural events. He insists that it be seen as a verbal record of a natural event recorded and preserved in the memory of generations:

> What meaning are we intended to find in the words that God came down in fire, to the sound of thunder and horn, to the mountain which smoked like

a furnace, and spoke to his people? It can mean, I think, one of three things. Either it is figurative language used to express a 'spiritual' process; or if biblical history does not recall actual events, but is metaphor and allegory, then it is no longer biblical, and deserves no better fate than to be surrendered to the approach of modern man, the historical, aesthetic and the like approaches. Or it is the root of a 'supernatural' event, one that severs the intelligible sequence of happenings we term natural by interposing something unintelligible. If that were the case, man of today in deciding to accept the Bible would have to make a sacrifice of intellect which would cut his life irreparably in two, provided he does not want to lapse into the habitual, lazy acceptance of something he does not really believe. In other words, what he is willing to accept would not be the Bible in its totality including all of life, but only religion abstracted from life.

But there is a third possibility: it could be the verbal trace of a natural event, i.e., of an event which took place in the world of the senses common to all men, and fitted into connections which the senses can perceive. But the assemblage that experienced this event experienced it as revelation vouchsafed to them by God, and preserved it as such in the memory of generations, an enthusiastic spontaneously formative memory. Experience undergone in this way is not self-delusion on the part of the assemblage: it is what they see, what they recognize and perceive with their reason, for natural events are the carriers of revelation, and revelation occurs when he who witnesses the event and sustains it experiences the revelation it contains. This means that he listens to that which the voice, sounding forth from this event, wishes to communicate to him, its witness, to his constitution, to his life, to his sense of duty. It is only when this is true that man of today can find the approach to biblical reality I, at any rate, believe that it is true.[30]

Secondly, he stresses the essentially mythic character of the Jewish scriptures and insists they are necessarily so because the non-rational and supra-rational truths they reveal can only be expressed mythically or symbolically. This assertion is fully consistent with the view put forward in his aesthetics that it is the function of art to give symbolic form to realities that cannot be comprehended rationally. Myth in defined once again, therefore, in terms of the phenomenon of immanence discussed in his aesthetic writings. He cites Plato in support of this elementary definition: 'To clarify our own understanding of the concept "myth" we can do no better,' he says, 'than to start with Plato's interpretation of this term: a narrative of some divine event described as corporeal reality.'[31] Buber proceeds then to identify myth-making with the disclosure of the non-rational, supracausal reality which is inaccessible to the powers of reason. He sees civilized man relying on causality to explain the nature of realities which primitive man believed he could not penetrate by 'investigation, duplication or verification' and therefore would have to mythicize:

Civilized man's understanding of the world is based on his comprehension of the functioning of causality, his perception of the processes of the universe in an empirical context of cause and effect. Only through an understanding of this functioning can man orient himself, find his way, in the infinite multiplicity of events; at the same time, however, the significance of the personal experience is diminished, because it is grasped only in its relation to other experiences, and not wholly from within itself. Primitive man's comprehension of the functioning of causality is still rather poorly developed. It is practically nonexistent in his approach to such phenomena as dreams or death, which for him denote a realm he is powerless to penetrate by investigation, duplication, or verification. It is also nonexistent in his relations with such men as sorcerers or heroes, who intervene in his life with a peremptory, demoniacal power that he is unable to interpret by analogy with his own faculties. He does not set these phenomena within a causal relationship, as he sets the small incidents of his day; does not link the actions of these men, as he links his own actions and the actions of the men he knows, to the chain of all happenings; does not register them with the equanimity of experience as he registers the familiar and the comprehensible. Instead, unimpeded by a sense of causal operations, he absorbs with all the tension and fervor of his soul, these events in their singularity, relating them not to causes and effects but to their own meaning-content, to their significance as expressions of the unutterable, unthinkable meaning of the world that becomes manifest in them alone.

As a result primitive man lacks the necessary empiricism and sense of purpose to cope with such elemental experiences, but at the same time he has a heightened awareness of the nonrational aspect of the single experience, an aspect that cannot be grasped within the context of other events but is to be perceived within the experience itself; of the significance of the experience as a signum of a hidden, supracausal connection; of the manifestness of the absolute. He assigns these events to the world of the absolute, the Divine; he mythicizes them. His account of them is a tale of a corporeally real event, conceived and represented as a divine, an absolute event, a myth.[32]

For all the reliance of civilized man on scientifically determined causality to explain the nature of reality, the need for myth persists. It persists because science itself points even more strongly than the superstitions of primitive man to the reality of the supracausal. Buber, in a discussion of Einsteinian physics in 'Man and His Image Work,' spoke of the greater mysteriousness of the universe confronting the scientist in the wake of the advances made by physicists. He quoted Einstein's words on this: 'what we (and by this ''we'' he meant we physicists) strive for,' he cried, 'is just to draw his lines after Him.' 'Since then', he wrote, 'the questionableness of such strivings has become far more serious still.'.[33] It remains more necessary than ever, he declared, to find ways to render undisclosed realities 'supracausally meaningful' in terms of their sensible representations. And this, he asserts, is the 'eternal function of myth':

> This myth-making faculty is preserved in later man, despite his more fully developed awareness of causal functioning. In times of high tension and intense experience the shackles of this awareness fall off man: he perceives the world's processes as being superacausally meaningful, as the manifestation of a central intent, which cannot, however, be grasped by the mind but only by the wide awake power of the senses, the ardent vibrations of one's entire being — as palpable, multifaceted reality. And this, more or less, is how the man who is truly alive still relates to the power and the fate of a hero; though capable of placing him within causality, he nevertheless mythicizes him, because the mythical approach discloses to him a deeper, fuller truth than the causal, and by so doing first reveals to him the very being of the beloved, beatific future. Myth, then, is an eternal function of the soul.[34]

Since the unalterable reality of the unconditioned and eternal can only be disclosed symbolically or mythically, and since these are the realities ultimately addressed in the religious relationship, it follows that religious meaning is necessarily a mythicized meaning. It is this truth which underlies Buber's assertion that myth is 'the nurturing source of all genuine religiosity.'[35] An important comparison is made in 'Myth in Judaism' between the different findings of myth in the Jewish and Hindu religions. In the Jewish tradition matter is seen as an immanent manifestation of divine reality (manifested in the act of divine creation) whereas in the latter it is merely an illusory reality. This difference accounts for the greater importance of the mythic in the Jewish religion and for its centrality in the whole Judaeo-Christian tradition:

> It is fundamental to Jewish religiosity, and central to Jewish monotheism — which is so widely misunderstood and so cruelly rationalized — to view all things as utterances of God and all events as manifestations of the absolute. Whereas to the other great monotheist of the Orient, the Indian sage as he is represented in the Upanishads, corporeal reality is an illusion, which one must shed if he is to enter the world of truth, to the Jew corporeal reality is a revelation of the divine spirit and will. Consequently, all myth is for the Indian sage, as later for the Platonist, a metaphor, whereas for the Jew it is a true account of God's manifestation on earth. The Jew of antiquity cannot tell a story in any other way than mythically, for to him an event is worth telling only when it has been grasped in its divine significance. All story-telling books of the Bible have but one subject matter: the account of YHVH's encounters with His people. And even later, when from the visibility of the pillar of fire and the audibility of the thunder over Sinai He passed into the darkness and the silence of the noncorporeal realm, the

continuity of mythic story-telling is not broken; true YHVH Himself can no longer be perceived, but all His manifestations in nature and in history can be so perceived. And it is of these that the inexhaustible subject matter of post- biblical myth is composed.[36]

Turning to the educational implications of all this it appears, firstly, that the scriptures must be regarded as essential subject matter for school study on the same grounds as the historical subject matter discussed earlier. As part of the mythic cultural inheritance — perhaps the definitive cultural inheritance — the study of scripture is crucial for the attainment of a genuine self-understanding by modern man. In an earlier chapter it was argued that the present becomes meaningful only when given its appropriate place in the continuum of past, present and future time. Like all those elements inherent in man's consciousness, the historical and cultural cannot ultimately be evaded. The consequence of an attempted isolation in the present would be the severest sense of self-alienation and meaninglessness. Similarly, Buber argues, man's instinct towards religiosity — an instinct which is rooted in his propensity towards the interpersonal — must be grounded also in the mythic-symbolic inheritance informing his own consciousness. For modern man, the religious spirit must be informed by the Judaeo-Christian inheritance of religious symbol and myth to which it is necessarily related. The alternative is the kind of superficial emotionalism condemned by Buber in this passage from 'Herut':

> One can be a rationalist, a freethinker, or an atheist in a religious sense, but one cannot, in a religious sense, be a collector of 'experiences,' a boaster of moods, or a prattler about God. When the teeming swarms of the marketplace have scattered into the night, the stars shine over the new stillness as over a mountain silence; but no eternal light can penetrate the fumes of the chatter-filled public house.
>
> But how can youth be saved from this error? Or rather, how can youth save itself from it? It has a great helper by its side: the living community of the people. Only the disengaged man, incapable of drawing upon any source deeper than that of his private existence, will degrade the unconditional's impact to an 'experience' and respond with literary effusions to the music of the spheres. The man who is truly bound to his people cannot go wrong, not because he has at his disposal the symbols and forms that millenia of his people's existence have created for envisioning as well as for serving the unconditional, but because the faculty to create images and forms flows into him from this bond to his people. I said: the man who is truly bound to his people. Right here it must be pointed out that a declaration of solidarity with one's people does not yet mean that one is truly bound to it.[37]

While arguing that man's innate religiosity is necessarily grounded in the received traditions of religious symbolism and myth, Buber insists, however, that religious mythicizing is a continuing, dynamic process. He speaks of the 'memory of the generations' as a 'spontaneously formative memory' in 'The Man of Today and the Jewish Bible'.[38] Throughout his essay on religion and youth he argues that 'myth making' and the symbolization of religious truth is never static: that it 'neither belongs to nor is finished with any single historical moment in time'. 'We must therefore reject commitment to a claim that Jewish teaching is something unfinished and unequivocal' he writes. 'For it is neither. It is rather a gigantic process, still uncompleted, of spiritual creativity and creative response to the unconditioned.'[39] He urges that man be encouraged to participate in this process with his 'conscious active life'. Implicit in all this is the same paradox identified earlier in a discussion of the teaching of traditional truths: that while the individual is necessarily bound to his past he relates to it freely through the process of dialogic reciprocity. Using the analogy of a rebirth, Buber spoke of every encounter with tradition as simultaneously a process of self-renewal on the part of the subject and of a transformation also of the traditions addressed dialogically. And this same principle applies to the interpretation of the scriptures at any period in time. 'Each generation,' he declares, 'must struggle with the Bible in its turn and come to terms with it'.[40] Initially, however, the educator's function is to induce in his pupils that openness to scripture which is the first crucial condition for its assimilation through dialogue:

> The man of today has no access to a sure and solid faith, nor can it be made accessible to him. If he examines himself seriously, he knows this and may not delude himself further. But he is not denied the possibility of holding himself open to faith. If he is really serious, he too can open up to this book and let its rays strike him where they will. He can give himself up and submit to the test without preconceived notions and without reservations he can absorb the Bible with all his strength, and wait to see what will happen to him, whether he will not discover within himself a new and unbiased approach to this or that element in the book. But to this end, he must read the Jewish Bible as though it were something entirely unfamiliar, as though it had not been set before him ready-made, at school and after in the light of 'religious' and 'scientific' certainties; as though he had not been confronted all his life with sham concepts and sham statements which cited the Bible as their authority. He must face the book with a new attitude as something new. He must yield to it, withhold nothing of his being, and let whatever will occur between himself and it. He does not know which of its sayings and images will overwhelm him and mould him, from where the spirit will ferment and enter into him, to incorporate itself anew in his body. But he holds himself open. He does not believe anything a priori; he does not disbelieve anything a priori. He reads aloud the words written in the book in front of him; he hears the word he utters and it reaches him. Nothing

is prejudged. The current of time flows on, and the contemporary character of this man becomes itself a receiving vessel.[41]

The passage identifies certain fundamental learning processes that can be cultivated by the religious educator: a personal engagement with the Biblical text, attention to the word, an unbiased hearing of the Biblical voice, and a total yielding of the spirit to the message disclosed. There is a further implication for the educator arising from Buber's assertion that religious myth-making is a continuous process and that the symbolism of the scriptures must be reinterpreted by successive generations. That process of symbolic reinterpretation is enacted powerfully in every generation by its artists, dramatists, musicians, novelists, poets, painters and sculptors. As Richard Wagner wrote: 'When religious forms become artificial then it is up to art to rescue the quintessence of religion.'[42] Pasternak, contemplating the paradox that 'literature is always meditating upon death and always thereby creating life', reflects that 'this was true of that work of art which is called the Revelation of Saint John and of all those works *that have been completing it throughout the ages*'[43] (my italics). The process is represented by Mandelstam as 'continuous imitation' of the prototypical act of creation: the redemption of man by Christ:

> Christian art is always based on the great idea of redemption. It is an 'imitation of Christ' infinitely varied in all its manifestations, an eternal return to the single creative act that began our historical era. Christian art is free. It is 'art for art's sake' in its fullest meaning. No necessity of any kind, not even the highest darkens its bright inner freedom, for its prototype, that which it imitates, is the very redemption of the world by Christ. Thus, neither sacrifice, nor redemption in art, but rather the free and joyous imitation of Christ is the keystone of Christian aesthetics. Art cannot be sacrifice, because a sacrifice has already been made; it cannot be redemption because the world, along with the artist, has already been redeemed. What remains? Joyous communion with God.... Our entire two thousand year old culture, thanks to the marvellous charity of Christianity is the world's release into freedom for the sake of play, for spiritual joy, for the free 'imitation of Christ'.[44]

Religious art must command the attention of the educator for its re-interpretation of those symbols and, above all, for its existential application of their meaning to the circumstances and needs of the present time. Should the religious educator turn to twentieth century art, literature and music, with this purpose in mind, he will have available to him an abundance of material from religious painters such as Rouault, Nolde and Chagall, musicians such as Britten, Messiaen and Stravinsky, and writers such as Auden, Eliot, Mandelstam, Akhmatova, Pasternak, Brodsky, Mauriac, Reverdy, Silone,

Celan, Bernanos, Claudel, Beckett and Greene — to mention only some of the major figures in twentieth century art, literature and music who have been centrally and continuously preoccupied with the contemporary meaning of the scriptures.

## 3 The Ethical and the Religious

Religious and moral education are being considered jointly in this chapter because of Buber's insistence on the inseparability of religious and moral truth. Repeatedly, he emphasized the need to root the ethical in the religious, and he ascribed much of the moral nihilism and disorder of the present time to the separation of religious and ethical values and to the prevalence of secularised and relativist systems of morality. His ethical principles, however, are not grounded in any form of religious orthodoxy; on several occasions he insisted that he had not attached himself formally to any religious creed, though his religious convictions were deeply informed, nonetheless, by the specific cultural traditions of Judaism (see Chapter 2). To say that his ethics are grounded in his religious beliefs is simply to point to their roots in the interpersonal dialogic of the I-Thou, which reaches towads the perfection of the unconditioned, eternal and infinite and is, therefore, ultimately to be seen as a religious relationship. His essential affirmation is that ethical values are strictly non-relativist, being necessarily related to the Absolute reality of the eternal Thou, like the religious values to which they are inextricably bound. This is the fundamental theme of Buber's essay, 'Religion and Ethics'.[45]

The essay is his definitive statement on the interrelation of the ethical and the religious. On the nature of the ethical he offers this rudimentary clarification: 'We mean by the ethical in this strict sense the yes and no which man gives to the conduct and actions possible to him, the radical distinction between them which affirms or denies them not according to their usefulness or harmfulness for individuals and society, but according to their intrinsic value or disvalue.'[46] The criterion of intrinsic value or disvalue, he writes, is the individual's awareness of his own value and potentiality, on the basis of which he decides 'what is right and what is wrong in this his own situation.' His ethical decision-making involves a critical action of self-reflection which is based on his 'awareness of what he is in truth, of what in his unique and non-repeatable existence he is intended to be'.[47] That awareness is related, in turn, to the Absolute reality towards which his nature aspires; the reality of the interpersonal in its unconditioned form. The religious relationship embodies this reaching out towards the reality of the Absolute:

> We mean by the religious in this strict sense, on the other hand, the relation of the human person to the Absolute, when and insofar as the person enters and remains in this relation as a whole being. This presupposes the existence

of a Being who though in Himself unlimited and unconditioned, lets other beings, limited and conditioned indeed, exist outside Himself. He even allows them to enter into a relation with Him such as seemingly can only exist between limited and conditioned beings. Thus in my definition of the religious 'The Absolute' does not mean something that the human person holds it to be, without anything being said about its existence, but the absolute reality itself, whatever the form in which it presents itself to the human person at this moment. In the reality of the religious relation the Absolute becomes in most cases personal, at times admittedly, as in the Buddhism which arose out of a personal relation to the 'Unoriginated', only gradually and, as it were, reluctantly in the course of the development of a religion. It is indeed legitimate to speak of the person of God within the religious relation and in its language, but in so doing we are making no statement about the Absolute which reduces it to the personal. We are rather saying that it enters into the relationship as the Absolute Person whom we call God. One may understand the personality of God as His act. It is, indeed, even permissible for the believer to believe that God became a person for love of him, because in our human mode of existence the only reciprocal relation with us that exists is a personal one.[48]

The correspondence of the ethical and the religious, however, is not represented by Buber as a logical correspondence of two kinds of truth, but as a unity which is known and experienced existentially. Both interpenetrate in the concrete situation confronting the individual and requiring his decision-making and his action. But, at both levels, the principle of a purely personal relationship is asserted. Thus, while ethical values and decisions are seen by Buber as being rooted in the Absolute reality on which the religious relationship is focussed, they are values which are defined *relationally* at the level of personal and interpersonal dialogue:

> Only out of a personal relationship with the Absolute can the absoluteness of the ethical coordinates arise without which there is no complete awareness of self. Even when the individual calls an absolute criterion handed down by religious tradition his own, it must be reforged in the fire of the truth of his personal essential relation to the Absolute if it is to win true validity. But always it is the religious which bestows, the ethical which receives.
>
> It would be a fundamental misunderstanding of what I am saying if one assumed that I am upholding so-called moral heteronomy or external moral laws in opposition to so-called moral autonomy or self-imposed moral laws. Where the Absolute speaks in the reciprocal relationship, there are no longer such alternatives. The whole meaning of reciprocity, indeed, lies in just this that it does not wish to impose itself but to be freely apprehended. It gives us something to apprehend, but it does not give us the apprehension. Our act must be entirely our own for that which is to be disclosed to us to be

disclosed, even that which must disclose each individual to himself. In theonomy the divine law seeks for your own, and true revelation reveals to you yourself.[49]

Reviewing the fluctuating relations between ethics and religion throughout history, Buber speaks of two periods when the relationship was especially close.[50] The first was in Oriental and Greek antiquity when the moral order was linked with the cosmic order; he instances the period of the Tao in China, of Rita in India, of Urta in Iran, of Dike in Greece, and the subsequent association of the eternal Ethos with the Absolute in Platonist thought. The second period he mentions is that of the Hebrew prophets when the moral law was derived from the divine law and man was urged to practise the holiness that would elevate him to the condition of the divine order — the order where the ethical merges totally with the religious. Buber sees the severance of the ethical-religious relationship as an inexorable process of degeneration occurring from the Enlightenment to the present age. On the current separation of the ethical from the religious, and the consequent relativizing of moral values, he was deeply pessimistic:

> Ours is an age in which the suspension of the ethical fills the world in a caricaturized form. False absolutes rule over the soul which is no longer able to put them to flight through the images of the true. Everywhere, over the whole surface of the human world — in the East and in theWest, from the left and from the right.
>
> There is no escape from it until the new conscience of men has arisen that will summon them to guard with the innermost power of their souls against the confusion of the relative with the Absolute, that will enable them to see through illusion and to recognize this confusion for what it is. To penetrate again and again into the false absolute with an incorruptible, probing glance until one has discovered its limits, its limitedness — there is today perhaps no other way to reawaken the power of the pupil to glimpse the never-vanishing appearance of the Absolute.[51]

While clearly rejecting the relativist and secularised ethics of the present time — such as the subjectively defined values of Sartre, the Deweyan pragmatist values , the Freudian values of the superego, or the naturalist values of positivist morality — Buber insisted, therefore, that his own ethical values be justified on principles that are religious, non-relativist and relationally oriented. The principles of ethical justification are ultimately rooted, he declared, in the absolute truths of the interpersonal dialogic. His ethical formulations, therefore, offer the stability and freedom of a conception of moral truth which is simultaneously located in the depth of the religious Absolute and in the authentic exercise of individual conscience and choice. His specification of the principles of ethical conduct is firmly grounded in this paradox of freedom and necessity which is one of the central truths of his entire dialogic philosophy. Three principles characterizing the essential nature of moral conduct are identified in his ethical writings. Moral conduct is identified, firstly, he says, by the responsible exercise of personal freedom; secondly, by its radical authenticity and, thirdly, by its response to the dictates of individual conscience.

The responsible exercise of freedom requires both an awareness of the dialogic potentiality of existence and an active responding to its demands in every hour and every situation the individual encounters. 'The idea of responsibility is to be brought back from the province of specialised ethics, of an ''ought'' that swings free in the air, into that of lived life,' he declares. 'Genuine responsibility exists only where there is real responding.' 'Let us realise the true meaning of being free of a bond,' he writes; 'it means that a quite personal responsibility takes the place of one shared with many generations. Life lived in freedom is personal responsibility or it is a pathetic farce.'[52] The responsible exercise of freedom through a wholehearted personal response to the demands of interpersonal dialogue is linked inextricably with an active witnessing of personal faith. Similarly, an evasion of personal responsibility is seen by him as an evasion of faith. In this passage he sees the delegation of personal responsibility by the individual to another person or group as exemplifying this kind of evasion:

> The attitude which has just been described means for the man of faith (I wish to speak only of him here), when he encounters it, his fall from faith — without his being inclined to confess it to himself or to admit it. It means his fall in very fact from faith, however loudly and emphatically he continues to confess it not merely with his lips but even with his very soul as it shouts down inmost reality. The relation of faith to the one Present Being is perverted into semblance and self-deceit if it is not an all-embracing relation. 'Religion' may agree to be one department of life beside others which like it are independent and autonomous — it has thereby already perverted the relation of faith. To remove any realm basically from this relation, from its defining power, is to try to remove it from God's defining power which rules over the relation of faith. To prescribe to the relation of faith that 'so far and no further you may define what I have to do; here your power ends and that of the group to which I belong begins' is to address God in precisely the same way. He who does not let his relation of faith be fulfilled in the uncurtailed measure of the life he lives, however much he is capable of at different times, is trying to curtail the fulfilment of God's rule of the world.[53]

Buber insists furthermore that a responsible answering to the voice of the dialogic Thou is one which occurs in the immediate, concrete situations of everyday existence, and in every instant of that existence. In 'Religion and

Ethics' he writes: 'We find the ethical in its purity only where the human person confronts himself with his own potentiality and distinguishes and decides in this confrontation without asking anything other than what is right and what is wrong *in this his own situation*'[54] (my italics). The ethical must be discovered in every hour, not from the rules or conventions of abstract thought systems, but from a personal appraisal of the demands of every situation and by way of a personal response to those demands:

> Certainly the relation of faith is no book of rules which can be looked up to discover what is to be done now, in this very hour. I experience what God desires of me for this hour — so far as I do experience it — not earlier than in the hour. But even then it is not given me to experience it except by answering before God for this hour as my hour, by carrying out the responsibility for it towards him as much as I can. What has now approached me, the unforeseen, the unforeseeable, is word from him, a word found in no dictionary, a word that has now become word — and it demands my answer to him. I give the word of my answer by accomplishing among the actions possible that which seems to my devoted insight to be the right one. With my choice and decision and action — committing or omitting, acting or persevering — I answer the word, however inadequately, yet properly; I answer for my hour. My group cannot relieve me of this responsibility, I must not let it relieve me of it: if I do, I pervert my relation of faith, I cut out of God's realm of power the sphere of my ground.[55]

Moral values cannot be conceived independently, therefore, of the freely chosen acts of the individual person. Being essentially situational and being rooted both in the personal exercise of freedom and the demands of dialogic reciprocation, they are deeply bound up with the dictates of an existence lived authentically. The concept of authentic living is one given repeated emphasis by Buber. It is a notion which grows out of radical understanding of what existence is. Since the central truth of human existence is its dialogic character, the primary ethical goal must be the realization of dialogic potentiality. The Good is identified, therefore, with the realization of this goal, and its opposite, Evil, is identified with the failure to realize dialogic potentiality. The whole notion is clearly informed by Buber's Hasidic writings, from which this comment in particular deserves to be reiterated: 'Man cannot reach the divine by reaching beyond the human; he can approach Him through becoming human. To become human is what he, this individual man, has been created for. . . . You cannot really love God if you do not love men, and you cannot really love men if you do not love God.'[56] The idea of authentication, in the Hasidic tradition, stands for the unity of the religious and the secular—a unity which must be realized in the particular existential situations of everyday life: 'Above and below — the decisive importance is ascribed to the "below". Here on the outermost margin of having become, the fate of the aeons is decided. The human world is the world of authentication.'[57] Authentic action is concerned, therefore, with the sanctification of all life — i.e. every thought, purpose and deed — in the actual moment of their occurrence. An authenticating faith is one applied actively to the whole world of common activity: 'Basically the holy in our world is nothing other than what is open to transcendence as the profane is nothing other than what is closed off from it. . . . God can be beheld in each thing, and reached through each pure deed.'[58] A further elaboration of the theme of authentic living and sanctification is provided in the notion of redemptive action, i.e. the idea that the individual is ultimately responsible for his own self-fulfilment or salvation. While severely criticizing Paulinist Christianity for its diminished sense of individual responsibility and its excessive emphasis on redemption through Christ's sacrifice on Calvary, Buber cites the more radical evidence of New Testament Christianity in support of the principle of self redemption (I am quoting the relevant passage at some length since it emphasizes the essential compatibility of Buber's ethics with the traditions of the Christian faith):

> It was only in the syncretistic Christianity of the West that faith, as it is known to the occidental, assumed primary importance; to earliest Christianity, the deed was central. As for the meaning-content of this striving towards the deed, it is clearly attested in one of the most original parts of the Gospels, which points most indubitably to a creative personality. In the first chapter of the Sermon on the Mount, it is stated: 'Do not think that I have come to abolish the law or the prophets; I have not come to abolish but to fulfill' (Matthew 5:17). The meaning of this statement emerges from the subsequent comparison between the old and new teaching; it is not at all the intention of the new teaching to be new; it wants to remain the old teaching, but a teaching grasped in its absolute sense. It wants to restore to the deed the freedom and sanctity with which it had originally been endowed, a freedom and sanctity diminished and dimmed by the stern rule of the ritual law, and to release it from the straits of prescriptions that had become meaningless, in order to free it for the holiness of an active relationship with God, for a religiosity of the deed. And to rule out any misunderstanding, Matthew adds: 'For I say to you truly: until heaven and earth vanish, neither the smallest letter nor a tittle of the law shall vanish, until all of this be done.' This means: until the teachings of unconditionality (Unbedingtheit) are fulfilled in all their purity, and with all the power of one's soul; until the world is sanctified, is God-informed, through the absolute deed.
>
> Early Christianity teaches what the prophets taught: the unconditionality of the deed. For all great religiosity is concerned not so much with what is being done as with whether it is being done in human conditionality or

divine unconditionality. And this chapter, the original Sermon on the Mount, closes with the words which, significantly, paraphrase a verse of Leviticus: 'Therefore you shall be perfect, even as your Father in heaven is perfect.' (11:14).[59]

Ethical action, therefore, is bound up with dialogic responses and with the process of self-authentication and self-redemption which are the common manifestations of its application to the circumstances of everyday life. And these processes are related, in turn, by Buber, to the personal, freely directed decision- making and choosing he associates with the individual's response to the voice of his own conscience. While allowing for the place of tradition or guidance from external sources in the act of moral choice — 'I do not in the least mean that a man must fetch the answer alone and unadvised out of his breast'[60] — he insists that the ultimate imperatives for action are those emanating from the personal dictates of individual conscience. The individual, he declares, 'must find his way to that responsibility armed with all the "ought" that has been forged in the group but exposed to destiny so that in the demanding moment all armour falls away from him.'[61] He finds the direction for action in the depth of his own being, in the matured imperatives of conscience:

> God tenders me the situation to which I have to answer; but I have not to expect that he should tender me anything of my answer. Certainly in my answering I am given into the power of his grace, but I cannot measure heaven's share in it, and even the most blissful sense of grace can deceive. The finger I speak of is just that of the 'conscience,' but not of the routine conscience, which is to be used, is being used and worn out, the play-on-the-surface conscience, with whose discrediting they thought to have abolished the actuality of man's positive answer. I point to the unknown conscience in the ground of being, which needs to be discovered ever anew, the conscience of the 'spark'; for the genuine spark is effective also in the single composure of each genuine decision. The certainty produced by this conscience is of course only a personal certainty; it is uncertain certainty; but what is here called person is the very person who is addressed and who answers.[62]

Significantly, Buber here emphasises the need to 'discover' the voice of conscience, a process he sees as one of self- illumination which is attained through confrontation of one's guilt. This is the theme of 'Guilt and Guilt Feelings' where he distinguishes a neurotic, groundless guilt from the universally experienced 'existential guilt' which derives from man's failure to enter into or sustain genuine dialogic relation. Where there is responsibility, he writes, there is also guilt: the guilty sense of a failure to respond with one's whole being to the possibilities for dialogue encountered in daily existence. Self-illumination, in this context, involves a genuine confrontation of personal failure in the moment of its occurrence. It is concerned essentially with the failure to relate: 'Injuring a relationship means that at that place the human order of being is injured,' he writes. 'No one other than he who inflicted the wound can heal it.'[63] Buber distinguishes further between the 'vulgar' conscience which torments and harasses but cannot penetrate the 'ground and abyss of guilt' and the 'great' or 'high' conscience which can reach the depths of personal self-consciousness and awareness of guilt:

> For this summoning a greater conscience is needed, one that has become wholly personal, one that does not shy away from the glance into the depths and that already in admonishing envisages the way that leads across it. But this in no way means that this personal conscience is reserved for some type of 'higher' man. This conscience is possessed in every simple man who gathers himself into himself in order to venture the breakthrough out of the entanglement in guilt. And it is a great, not yet sufficiently recognized, task of education to elevate the conscience from its lower common form to conscience-vision and conscience-courage. For it is innate to the conscience of man that it can elevate itself.
>
> From this position a man can understand the threefold action to which I have referred: first, to illuminate the darkness that still weaves itself about the guilt despite all previous action of the conscience — not to illuminate it with spotlights but with a broad and enduring wave of light; second, to persevere, no matter how high he may have ascended in his present life above that station of guilt — to persevere in that newly won humble knowledge of the identity of the present person with the person of that time; and third, in his place and according to his capacity, in the given historical and biographical situations, to restore the order-of-being injured by him through the relation of an active devotion to the world — for the wounds of the order-of-being can be healed in infinitely many other places than those at which they were inflicted.
>
> In order that this may succeed in that measure that is at all attainable by this man, he must gather the forces and elements of his being and ever again protect the unity that is thus won from the cleavage and contradiction that threaten it. For, to quote myself, one cannot do evil with his whole soul, one can do good only with the whole soul. What one must wrest from himself, first, is not yet the good; only when he has first attained his own self does the good thrive through him.[64]

One of the functions of the educator, as the passage indicates, is to elevate conscience from its lower 'vulgar' form into its higher form as 'great conscience' or 'conscience vision'. Every individual has the capacity to bring about such a transformation. The teacher's role in facilitating this will be considered presently. In 'Guilt and Guilt Feelings' Buber describes the role of the therapist in helping his patients to develop their power of conscience vision. Since his conception of the roles of therapist and teacher/counsellor are closely intertwined, his comments have considerable significance for the educator. The therapist, he writes, 'is no pastor of souls and no substitute for one. It is never his task to mediate a salvation: his task is always only to further a healing.' His role is to facilitate self-illumination in his patients:

> There, to be sure, it is still denied him to treat 'the essential' in his patients, but he may and should guide it to where an essential help of the self, a help till now neither willed nor anticipated, can begin. It is neither given the therapist nor allowed to him to indicate a way that leads onward from here. But from the watchtower to which the patient has been conducted, he can manage to see a way that is right for him and that he can walk, a way that it is not granted the doctor to see. For at this high station all becomes personal in the strictest sense. . . .
>
> When the therapist recognizes an existential guilt of his patient, he cannot — that we have seen — show him the way to the world, which the latter must rather seek and find as his own personal law. The doctor can only conduct him to the point from which he can glimpse his personal way or at least its beginning. But in order that the doctor shall be able to do this, he must also know about the general nature of the way, common to all great acts of conscience, and about the connection that exists between the nature of existential guilt and the nature of this way.[65]

The counselling of the guilty has a purpose beyond that of self-illumination, as a previously quoted passage will indicate.[66] It is concerned also with the further activities of perseverance in the act of self-illumination and ultimately with the reparation of the injury which was the initial source of guilt. On the issue of perseverance, Buber writes of the common tendency to resist self-illumination: 'Only when the human person himself overcomes this lower resistance can he attain to self-illumination.'[67] But self-illumination remains a mere prelude to the ultimate form of ethical action which is the active reparation of one's guilt. The reparation of guilt is concerned essentially with reconciliation in the sphere of the interpersonal:

> If a man were only guilty toward himself, in order to satisfy the demanding summons that meets him at the height of conscience, he would only need to take this one road from the gate of self-illumination, that of persevering. But a man is always guilty toward other beings as well, towards the world, toward the being that exists over against him. From self-illumination he must, in order to do justice to the summons, take not one road but two roads, of which the second is that of reconciliation. By reconciliation is understood here that action from the height of conscience that corresponds on the plane of the law to the customary act of reparation. In the realm of existential guilt one cannot, of course, make reparation in the strict sense — as if the guilt with its consequences could thereby be recalled, as it were. Reconciliation

means here, first of all, that I approach the man toward whom I am guilty in the light of my self-illumination (in so far as I can still reach him on earth) acknowledge to his face my existential guilt and help him, in so far as possible, to overcome the consequences of my guilty action. But such a deed can be valid here only as reconciliation if it is done not out of a premeditated resolution, but in the unarbitrary working of the existence I have achieved. And this can happen, naturally, only out of the core of a transformed relationship to the world, a new service to the world with the renewed forces of the renewed man.[68]

## 4   The Education of Character

These are the main ethical principles informing Buber's theories of moral education. In his educational writings he reaffirms the religious orientation of all ethical values, while radically revising traditionalist conceptions of the relationship between religion and morality. In these writings also he emphatically rejects the relativist and secular ethics adopted by some contemporary educationalists — he particularly mentions John Dewey in this context[69] — and re-emphasizes the orientation of his own ethical values towards an absolute truth, i.e. the absolute truth disclosed in the interpersonal dialogic. Moral education, he argued, aims to develop certain propensities in the student: it aims particularly to promote a responsible exercise of freedom and the continuing authentication of all intentions and deeds in the moment of their occurrence. Once again he insists that imperatives for moral action emanate primarily from the urgings of the individual's own conscience. The conscience of which he writes, however, is the 'high conscience' or 'conscience courage' which is informed through self-illumination. The educator is seen to exercise a particular responsibility in assisting his pupil towards the achievement of the highest possible degree of self-awareness and personal illumination. Ultimately, all moral action is oriented towards a deepening of individual capacities for interpersonal relation and for the reparation of injured or unfulfilled relations in the circumstances of everyday life.

These are the basic principles underlying Buber's two main treatises on moral education, 'Teaching and Deed' and 'The Education of Character'.[70] Both essays provide the pedagogic detail for the practical implementation of his ethical principles through the educational process. A recurring concern of both essays is the need to maintain a close interrelation between ethical thought and action. In 'Teaching and Deed' he writes: 'What counts is not the extent of spiritual possessions, not the thoroughness of knowledge, not the keenness of thought but to know what one knows and to believe what one believes so directly that it can be translated into the life one lives.'[71] The context in which this issue is considered, however, is one where the relativism and secularism of much contemporary theory is emphatically condemned and rejected. This matter is raised firstly in a discussion of Georg Kerschensteiner's[72] distinction between 'character in the general sense' — by which he simply meant the consistency between man's actions and his 'attitudes to his human surroundings' — and what he (Kerschensteiner) called 'real ethical character' — which involves the adoption of absolute, but abstractly formulated, values and norms. Buber questions the acceptability of the second of these conceptions in the circumstances of the present time:

> 'Absolute validity' can only relate to universal values and norms, the existence of which the person concerned recognizes and acknowledges. But to deny the presence of universal values and norms of absolute validity — that is the conspicuous tendency of our age. This tendency is not, as is sometimes supposed, directed merely against the sanctioning of the norms by religion, but against their universal character and absolute validity, against their claim to be of a higher order than man and to govern the whole of mankind. In our age values and norms are not permitted to be anything but expressions of the life of a group which translates its own needs into the language of objective claims, until at last the group itself, for example a nation, is raised to an absolute value — and moreover to the only value. Then this splitting up into groups so pervades the whole of life that it is no longer possible to re-establish a sphere of values common to mankind, and a commandment to mankind is no longer observed. As this tendency grows the basis for the development of what Kerschensteiner means by moral character steadily diminishes. How, under these circumstances, can the task of educating character be completed?[73]

Kerschensteiner's alternative notion of character as a 'voluntary obedience to the maxims which have been moulded in the individual by experience, teaching and reflection' is dismissed also by Buber as merely a form of self-control, a 'habit' of self-conquest. But this concept of habit, Buber argues, has been further developed by John Dewey in his work, *Human Nature and Conduct*, and forms the theoretical basis of his thinking on moral education. Character, he says, is seen by Dewey as an 'interpenetration of habits' and the 'continued operation of all habits in every act' is its everyday manifestation in human behaviour. This whole concept is dismissed by Buber as an inadequate basis on which to determine the principles of moral education:

> With this concept of character as an organization of self-control by means of the accumulation of maxims, or as a system of interpenetrating habits, it is very easy to understand how powerless modern educational science is when faced by the sickness of man. But even apart from the special problems of the age, this concept can be no adequate basis for the construction of a genuine education of character. Not that the educator could dispense with

employing useful maxims or furthering good habits. But in moments that come perhaps only seldom, a feeling of blessed achievement links him to the explorer, the inventor, the artist, a feeling of sharing in the revelation of what is hidden. In such moments he finds himself in a sphere very different from that of maxims and habits. Only on this, the highest plane of his activity, can he fix his real goal, the real concept of character which is his concern, even though he might not often reach it.[74]

Significantly, at the end of this passage, Buber points to the higher concept of self-illumination as the key to a more stable reconception of the process of moral education in an age of fluctuating standards and values. In genuine personhood, which is attained through authentic self-awareness, the individual discovers the reality of absolute values:

One has to begin by pointing to that sphere where man himself, in the hours of utter solitude, occasionally becomes aware of the disease through sudden pain: by pointing to the relation of the individual to his own self. In order to enter into a personal relation with the absolute, it is first necessary to be a person again, to rescue one's real personal self from the fiery jaws of collectivism which devours all selfhood. The desire to do this is latent in the pain the individual suffers through his distorted relation to his own self. Again and again he dulls the pain with a subtle poison and thus suppresses the desire as well. To keep the pain awake, to waken the desire — that is the first task of everyone who regrets the obscuring of eternity. It is also the first task of the genuine educator of our time.

The man for whom absolute values in a universal sense do not exist cannot be made to adopt 'an attitude which in action gives the preference over all others to absolute values.' But what one can inculcate in him is the desire to attain once more to a real attitude, and that is the desire to become a person following the only way that leads to this goal to-day.[75]

Moral education, therefore, is still oriented towards absolute values, but these values have to be discovered and authenticated at the level of personal self-awareness and in terms of the existential situations of everyday life. The more problematic issue, however, is how this ideal is to be achieved. Buber's essay, 'The Education of Character,' addresses the issue directly and specifies various curricular and pedagogic measures that are necessary for its achievement. An important distinction is made in the essay between pedagogy in a discipline such as mathematics, where learning is directed towards an identifiable body of subject content, and the kind of teaching required in the more problematic field of moral education. The instructional/didactic model which may be appropriate in the first instance is inadequate in the latter, he says, because of the pupils' inherent resistance to the challenge of moral formation, especially in the sphere of their own personal self-illumination:

If I have to teach algebra I can expect to succeed in giving my pupils an idea of quadratic equations with two unknown quantities. Even the slowest-witted child will understand it so well that he will amuse himself by solving equations at night when he cannot fall asleep. And even one with the most sluggish memory will not forget, in his old age, how to play with x and y. But if I am concerned with the education of character, everything becomes problematic. I try to explain to my pupils that envy is despicable and at once I feel the secret resistance of those who are poorer than their comrades. I try to explain that it is wicked to bully the weak, and at once I see a suppressed smile on the lips of the strong. I try to explain that lying destroys life, and something frightful happens: the worst habitual liar of the class produces a brilliant essay on the destructive power of lying. I have made the fatal mistake of giving instruction in ethics, and what I said is accepted as current coin of knowledge; nothing of it is transformed into character building substance.[76]

To be effective, moral education involves the spontaneous personal contact between teacher and pupil which is possible only when a wholehearted, trusting relationship has been established between them. 'Only in his whole being, in all his spontaneity can the educator truly affect the whole being of his pupil,' Buber declares. 'For educating characters,' he says, 'you do not need a moral genius but you do need a man who is wholly alive and able to communicate himself directly to his fellow beings. His aliveness streams out to them and affects them most strongly and purely when he has no thought of influencing them.'[77] 'The educator embodies in his own personality and life the responsibility and moral integrity he communicates to his pupil. His influence is expressed in terms of the notion of spontaneous 'impression', i.e. as the conscious, willed element of personal interpenetration in the character forming process':

The Greek word character means 'impression'. The special link between man's being and his appearance, the special connexion between the unity of what he is and the sequence of his actions and attitudes is impressed on his still plastic substance. Who does the impressing? Everything does: nature and the social context, the house and the street, language and custom, the world of history and the world of daily news in the form of rumour, of broadcast and newspaper, music and technical science, play and dream — everything together. Many of these factors exert their influence by stimulating agreement, imitation, desire, effort; others by arousing questions, doubts, dislike, resistance. Character is formed by the interpenetration of all those multifarious opposing influences. And yet, among this infinity of form-giving forces the educator is only one element among innumerable others, but distinct from them all by his will to take part in the stamping of character and by his consciousness that he represents in the eyes of the growing person a certain selection of what is, the selection of what is 'right', of what should be. It is in this will and this consciousness that his vocation as an educator finds its fundamental expression.[78]

The profile of the educator put forward in this essay is remarkably similar to that of the zaddik-teacher in Buber's Hasidic writings. Three requirements are specified for the moral educator. He must, firstly, be distinguished by his humility: his awareness that he is a single element only in the midst of all those influences 'impressing' the consciousness of his pupil. He must be distinguished, secondly, by his corresponding awareness of the intentional nature of his role: by the 'feeling of being the only existence that wants to affect the whole person, and by the feeling of responsibility for the selection of reality which he represents to the pupil.' Thirdly, he must recognize the importance of gaining access to his pupil by securing his trust, the trust that derives from the pupil's confidence in the meaningfulness of his own existence. 'For the adolescent who is frightened and disappointed by an unreliable world,' he writes, 'this confidence means the liberating insight that there is human truth, the truth of human existence. When the pupil's confidence has been won, his resistance against being educated gives way to a singular happening: he accepts the educator as a person.'[79] Beyond the creation of a trusting relationship, moral education consists essentially of a reciprocal exploration by teacher and pupil of the moral demands presented by all the situations confronting them. It is a meeting of two persons engaged in a responsible questioning and answering of the problematics of moral truth in the situations in which they present themselves:

> The teacher who is for the first time approached by a boy with somewhat defiant bearing but with trembling hands, visibly opened up and fired by a daring hope, who asks him what is the right thing in a certain situation — for instance, whether in learning that a friend has betrayed a secret entrusted to him one should call him to account or be content with entrusting no more secrets to him — the teacher to whom this happens realizes that this is the moment to make the first conscious step towards education of character; he has to answer, to answer under a responsibility, to give an answer which will probably lead beyond the alternatives of the question by showing a third possibility which is the right one. To dictate what is good and evil in general is not his businses. His business is to answer a concrete question, to answer what is right and wrong in a given situation. This, as I have said, can only happen in an atmosphere of confidence. Confidence, of course, is not won by the strenuous endeavour to win it, but by direct and ingenuous participation in the life of the people one is dealing with — in this case to the life of one's pupils — and, by assuming the responsibility which arises from such participation. It is not the educational intention but it is the meeting which is educationally fruitful. A soul suffering from the contradictions of the world of human society, and of its own physical existence,

approaches me with a question. By trying to answer it to the best of my knowledge and conscience I help it to become a character that actively overcomes the contradictions.[80]

While emphasizing the importance of confidence and trust, Buber does not suggest that the relationship between teacher and pupil is one of unconditional agreement. He sees conflict and disagreement as the inevitable consequences, in fact, of the kind of dialogic questioning he advocates. Conflict, he suggests, is one of the great tests for the educator, since it must be conducted in the spirit of reciprocal dialogue if it is to be truly educative. 'If he (the educator) is the victor,' he says, 'he must help the vanquished to endure defeat; and if he cannot conquer the self-willed soul that faces him . . . then he has to find the word of love which, alone, can help to overcome so difficult a situation.'[81] Equally, he stresses the importance of discipline and order in classroom relationships. The educator, he says, must strive to make that discipline 'inward and autonomous'; self-discipline as well as self-awareness are essential if the 'vulgar' unenlightened conscience is to be elevated to the plane of the 'high' or 'great' conscience which enables the pupil to assess his own ethical responsibility in every situation. This ultimately becomes the goal of all moral education:

The great character can be conceived neither as a system of maxims nor as a system of habits. It is peculiar to him to act from the whole of his substance. That is, it is peculiar to him to react in accordance with the uniqueness of every situation which challenges him as an active person. Of course there are all sorts of similarities in different situations; one can construct types of situations, one can always find to what section the particular situation belongs, and draw what is appropriate from the hoard of established maxims and habits, apply the appropriate maxim, bring into operation the appropriate habit. But what is untypical in the particular situation remains unnoticed and unanswered. To me that seems the same as if, having ascertained the sex of a new-born child, one were immediately to establish its type as well, and put all the children of one type into a common cradle on which not the individual name but the name of the type was inscribed. In spite of all similarities every living situation has, like a new-born child, a new face, that has never been before and will never come again. It demands of you a reaction which cannot be prepared beforehand. It demands nothing of what is past. It demands presence, responsibility; it demands you. I call a great character one who by his actions and attitudes satisfies the claim of situations out of deep readiness to respond, with his whole life, and in such a way that the sum of his actions and attitudes expresses at the same time the unity of his being in its willingness to accept responsibility. As his being is unity, the unity of accepted responsibility, his active life, too, coheres into unity. And one might perhaps say that for him there rises a unity out of the situations he has responded to in responsibility, the indefinable unity of a moral destiny.[82]

Ironically, it is in this context of situationally addressed, personally defined ethical values, that traditional ethical norms and standards become meaningful. While emphasizing the personal impact of conscience on the process of decision making, and therefore emphasizing also the radical freedom of the act of ethical choice, Buber sees moral traditions and norms as impinging nonetheless on individual decisions and choices. But he sees the individual's engagement with the past as part of the dialogic process; while individual decisions and choices are deeply informed by the inherited values and norms, the traditions they represent have to be addressed dialogically (i.e. critically and questioningly) and appropriated at the level of personal meaning-making. In 'Guilt and Guilt Feelings' Buber acknowledges that 'the content of conscience is in many ways determined by the commands and prohibitions of the society to which its hearer belongs or those of the traditions of faith to which he is bound.'[83] But the individual's relationship with those traditions has to be one of critical dialogue, by virtue of which traditional dogmas and norms are freely appropriated and assimilated in the particular circumstances of the situations to which they are applied:

> No responsible person remains a stranger to norms. But the command inherent in a genuine norm never becomes a maxim and the fulfilment of it never a habit. Any command that a great character takes to himself in the course of his development does not act in him as part of his consciousness or as material for building up his exercises, but remains latent in a basic layer of his substance until it reveals itself to him in a concrete way. What it has to tell him is revealed whenever a situation arises which demands of him a solution of which till then he had perhaps no idea. Even the most universal norm will at times be recognized only in a very special situation. I know of a man whose heart was struck by the lightning flash of 'Thou shalt not steal' in the very moment when he was moved by a very different desire from that of stealing, and whose heart was so struck by it that he not only abandoned doing what he wanted to do, but with the whole force of his passion did the very opposite. Good and evil are not each other's opposites like right and left. The evil approaches us in a whirlwind, the good as a direction. There is a direction, a 'yes', a command, hidden even in a prohibition, which is revealed to us in moments like these. In moments like these the command addresses us really, in the second person, and the Thou in it is no one else but one's own self. Maxims command only the third person, the each and the none.[84]

The image of rebirth is used by Buber in 'Teaching and Deed' to convey the nature of the individual's dialogue with the past. 'Let me reiterate that such continuity does not imply the preservation of the old,' he writes; rather it is a 'ceaseless begetting and giving birth to the same single spirit and its continuous integration into life.'[85] The same notion is developed further in his esssay, 'What Are We To Do About the Ten Commandments', where the concepts of individual freedom and the dialogic assimilation of tradition and authority are closely linked. This passage particularly expresses the nature of this dialogic encounter:

> You want to know what I think should be done about the Ten Commandments in order to give them a sanction and validity they no longer possess.
> In my opinion the historical and present status of the Decalogue derives from a twofold fact.
> 1) The Ten Commandments are not part of an impersonal codex governing an association of men. They were uttered by an I and addressed to a Thou. They begin with the I and every one of them addresses the Thou in person. An I 'commands' and a Thou — every Thou who hears this Thou — 'is commanded.'
> 2) In the Decalogue, the word of Him who issues commands is equipped with no executive power effective on the plane of predictable causality. The word does not enforce its own hearing. Whoever does not wish to respond to the Thou addressed to him can apparently go about his business un-impeded. Though He who speaks the word has power (and the Decalogue presupposes that he had sufficient power to create the heavens and the earth) he has renounced this power of his sufficiently to let every individual actually decide for himself whether he wants to open or close his ears to the voice, and that means whether he wants to choose or reject the I of 'I am'. He who rejects Him is not struck down by lightning; he who elects Him does not find hidden treasures.[86]

A comment in 'Teaching and Deed' brings us to the final issue in this discussion of the aims and methods of moral education. On the question of revivifying traditional values, Buber declares: 'Only the teachings truly rejuvenated can liberate us from limitations and bind us to the uncon-ditional.'[87] Earlier in this chapter I cited his view that the reality of absolute truths and values is ultimately disclosed, not through authority or any external source, but from the depth of individual personhood. 'In order to enter into a personal relation to the absolute,' he wrote, 'it is first necessary to be a person again.'[88] His final conclusion, therefore, is that the eternal, i.e. religious, nature of ethical values is disclosed ultimately through the pro-cesses that have been described as contributing to the deepening of that sense of personhood: i.e., through self illumination, critical dialogue, attention to the voice of conscience, and the authentication of all action in the uniqueness of its occurrence:

> He who knows inner unity, the innermost life of which is mystery, learns to honour the mystery in all its forms. In an understandable reaction against the former domination of a false, fictitious mystery, the present generations are obsessed with the desire to rob life of all its mystery. The fictitious mystery will disappear, the genuine one will rise again. A generation which honours the mystery in all its forms will no longer be deserted by eternity. Its light seems darkened only because the eye suffers from a cataract; the receiver has been turned off, but the resounding ether has not ceased to vibrate. To-day, indeed, in the hour of upheaval, the eternal is sifted from the pseudo-eternal. That which flashed into the primal radiance and blurred the primal sound will be extinguished and silenced, for it has failed before the horror of the new confusion and the questioning soul has unmasked its futility. Nothing remains but what rises above the abyss of to-day's monstrous problems as above every abyss of every time; the wing-beat of the spirit and the creative word. But he who can see and hear out of unity will also behold and discern again what can be beheld and discerned eternally. The educator who helps to bring man back to his own unity will help to put him again face to face with God.[89]

# VI

# Aesthetic Education

## 1  The Nature of Aesthetic Creativity

Man fulfils his destiny, Buber said, through the four main relational potencies of his existence: the potencies of loving, knowing, believing and creating. Through his love, his faith, his knowledge and his art he strives for the perfection of relation in its unconditioned, intemporal and infinite forms. While stressing the interrelatedness of all four potencies, Buber also stressed their essentially autonomous character. Each, he said, discloses in a special way the reality of relation in its ultimate form. Thus, when he discussed the nature of creativity, he first rejected what he called the modern tendency to see it as a derivatory potentiality and insisted that it is rooted in the wholeness of man's nature. In his Heidelberg lecture he declared: 'We must continually point out that human inwardness is, in origin, a polyphony in which no voice can be "reduced" to another, and in which the unity cannot be grasped analytically, but only heard in the present harmony.'[1] He insisted that the 'originative instinct', like the potencies of loving, knowing and believing, is grounded in the reality of man's nature as essentially a relating, reciprocating, rather than self fulfilling, or socially oriented being. Thus, he rejected the 'expressive' concept of creativity (i.e. the concept in which creativity is identified with self-expression) as one grounded falsely in the singleness of selfhood. Creativity, he declared, like the other relational potencies, springs from the depth of the interpersonal: from man's relation to fellowman, to the surrounding universe, to his heritage of religion, culture and art.

It is significant that Buber defined creativity both as an aesthetic potentiality and as one which is possessed universally. In the Heidelberg lecture he said: 'Everyone is elementally endowed with the basic powers of the arts, with that of drawing, for instance, or music; these powers have to be developed and the education of the whole person is to be built up on them as on the natural activity of the self.'[2] There are two crucial qualifications in the passage from which these words are taken. The first lies in the assertion that aesthetic potentiality is something which dwells to some extent in all men; the second involves the use of the qualifying term 'elementally'. Both suggest that while the potentiality exists in all men, it is fulfilled only in the case of the few. This becomes clearer when he further states that 'art is only the province in which the faculty of production which is common to all reaches completion.'[3] There is a distinction here which has a vital bearing on Buber's entire approach to aesthetic education and the nurturing of creativity. It is a distinction more commonly expressed through the terms 'aesthetic' and 'artistic'. Aesthetic potentiality, he says, manifests itself primarily in the creation of art, but for those ungifted with artistic talent it is fulfilled through personal encounters both with the existential evidence of beauty and with its embodied forms in the heritage of art. It manifests itself both as origination and response: in the first as artistic creation; in the second as the more universal faculty of aesthetic or receptive appreciation. The notion is used consistently throughout Buber's work in both these senses.

It is essential, therefore, when considering his aesthetic theories and their implications for education, that the aesthetic encounter be seen to comprehend both the functions of origination and response. The main sources for a discussion of his aesthetics are the essay, 'Education', from *Between Man and Man*, certain passages from *I and Thou*, and a major essay he completed shortly before his death, 'Man and his Image-Work'. Additionally, there are various commentaries on the different art-forms — on poetry, drama, fiction, music and painting — scattered throughout his writings. In all these works he consistenly emphasized the notion of creativity as encounter. Whether it is realized in the creation of art or in the receptive contemplation of art and beauty, the aesthetic experience is represented by Buber as essentially a relational encounter, and specifically, an encounter with form. In *Between Man and Man* he writes: 'Here is pure gesture which does not snatch the world to itself, but expresses itself to the world. Should not the person's growth into form, so often dreamed of and lost, at last succeed from this starting-point.'[4] The notion of form has a twofold significance in his writings. It is, firstly, the objectified, structured character of the reality which is external to man as the perceiving subject — it is 'the being of the world as an object'.[5] It is the sensible structure of the reality the subject perceives. The artist penetrates the form of this external reality and reinvokes its structure in his art. Secondly, the idea of form connotes the personhood of the sensible reality which the subject perceives and which again is embodied by the artist in his art. The aesthetic encounter, therefore, aspires ultimately to the condition of dialogue, to the reciprocity of the I-Thou. This is how it is conceived by Buber in *Between Man and Man* and in *I and Thou*. 'The being of the world as an object is learned from within,' he writes, 'but not its being as a subject, its saying I and Thou. What teaches us the saying of Thou is not the originative instinct but the instinct for communion.'[6] What is stressed in all these writings, therefore, is the radically relational character of the aesthetic potency. This passage from *I and Thou* expresses the point clearly and succinctly:

This is the eternal origin of art that a human being confronts a form that wants to become a work though him. Not a figment of his soul but something that appears to the soul and demands the soul's creative power. What is required is a deed that a man does with his whole being: if he commits it and speaks with his being the basic word to the form that appears, then the creative power is released and the work comes into being.

The form that confronts me I cannot experience or describe; I can only actualize it. And yet I see it, radiant in the splendour of the confrontation, far more clearly than all clarity of the experienced world. Not as a thing among the 'internal' things, not as a figment of the 'imagination', but as what is present. Tested for its objectivity, the form is not 'there' at all; but what can equal its presence ? And it is an actual relation: it acts on me as I act on it. Such work is creation, inventing is finding. Forming is discovery.[7]

To inquire more closely into the nature of aesthetic encounter we can turn to Buber's essay, 'Man and his Image-Work', which is his most mature statement on the subject. Five main positions are articulated in this essay. These are; firstly, the idea of art as a relationship in which spiritual and sensible elements interpenetrate; secondly, the idea of creation as a 'drawing forth' or a discovery of meaning beyond the sphere of the phenomenal; thirdly, the notion of image-making as an intentional, meaning-conferring activity; fourthly, the idea of art as a transcendence of the spheres of utility and need; and fifthly, the notion of artistic creation as revelation of dialogic truth.

Buber formulates the fundamental question of the essential nature of art in terms that are strictly anthropological. He considers the connection between the nature of art and the nature of man. The question to be addressed, he says, is this: 'What can be said about art as about a being that springs from the being of man?' Initially he defines art as a dependent relation: it embraces a dependence by man on that which exists independently of him. But he defines it more specifically as a relation which is characterized by the interpenetration of spiritual and sensible elements. Like all encounters between man and the realities that are external to his own subjectivity, the artistic encounter is sensibly and immanently informed:

> The path of our question must begin in the sphere in which the life of the human senses dwells; it is that in which the dependence of man on the existent properly constitutes itself and that which determines the reality-character of all art so that no mental and no emotional element may enter into art otherwise than through becoming a thing of the senses. Another path could be taken only by a radical idealism that would understand all notion of the senses as product of the sovereign subject. We can no longer do this, we who are unavoidably set before a world that is, certainly, again and again, immanent in our souls but is not originally immanent in it, a world which

manifests itself as transcending the soul precisely in the course of that becoming immanent in it which is happening at any given time. The artist is not a slave to nature, but free as he may hold himself of it and far as he may remove himself from it, he may establish his work only by means of what happens to him in the sphere of the bound life of the senses — in the fundamental events of perception, which is a meeting with the world and ever again a meeting with the world.[8]

In the same context Buber insists on the basic anthropological truth of the reality of man's composite nature and its involvement in all his encounters with the world: 'What is specifically human, what decisively sets man apart from all other living beings cannot', he writes, 'be grasped by the concept of spirituality'. 'The whole body-soul person', he declares, 'is the human in man; it is this wholeness which is involved in his meeting with the world.'[9] This position is further advanced in his discussion of the ideas of the German aesthetician, Conrad Fiedler. He writes of the transitional significance of Fiedler's thought: his anticipation of the anthropological conception of art by looking to the nature of man to determine why he creates artistically. But ultimately he sees Fiedler as being imprisoned by the traditions of German idealism and to this he attributes his (Fiedler's) conception of art as fundamentally cognitional. While allowing for certain interconnections between artistic creation and cognitional thought, Buber sees them ultimately as parallel modes of relation. 'Thinking and art certainly supplement one another but not as two connected organs,' he writes; 'rather they are like the electric poles between which the spark jumps.'[10] While discussing this issue he points to the struggle which artistic discovery entails, emphasizing the hiddenness and mysteriousness of the sensible, formal reality which the artist draws forth:

> To the simple reader to whom Dürer speaks, and I dare to confirm his simple understanding in opposition to so grandiose a deed of violence, it says to him that what is imprisoned in another substance at times cannot be gently drawn from it but must be 'torn' out of it by force, and such an action Albrecht Durer believes the composed force of the strong artist capable of. The reader whom he really addressed, the young painter, shall feel: 'So deep as it is thus hidden, so resistant as it is delivered up, so strong and well must I work.'
>
> What Dürer here means by art and immediately after explains as 'learned art which is propagated by seed, grows up and brings fruit of its kind', that is the knowledge, handed down from the teaching to the learning artist, about that intercourse with nature which draws forth. Only through it and out of it is 'the collected hidden treasure of the heart' legitimately and without arbitrariness 'revealed through the work and the new creature'.[11]

The sphere of form and structure resists discovery because it is not totally explicable. Buber writes of the disparity between the 'penetrating images of our perception', which are bound up with our relations with existent being, and the substratum of existence that is not perceived and is not 'accessible to us as a reality'.[12] He speaks of an existence beyond the phenomenal, stressing the radical mysteriousness of the undisclosed: 'It, nature, that which incessantly speaks to us, does not, to be sure, divulge its mystery to us.'[13] Contemporary advances in science, he says, have only deepened our awareness of the hiddenness of the transphenomenal. 'As the consequence of the new situation in physics,' he writes, 'even the words "to be" and "to know" have lost their simple meaning.' We are obliged, he says, to attest constantly to the 'uncanny strangenness of the world'.[14] In an anecdote about Einstein Buber illustrates man's everpresent need to penetrate this hidden strangeness of being. Significantly, he identifies the quest directly with the process of artistic creativity:

> I recall an hour that I spent over forty years ago in conversation with Albert Einstein. I had been pressing him in vain with a concealed question about his faith. Finally he burst forth. 'What we (and by this "we" he meant we physicists) strive for', he cried, 'is just to draw his lines after Him.' To draw after — as one retraces a geometrical figure. That already seemed to me then an innocent hubris; since then the questionableness of such strivings has become far more serious still. The fundamental impossibility of investigating the electron, the 'complementarity' of contradictory explanations — and the lines of being that God has drawn! And nonetheless we must proceed from this unimageable, unrealizable, uncanny, unhomelike world if we want to find the nature of which we ourselves may say that art is hidden in it and is to be 'torn' out of it.[15]

Ultimately, therefore, Buber sees artistic creation as a search to find immanent forms to correspond to the unknown and the mysterious in existence: to find images for the sphere he designates the 'ontic x'. The process is characterized as essentially an intentional, meaning-conferring activity: one which is concerned with the reality that exists beyond that which is conveyed through sensible form. The artist *imagines* this reality; he *confers* meaning on it through his images and symbols:

> Even when I wander in the desert and nowhere a form offers itself to my eye, even when a crude noise strikes my ear, there takes place in my perception binding and limiting, joining and rhythmizing, the becoming of a formed unity. The truer, the more existentially reliably it takes place, so much the more, in all realms of sense, is observation transformed into vision. Vision is figurating faithfulness to the unknown and does its work in cooperation with it. It is faithfulness not to the appearance, but to being — to the inaccessible with which we associate.[16]

The artist's 'figurating vision' gives the insensible reality of the 'x world' (the world of the undisclosed) a present, i.e. sensible correspondence (The word 'vision' is used in this context by Buber to signify the process of apprehending through sense). All that can be apprehended, he says, has a 'direction towards figuration',[17] i.e. towards immanent representation as image. The form-revealing and form-embodying processes of art, therefore, are essentially transcendent activities. They are activities transcending the ordinary realm of need. Perception, in its ordinary forms, draws out from being 'the world that we need',[18] he writes; the artist seeks out and reveals the wholeness of the world, including the sphere of the undisclosed which lies beyond the realm of perceived need. His image-making, therefore, is a transformative activity in which the encounter between his being as a subject and the being of the unknown is given meaning and immanent form. Through his radical activity of 'formation' he participates in the unifying processes by which the undisclosed is linked with the disclosed:

> The artist is the man who instead of objectifying what is over against him forms it into an image. Here the nature of the action in which perception takes place no longer suffices: the working must play a substantial part if that which stands over against him is to become image. That which stands over against, I say; that does not mean this or that phenomenon, this or that piece of the external world, some complex of appearance given to the sight or the hearing in the actual experience, but whatever in the whole possible world-sphere enters into that sense with which this particular art is associated, the whole possible world-sphere of sight, the whole possible world-sphere of hearing. This and nothing less than this is that by which the artist exercises what Jean Paul — in distinction from the power of imagination, 'which animals also have since they dream and they fear' — calls the power of formation, that which 'makes all parts into a whole' and establishes the freedom 'whereby the beings move in their ether like suns'.[19]

This conception of art as a transcendent activity points to a more fundamental question: from where does the urge towards creativity spring? Why has the species man not been content to allow the formed universe penetrate his consciousness spontaneously through the ordinary process of perception? Why does he seek to represent undisclosed meaning through the creation of sensible form? Why does he seek to extend his perceptions into the realm beyond the phenomenal? Buber's response to these questions is this brief and rather cryptic statement, 'He exceeds the needed for the sake of the intended'.[20] The urge to transcend, he says, is present in all the four potencies of man's existence. It springs, firstly, from man's dissatisfaction with the constrictions of the spheres of utility and need, and secondly, from his longing for the perfection of relation. In his knowing, for instance, he seeks to transcend the world he knows as object by transforming it into the realm of the I-Thou, i.e. by conferring on it a personal meaningfulness. He seeks the perfection of the knowing potency through his act of intentional meaning-making; thus he 'exceeds the needed for the sake of the intended'. The same principle is applied in the sphere of artistic creation:

> All this dissatisfaction and longing, exclusiveness and inclusiveness, we find again in the realm of art. The artist, whose meetings with x are of an intensity peculiar to him, does not content himself with beholding what the common human world of the senses makes perceptible to him. He wants, in that sphere among the senses to which his art is oriented, to experience and realize the perfection of the relation to the substratum of the sense things: through the figuration in vision and in work. He does not portray the form, he does not really remould it; he drives it — not just in the individual object, but in the whole fullness of possibility of this one sense, in so far as it opens itself to him; he drives it into its perfection in its fully figured reality, and the whole optical, the whole acoustical field becomes refashioned ever anew. And already the power of exclusiveness has become apparent to us: the working of all other senses must be cut in order that the working of this one may attain to such perfection in the imprint of its art. But the life of all the other senses is secretly included in the working and the work; deep correspondences, magical evocations exist here, and our concrete understanding is enriched when we succeed, say, in becoming aware of the rhythm in a work of sculpture.[21]

Art, therefore, is a mode of disclosing the ultimate reality and truth of betweenness: it is 'the realm of the between which has become form'.[22] All art, Buber declares in his essay, 'Dialogue', 'is from its origin essentially of the nature of dialogue.'[23] Repeatedly, he stresses the radical mysteriousness of artistic truth: 'All music calls to an ear not the musician's own, all sculpture to an eye not the sculptor's, architecture in addition calls to the step not in the building. They all say, to him who receives them, something (not a feeling but a perceived mystery) that can be said only in this one language.'[24] In 'Distance and Relation' he locates the creative process in the ultimate sphere of the 'really real':

> Art is neither the impression of natural objectivity nor the expression of spiritual subjectivity, but it is the work and witness of the relation between the substantia humana and the substantia rerum, it is the realm of 'the between' which has become a form. Consider great nude sculptures of the ages: none of them is to be understood properly either from the givenness of the human body or from the will to expression of an inner state, but solely from the relational event that takes place between two entities which have gone apart from one another, the withdrawn 'body' and the withdrawing 'soul'. In each of the arts there is something specifically corresponding to

the relational character to be found in the picture. Music, for example, can be understood in terms of categories only when it is recognized that music is the ever renewed discovering of tonal being in the movement of 'distancing' and the releasing of this tonal being in the movement of relation by bodying it forth.[25]

While defining art as the fulfilment of a specific relational potency, Buber, however, continually stressed its links with the associated potencies of knowing, loving and believing. In this key passage from *I and Thou*, for instance, where he employs familiar idioms from scripture and the familiar imagery of music, he emphasizes the interdependent nature of the activities of creating, knowing and understanding:

> . . . as he beholds what confronts him, the form discloses itself to the artist. He conjures it into an image. The image does not stand in the world of gods but in this great world of men. Of course it is 'there' even when no human eye afflicts it; but it sleeps. The Chinese poet relates that men did not want to hear the song that he was playing on his flute of jade; then he played it to the gods, and they inclined their ears; and ever since men too have listened to the song — and thus he went from the gods to those with whom the image cannot dispense. As in a dream it looks for the encounter with man in order that he may undo the spell and embrace the form for a timeless moment. And there he comes and experiences what there is to be experienced: that is how it is made, or this is what it expresses, or its qualities are such and such, and on top of that perhaps also how it might rate. Not that scientific and aesthetic understanding is not necessary — but it should do its work faithfully and immerse itself and diasappear in that truth of the relation which surpasses understanding and embraces what is understandable.[26]

And this points, finally, to the question of the kind of mutuality which exists in the dialogic relation of art. In any consideration relating to dialogic encounter the precise nature of the reciprocation involved should be specified. Where art is clearly seen to embody the experience of the interpersonal — in romantic love poetry, for example — the nature of the reciprocation involved is self-evident. But where the artist addresses inanimate nature the issue becomes more complex, since one assumes the inanimate world does not reciprocate the artist's Thou-saying. The issue arises also in the context of the appreciation of art, since the work of art once again does not reciprocate the appreciation of the viewer, listener or reader. On this matter considerable illumination can be found in the passsage from the Afterword to *I and Thou* where Buber describes the dialogue between man and nature:

> It is part of our concept of the plant that it cannot react to our actions upon it, that it cannot reply. Yet this does not mean that we meet with no

reciprocity at all in this sphere. We find here not the deeds of posture of an individual being but a reciprocity of being itself — a reciprocity that has nothing except being. The living wholeness and unity of a tree that denies itself to the eye, no matter how keen, of anyone who investigates, while it is manifest to those who say You, is present when they are present: they grant the tree the opportunity to manifest it, and now that tree that has being manifests it. Our habits of thought make it difficult for us to see that in such cases something is awakened by our attitude and flashes towards us from that which has being. What matters in this sphere is that we should do justice with an open mind to the actuality that opens before us. This huge sphere that reaches from the stones to the stars I should like to designate as the pre-threshold, meaning the step that comes before the threshold.[27]

From this it would appear that, while the reciprocation normally embracing the dialogic between man and man is not possible in the relation between man and inanimate being, a certain order of inclusion may exist in the latter just the same. That limited inclusion derives from the fact of the subject addressed being present to the beholder when he himself is fully present to that subject. They key word in this, perhaps, is 'subject'; it implies the personhood that is brought forth in the contemplated existent by virtue of the dialogic intensity with which it is addressed. And this, it would appear, is Buber's meaning also when he speaks of the artist 'bringing into being the form that confronts him',[28] and when he emphasizes the 'presence' of the perceived form and its capacity to 'act' on the perceiving subject, i.e. the artist:

> This is the eternal origin of art that a human being confronts a form that wants to become a work through him. Not a figment of his soul but something that appears to the soul and demands the soul's creative power. What is required is a deed that a man does with his whole being: if he commits it and speaks with his being the basic word to the form that appears, then the creative power is released and the work comes into being.
>
> The form that confronts me I cannot experience nor describe; I can only actualize it. And yet I see it, radiant in the splendour of the confrontation, far more clearly than all clarity of the experienced world. Not as a thing among the 'internal' things, not as a figment of the 'imagination', but as what is present. Tested for its objectivity, the form is not 'there' at all, but what can equal its presence? And it is an actual relation: *it acts on me as I on it*. Such work is creation, inventing is finding. Forming is discovery[29] (my italics).

## 2  The Language of Art

The foregoing section has attempted to define Buber's conception of the nature of aesthetic creativity. It has emphasized its dual character as an activity embracing the complementary functions of origination and response.

It has identified creativity as something in which all can participate: some as art-makers, some through the receptive activities of critical judgement , assessment and appreciation. It has been suggested that all those participating in the creative process, whatever the nature and level of their involvement, are engaged in a specific and distinctive mode of relation: a mode characterized by its interpenetration of the realms of sprit and sense; by its grasp of the transphenomenal; by its intentional concern with symbolic meaning-making; by its transcendence of the realms of utility and need; and by its capacity to invoke the reality of the undisclosed.

The whole matter can be examined in more detail, and its applications to education can be specified more closely, if these principles are considered in the context of a particular art-form. Buber has discussed various art-forms in his aesthetic writings. Several aspects of architecture, music, painting and sculpture are considered throughout his work. His most fully developed views, however, are in the sphere of the language arts and it is to his writings on poetry, drama and fiction, therefore, we must turn for a fuller understanding of his treatment of the creative and imaginative processes. His philosophy of language and his literary aesthetics are developed both from the standpoint of the philosophical theorist and from his own artistic vantage point as dramatist, novelist and poet. It will be recalled that he was the author of a Biblical drama, *Elijah*, a novel, *For the Sake of Heaven*, and a large number of poems. His status as an artist lends a special depth of insight to his theories of literary creativity. These theories are grounded firmly, however, in his philosophical descriptions of the nature of language.

The most fully elaborated of these descriptions occurs in his essay, 'The Word that is Spoken'. Here he identifies three 'modes-of-being of language':[30] the modes of present continuance, potential possession and actual occurrence. The first of these modes, that of present continuance, is defined in the essay as the totality of what can be spoken in a particular realm of language at a particular period in time. The second, that of potential possession, is defined as the totality of what has ever been expressed in a particular realm of language, from the most sophisticated to the most trivial forms of utterance. The third mode, that of actual occurrence, is the living speech of everyday usage.

All three modes are linked closely by Buber. The first and second, the continuing potential of language and the linguistic heritage, are enlivened and sustained, he says, by the dynamic spokenness of language in its mode of actual occurrence. They are linked also by their need for intentional or subjective relevance. Thus, in defining 'present continuance' as 'the totality of what can be spoken', Buber adds the important qualifying clause — 'as regarded from the point of view of the person who is able to say what is to be said.'[31] Similarly, he defines 'potential possession' as 'the totality of what has ever been uttered', but adds the words, 'in so far as it proves itself capable of being included in what men intend to utter and do utter.'[32] The living spokenness of language is related, in turn, to its dialogic character: to its origins in interhuman mutuality. Language, he writes, expresses the 'being-with-one-another' which is present between its speakers and its hearers. Their dialogic being is actualized in the language they intend and utter; it manifests itself in the living texture of their speech:

> The importance of the spoken word, I think, is grounded in the fact that it does not want to remain with the speaker. It reaches out toward a hearer, it lays hold of him, it even makes the hearer into a speaker, if perhaps only a soundless one. But this must not be understood as if the place of the occurrence of language is the sum of the two partners in dialogue or, in the terminology of Jacob Grimm, of the two 'fellows in speech'; as though the occurrence of language were to be understood through the psychophysical comprehension of two individual unities in a given period of time. The word that is spoken is found rather in the oscillating sphere between the persons, the sphere that I call 'the between' and that we can never allow to be contained without a remainder in the two participants. If we could take an inventory of all the physical and psychic phenomena to be found within a dialogic event, there would still remain outside something *sui generis* that could not be included — and that is just what does not allow itself to be understood as the sum of the speech of two or more speakers, together with all the accidental circumstances. This something *sui generis* is their dialogue.[33]

The two fundamental concepts of 'betweenness' and 'spokenness' are linked together inextricably in this passage from 'The Word That Is Spoken'. Buber points to a fundamental anthropological dependence between linguistic dialogue and the essentially relational character of man's own being. Linguistic utterance, he says, is possible only by virtue of men addressing each other; the spokenness of their language attests existentially to its radically dialogic character. Historically, language came into existence in the context of relational dialogue:

> A precommunicative stage of language is unthinkable. Man did not exist before having a fellow being, before he lived over against him, toward him, and that means before he had dealings with him. Language never existed before address; it could become monologue only after dialogue broke off or broke down. The early speaker was not surrounded by objects on which he imposed names, nor did adventures befall him which he caught with names: the world and destiny became language for him only in partnership. Even when in solitude beyond the range of call the hearerless word pressed on his throat, this word was connected with the primal possibility, that of being heard.[34]

Two further features of linguistic utterance are stressed in the essay: its becoming, dynamic character and the problematic nature of its existence. Buber adopts the same distance-relation formulation for the process of linguistic growth as he does for the dialogic process itself. He sees it as a dynamic manifestation of the continuing oscillation of the two movements of distance and relation characterizing all human existence. Nowhere, he declares, is this dual process manifested so comprehensively as in language:

> Unlike all other living beings, man stands over against a world from which he has been set at a distance, and, unlike all other living beings, he can again and again enter into relationship with it. This fundamental double stance nowhere manifests itself so comprehensively as in language. Man — he alone — speaks, for only he can address the other just as the other being standing at a distance over against him; but in addressing it, he enters into relationship. The coming-to-be of language also means a new function of distance. For even the earliest speaking does not, like a cry or a signal, have its end in itself; it sets the word outside itself in being, and the word continues, it has continuance. And this continuance wins its life ever anew in true relation, in the spokenness of the word. Genuine dialogue witnesses to it, and poetry witnesses to it. For the poem is spokenness, spokenness to the Thou, wherever this partner might be.[35]

In the same context Buber proceeds to define language as a phenomenon characterized by conflicting or dialectic tensions. He rejects the notion of monadic speech: the givenness of the Thou, he says, implies the givenness of an other for the addressing subject. Since the speaking subject and the addressed or responding other cannot use language with *identical* meaning or intention, their speaking is charged inevitably with the tension of potential disagreement, conflict and contradiction. It is this very tension and ambiguity which is inherent in linguistic utterance that constitutes its living, dynamic spokenness. The problematic character of living speech affords new possibilities for understanding and simultaneously for the growth of language itself. It achieves both by intensifying the generating force of the twin movements of distance and relation embracing human mutuality:

> When two friends discuss, say, the concept of thought, then the concept of the one and that of the other may be very similar in meaning; but we are not allowed to regard them as identical in meaning. This does not cease to be true even when the two of them begin by agreeing on a definition of the concept: the great fact of personal existence will penetrate even into the definition unless the two 'fellows in speech' join in betraying the logus for logical analysis. If the tension between what each means by the concept becomes too great, there arises a misunderstanding that can mount to destruction. But below the critical point the tension need by no means become inoperative; it can become fruitful, it always becomes fruitful

where, out of understanding each other, genuine dialogue unfolds.

From this it follows that it is not the unambiguity of a word but its ambiguity that constitutes living language. The ambiguity creates the problematic of speech, and it creates its overcoming in an understanding that is not an assimilation but a fruitfulness. The ambiguity of the word, which we may call its aura, must to some measure already have existed whenever men in their multiplicity met each other, expressing this multiplicity in order not to succumb to it. It is the communal nature of the logos as at once 'word' and 'meaning' which makes man man, and it is this which proclaims itself from of old in the communalizing of the spoken word that again and again comes into being.[36]

Throughout the essay, 'The Word that is Spoken', Buber consistently stresses the dynamic spokenness of language and its disclosure of the inherently dialogic character of interhuman utterance. The principle is maintained throughout his writings on poetry, drama and fiction. He sees poetry as the highest and most accomplished expression of the spokenness of living speech and of the dialogic nature of linguistic utterance. 'For the poem is spokenness', he writes, 'spokenness to the Thou, wherever this partner might be.'[37] Three fundamental charactertistics of poetry are identified in these writings: firstly, its transcendence of specific sensible structure; secondly, the irreducible quality of its spokenness; thirdly, the special 'faithfulness' evidenced in its continuity of word and meaning. In 'Man and his Image-Work' Buber speaks of the power of poetic language to evoke the 'primal structure of man as man' by virtue of its transcendence of specific sensible structure.[38] Unlike the plastic and acoustical arts — which are determined by specific contexts of sense — poetry enjoys an autonomy and structural multiplicity which derives, he says, from its universal presence in the living speech of interhuman dialogue:

> Only *one* art has a sphere that is not sufficiently determined by one of the senses, but rather itself lives above the level of the senses; it is poetry. Poetry does not originate from one of the senses' standing over against the world, but from the primal structure of man as man, his primal structure founded upon sense experiences and overarched by the spirit's power of symbols, from language. Even when one tries to grasp the determination of the spheres objectively and instead of sight and hearing speaks of space and time, language remains for poetry as a third. The other arts create out of the spheres of space and time; they are obliged to them and do justice to them: painting by preserving the interrelations of things while renouncing their corporeality; the plastic arts by erecting in this space the corporeal individual being while renouncing its interrelations; architecture by transforming in this space the proportions, the functional relations, the geometric structures in the midst of the unmathematical reality which it

thereby also hides; music by embodying time itself in tones, as though, indeed, there were no space. But poetry is not obedient to anything other than language, whether it calls and praises, narrates, or allows the happening between men to unfold in dialogue.[39]

This universality of poetic spokenness points also to its irreducibility. The poem, Buber writes, 'imparts a truth which cannot come to words in any other manner than just this one, in the manner of this form.' He warns that 'every paraphrase of a poem robs it of its truth.'[40] This raises the more complex issue of the nature of poetic truth. For Buber it is essentially a continuity of language and meaning. 'The relation between meaning and saying,' he writes, 'points us to the intended relation between unity of meaning and saying, on the one side, and that between meaning and saying and the personal existence, on the other side.'[41] The crucial term here, perhaps, is 'intended'. The poet intends a unity of meaning and word: a faithfulness to the word which is manifested in its highest form in his poetry. It is a threefold faithfulness: faithfulness, first, to the reality perceived, secondly, to the person addressed, and thirdly, to the authentic reality of the word. A remarkable passage from 'The Word That Is Spoken' describes these three processes:

> The truth that is concerned in this fashion is not the sublime 'unconcealment' suitable to Being itself, the *aletheia* of the Greeks; it is the simple conception of truth of the Hebrew Bible; whose *etymon* means 'faithfulness', the faithfulness of man or the faithfulness of God. The truth of the word that is genuinely spoken is, in its highest forms — in poetry and incomparably still more so in that message-like saying that descends out of a stillness over a disintegrating human world — indivisible unity. It is a manifestation without a concomitant diversity of aspects. In all its other forms, however, three different elements must be distinguished in it. It is, in the first place, faithful truth in relation to the reality which was once perceived and is now expressed, to which it opens wide the window of language in order that it may become directly perceptible to the hearer. It is, second, faithful truth in relation to the person addressed, whom the speaker means as such, no matter whether he bears a name or is anonymous, is familiar or alien. And to mean a man means nothing less than to stand by him and his insights with the elements of the soul that can be sent forth, with the 'outer soul', even though at the same time one fundamentally remains and must remain with oneself. Third, it is the truth of the word that is genuinely spoken, faithful truth in relation to its speaker, that is, to his factual existence in all its hidden structure. The human truth of which I speak — the truth vouchsafed men — is no pneuma that pours itself out from above on a band of men now become superpersonal: it opens itself to one just in one's existence as a person. This concrete person, in the life-space

allotted to him, answers with his faithfulness for the word that is spoken to him.[42]

If poetry, in the spirit of 'faithful truth' which is described in this passage, attests to the deep reality of human encounter, then it must attest also to the ultimately religious character of that encounter. In the third section of *I and Thou* Buber describes how the interhuman relation extends into the realms of the unconditioned, the infinite and intemporal: that is, into the sphere of religious dialogue where the subject addresses the eternal Thou. Ultimately, this is the truth to which the poet attests in his poetry, as is made evident by Buber in his writings on Goethe and Hölderlin. In *I and Thou* Goethe, Socrates and Christ are linked in a passage describing the dialogic I-saying. 'How powerful, even over-powering is Jesus' I-saying', the passage says. It continues: 'But it is the I of the unconditioned relation in which man calls his you "Father" in such a way that he himself becomes nothing but a son. Whenever he says I, he can only mean the "I" of the holy basic word that has become unconditional for him.'[43] Buber suggests a comparison between the I-saying of Christ to his Father and the poet's I-saying to nature. He takes Goethe as an example of one whose poetry addresses the Thouness of the other in a spirit of faithfulness which is comparable to Christ's I-saying to his Father:

> How beautiful and legitimate the full I of Goethe sounds! It is the I of pure intercourse with nature. Nature yields to it and speaks ceaselessly with it; she reveals her mysteries to it and yet does not betray her mystery. It believes in her and says to the rose: 'So it is You' — and at once shares the same actuality with the rose. Hence, when it returns to itself, the spirit of actuality stays with it; the vision of the sun clings to the blessed eye that recalls its own likeness to the sun, and the friendship of the elements accompanies man into the calm of dying and rebirth. Thus the 'adequate, true and pure' I-saying of the representatives of association, the Socratic and the Goethean persons, resounds through the ages.[44]

In Goethe's poetry Buber found powerful confirmation for his conviction that a deep concern for humanity opens up a relation with the infinite, unconditioned and eternal and therefore extends the interhuman into the sphere of religious dialogue A verse from Goethe affirming this conviction was quoted on the opening page of the first edition of *I and Thou*. It read: 'So waiting I have won from thee the end/ God's presence in each element.'[45] In an essay, 'Goethe's Concept of Humanity', Buber declares that while the unconditioned can never be contemplated directly, it is disclosed through 'any relationship effected with a man's whole being.'[46] It can be contemplated, in other words, in its immanent and symbolic manifestations. He sees Goethe's poetry as being fervently expressive of this truth:

Any genuine life-relationship to divine being — i.e., any such relationship effected with one's whole being — is a human truth, and man has no other truth. To realize this does not mean to relativize truth. The ultimate truth is one, but it is given to man only as it enters, reflected as in a prism, into the true life-relationships of the human persons. We have it, and yet have it not, in its multicoloured reflection. 'The True, which is identical with the Divine, can never be perceived by us directly; we only contemplate it in its reflection, in the example, the symbol.' Human truth is not conformity between a thing thought and the thing as being; it is participation in Being. It cannot claim universal validity, but it is lived, and it can be lived exemplary, symbolically. Beyond acts of discerning, choosing and judging, beyond acts of rewarding and punishing, we contemplate a pure humanity which expiates all human failings.[47]

In Hölderlin Buber found further support for his conception of poetry as attestation of religious dialogue. Holderlin's poem, 'Patmos', is mentioned several times in his writings and occupies a prominent place in his prose-work, *Daniel*. Buber particularly liked this line from 'Patmos' — 'Where danger is, the delivering power grows too.'[48] In 'What Is Common to All' Hölderlin's work is cited by Buber as an instance of the poetic expression of communal dialogue with the Divine. 'In our age,' he writes, 'this We standing before the divine countenance has attained its highest expression through a poet, through Friedrich Hölderlin. He says of the authentic past of man as man, "since we have been a dialogue and have been able to hear from one another". And after that comes the words, "But we are soon song."[49] In Hölderlin's poetry, he concludes, 'the self-contained communality of Heraclitus that overspans the opposites has here become the choral antiphony *which is directed upwards*'[50] (my italics).

The principle of dialogic spokenness is applied by Buber in a special manner to the dramatic arts. Drama, he says, represents the 'rising to artistic independence of the element of dialogue.'[51] He particularly emphasizes its expression of dialogic tension: it embodies 'the word as something that moves between being'; 'essential to it', he says, 'is the fact of tension between word and answer.'[52] He sees drama as particularly representing the problematic of linguistic utterance. Through its articulation of difference and conflict it gives artistic shape and form in a specially intensive way to the dual movements of distance and relation present in human existence:

Thus through the mere fact, given form by dialogue, of the *difference* between men there already exists, before any actual action, that dramatic entanglement which, woven with the unfathomableness of destiny, appears as 'tragedy', the same entanglement which drawn into the all-too-clear world of caprice and accident makes for 'comedy' How both, the tragic and the comic, can unite in pure actionless dialogue has been shown to us by

Plato in whose works his master and the many-named sophist confront each other like two types of the Attic theatre: the ironic man (*Eiron*), who does not say what he knows, and the boaster (*Alazon*), who says what he does not know — and what we finally experience is the fate of the spirit in the world. With the mere antagonistic existence of the persons that proclaims itself dialogically, the dramatic is essentially present; all action can only unfold it.[53]

Elaborating further on the nature of dramatic dialogue, Buber strongly echoes Pasternak's theme, conveyed in the story, 'Il Tratto di Apelle', that the theatrical impulse is rooted in the desire to assume the identity of another being.[54] 'It originates', Buber writes, 'in the elemental impulse to become this other being.'[55] As an art-form, he says, drama combines two basic dialogic principles: the 'spiritual' principle of poetic spokenness it manifests in its articulation of conflict through dramatic speech; and the 'natural'.principle of assumed otherness it manifests in its theatrical function of mimic transformation. In this passage from his essay, 'Drama and Theatre', where he is discussing some aspects of classical drama, he insists the two principles are as inseparable as body and spirit:

With this example of Greek tragedy, I have already anticipated. Here both principles are already joined, the spiritual principle of dialogue and the natural one of mimic transformation-play that relate to each other as love to sex, that need each other, as love needs sex in order to obtain body, and sex needs love in order to attain spirit. But one must understand, indeed, that though love certainly appears later in the history of man, it cannot be derived from sex. In the truth of being love is the cosmic and eternal power to which sex is sent as a sign and a means it employs in order that out of it love may be reborn on earth. Therefore, too, the theatre needs the drama more than drama needs the theatre. The drama that cannot become embodied in a theatre exists discarnate in lonely spirit. But the theatre that is not obedient to drama bears the curse of soullessness that, for all its luxuriant variegation, it can hardly stifle for the hour's duration of its magic show. An age of unperformed drama can be an heroic Eiron, yet an age in which the self-glorious theatre treats all drama as material and occasion for its phantasmagoria is a pitiful Alazon. In order that a faithless public, which allows 'diversions' to be set before it because it fears concentration, be redeemed from its fear to awe and elevated to belief in the reality of the spirit, great work, great education, great teaching are necessary.

The theatre can take part in this work first of all through submitting itself to the command of the word. The word that convulses through the whole body of the speaker, the word that serves all gestures in order that all the plasticity of the stage constructs and reconstructs itself as a frame, the stern over-againstness of I and Thou, overarched by the wonder of speech, that governs all the play of transformation, weaving the mystery of the spirit into every element — it alone can determine the legitimate relation between drama and theatre.[56]

One further aspect of the dialogic view of literature remains to be discussed. While the *tension* of interhuman dialogue finds expression particularly in drama and theatre, the *imperfection* of dialogue has been one of the foremost themes in literature, from its most primitive to its most sophisticated forms. Buber discusses this issue in the context of modern literature, and particularly in relation to the works of Dostoievsky and Kafka.[57] In the course of the discussion he points to the disparity between the human aspiration towards dialogic fulfilment and the limitations placed on the human potential for this fulfilment by the temporal and spatial constrictions of man's existence. This disparity between the perfection sought and the reality of what can be achieved is seen by Buber as one of the major sources of conflict and suffering in human life. Like his predecessors, Goethe and Dostoievsky, and his contemporary, Kafka, he sees the suffering and self-conflict resultant on the failure to relate as an endemic feature and condition of man's existence. Literature which so radically affirms the dialogic element in human life must testify also, he says, to the conflict and suffering arising from the inevitable frustrations and failures of the human aspiration towards its perfection.

In his essay, 'Guilt and Guilt Feelings' Buber traces the origins of man's 'existential guilt' to the failures inevitably arising from the various relationships in which he is engaged. These failures are traced in the essay to the disparity between man's aspirations and needs and the circumstances of his existence. He quotes Pascal: 'The greatness of man is bound up with his misery. Man is the being who is capable of becoming guilty and of illuminating his guilt.'[58] Buber points to an inherent resistance in man to the act of self-illumination which is the primary requirement for the purging of his guilt. He sees this resistance as being profoundly indicative of man's failure to achieve genuine dialogue and therefore as a cause of continuing misery and suffering in his existence. He cites Dostoievsky's Stavrogin and Kafka's Mr K. as two characters who fail to achieve self-illumination and become the victims of their own guilt. Goethe, he says, also traced the tragedy of man's existence to his yearning for the perfection of the unconditioned and intemporal while being embedded in the conditioned and the temporal. He (Buber) cites a passage from *The Sorrows of Werther* where the hero, shortly before his suicide, considers the nature of suffering and sees that it is endemic in his own human condition. When he asks 'the father' why he has forsaken him Werther finds himself 'thrown back entirely on himself and his own misery.'[59] Like Stavrogin and K., he cannot confront the source of this misery and becomes its victim. Again, like Dostoievsky and Kafka, Goethe affirms the permanence of suffering in mortal life. In his essay, 'Goethe's Concept of Humanity' Buber indicates the power and vividness with which this truth is conveyed by Goethe through his use of the archetypal Christian imagery in which the theme has traditionally been represented. Werther, he says...

> ... speaks as one who stands outside 'religion', by which he means not the belief in God but Christianity, and that not in a general sense, but as the condition of a man certain of being redeemed by the Mediator. He does not question the divinity of Christ; he calls him not only the Son of God but 'God from Heaven', and even, using an Old Testament appellation of the Father, Him 'who stretches out the heavens like a curtain.' The only idea he rejects, because his 'heart' bids him reject it, is that he should be one of those whom the Father, in the language of the Gospel of St John, has given to the Son: 'What if the Father wants — as my heart tells me he does — to keep me for Himself? But he who is thus retained by the Father is destined to be crucified by the world, i.e. to suffer, in his own actual life, not by way of imitation of Christ, what the Son of God has suffered. His is 'the human lot of having to bear one's full measure of suffering'. He has to drain, with lips that are nothing but human, the cup which 'was too bitter for the human lips of the God from Heaven.' And when at last he, too, asks the Father why he has forsaken him, then the voice in which he is speaking is 'that of creature, thrown back entirely upon himself, deprived of his self, and sinking into abysmal depths.'[60]

## 3 Creativity and Literacy

Buber's aesthetic theories are highly relevant to the contemporary debate on the nature of creativity and the methods that should be employed for its fostering in school classrooms. The nature and significance of his contribution to this particular sphere of educational theory and practice can be assessed most usefully in the context of this debate. This final section will attempt to show that his concept of creativity, with its carefully balanced identification of the place of expressive and receptive activities, offers a realistically conceived alternative to the polarized positions adopted on the issue by many contemporary theorists. Since the whole question of creativity is deeply bound up with the crucial matter of the development of literacy, further consideration will be given to the implications of Buber's aesthetics for the formulation of aims for an effective linguistic pedagogy.

On one side of the 'creativity debate' one finds an excessive emphasis on expressive potentialities to the detriment of the receptive capacities with which they must be linked. This emphasis has been associated particularly with the 'child art' movement in the visual arts and with the 'creative writing' movement in the language arts. In the sphere of the visual arts controversy has focussed mainly on the views of Herbert Read: on his promotion of the notion of creativity as self-expression, his virtual identification of art with play, his exaggerated claims for Jungian theories of symbolization and his inflated sense of the value of children's 'art'. There are a number of statements in *Education through Art* which clearly identify Read with the extremes of progressivist educational theory. At an early stage in the work he writes: 'It is assumed that the general purpose of education is to foster the growth of what is individual in each human being, at the same time harmonizing the individuality thus educated with the organic unity of the social group to which the individual belongs.'[61] This, on first reading, seems no more than a humanely inspired platitude, but later we find that the notion of growth is identified primarily with the free expression of individual impulses. 'Education', he says, 'is the fostering of growth, but apart from physical maturation growth is only made apparent in expression — audible or visual signs and symbols.'[62] This is taken a stage further again when self-expression is equated with artistic expression. The following is the quotation from *Education through Art* which has drawn the most vociferous condemnation of progressivist theory and the entire child art movement from a multitude of writers who see the equation of art with individual expression as debasing the complex and highly developed processes involved in the act of creation. 'All faculties, of thought, logic, memory, sensibility and intellect,' Read says, 'are involved in such processes (the expressive) . . . And they are all processes which involve art, for art is nothing but the good making of sounds, images, etc. . . . The aim of education is therefore the creation of artists — of people efficient in the various modes of expression.'[63]

A similar emphasis on 'free expression', uninhibited by any corresponding attention to the structures of language, and an emphasis on imaginative spontaneity without a corresponding emphasis on the mastery of symbolic language, were the hallmarks of the 'language through experience' movement of the 1950s and 1960s. Its advocates fall into two main groupings: those such as Langdon, Pym and Hourd[64] whose emphasis on self-expression is so excessive as to make a concern for the formal conventions of language seem peripheral to the entire process, and others, such as Peel and Maybury,[65] who have advocated a more balanced approach to the expressive and technical aspects of language. The following statement from a widely used pedagogic manual is fairly typical of the excesses of the first of these two approaches. On the need for instruction in the technical skills of writing the author advises: 'Correctness in spelling or tenses is unimportant. The spontaneity that is vital to much of this work will be lost if spelling creates inhibitions. . . . Indeed, so unimportant is the criterion of spelling, agreement and the like, that, in the case of the non-writer, the teacher must be prepared either for another pupil to write down the work at the author's dictation or make arrangements for the pupil to tape his own work, alterations and all.'[66] It should be stressed that this is indeed an extreme position and one carefully avoided by Maybury, Peel and others who advise various stages in the drafting of imaginative writing, with a planning stage at the outset being devoted to the ordering of subject-matter, and a revision stage at the end devoted to the correction of errors in grammar, syntax, punctuation and spelling.

Yet the main result of this continuing emphasis on spontaneity has been an imbalance in teaching between the expressive and structural aspects of writing, with the latter frequently being seen as subordinate and relatively unimportant features of the drive for expressive fluency. David Holbrook, for instance, while manifesting a clear concern for the development of the constructional skills of writing in *English for Maturity*,[67] has provided much support also for the idea that children who are emotionally, socially and linguistically deprived attain high levels of literacy, simply by an outpouring of emotion in a stream of disorganized and technically defective prose. Of one of the pupils in the case studies from *English for the Rejected*, for example, he said: 'Though she often spelt wrongly, and her punctuation was imperfect, these faults often arose simply because her courageous sallies into imaginative expression far outstripped her technical powers of handling words graphically. But she seemed to me the most literate of the children, in that her language, coming directly as she spoke, felt and thought, without conscious manipulation, had the power not only to move deeply but also to express profound truths of nature and reality'.[68] This, whatever the author's intention, is clearly open to serious misinterpretation and was indeed in conflict with research, already available at the time the book was written, which found greater confidence in linguistic expression amongst children instructed systematically in the technical skills.[69]

Predictably, there has been a strong reaction to all these views, and particularly to the identification of creativity with self-expression and the reduction of artistic creativity to the level of commonplace experience. Much of the reaction has come, however, from theorists taking a similarly extreme position by excessively emphasizing receptive and critical responses to art. G.H. Bantock and Mary Warnock have emphasized formal studies in the arts as forcefully as 'progressivist' thinkers emphasize expressive activities. Bantock, like Eliot and Leavis, contends that the great delusion of progressivist education is its universalization of the artistic function. 'Today's educational fetish is creativity for all', he writes. 'No greater error exists in current education than the belief that creativity can come out of a vacuum. The great masters have ever followed the tradition, defined by Gombrich in the terms "making comes before matching", which is another way of saying

that art (creativity) is the product of art rather than nature.'[70] While demon-
strating the enriching power of formal studies in literature, music and the
visual arts, and their simultaneous fostering of cognitive and affective
development, Bantock fails, however, to recognize the further enrichment
which mastery of their expressive capacities can provide. More significantly,
his proposal that a two-tier curriculum be designed to provide a traditional
programe in the arts for the intellectually and socially privileged elite, and a
diluted, less sophisticated programme for the rest, can hardly be defended,
in the face of evidence from education systems in Western and Eastern
Europe of the success of common courses in the arts for all students.[71]

Mary Warnock, in contrast to Bantock, has made an eloquent case for the
common culture curriculum in *Schools of Thought*,[72] though she shares his
notion of aesthetic development as almost exclusively the training of critical
and receptive sensitivities. In a work where she asserts her view that the
cultivation of imagination should be the chief aim of education, she states:

> I do not believe that children exercise imagination more by having a set of
> handbells put before them, or a glockenspiel, and being told to make their
> own music than by listening to music with a receptive ear. I do not believe
> that there is anything uniquely valuable ( though it may have value) in
> getting children to write or draw things which are to be 'original'. On the
> contrary, they may be deprived if they are not encouraged to read and to
> look at the works of other people . . . grown-ups or the work of nature. The
> fact is that if imagination is creative in all its uses, then children will be
> creating their own meanings and interpretations of things as much by
> looking at them as by making them.[73]

A more balanced approach to these issues may be seen in the work of Louis
Arnaud Reid and Elliot Eisner in the visual arts and of Peter Abbs and
Bernard Harrison in the language arts.[74] Reid, in a recent publication,
challenges the notion that 'child art' is to be valued for its spontaneity and
supposed originality. He sees early art education as a preliminary stage in
the training of perceptual and technical skills — from which artistic creativity
will be nurtured in exceptional instances — but which serves in most cases
to provide a preliminary awareness of the language of the particular art-form
studied. He says: 'Education in how to look at pictures or other works of art
is a must. . . . Very few children will become artists (and these may need
special attention). But educated introduction to the arts which have both
reflected and influenced great human cultures, is, surely, and particularly in
a materialistic world — a right and a necessity for all. But it does more than
that. Participation in art is an illuminated form of living.'[75]

This view is reasserted by Eisner whose work may be more significant than
Reid's in this respect, since he anticipated current reactions against

progressivism as long ago as the late 1950s. At that time he condemned progressivist theory for its naive conception of child development, its excessive emphasis on activity, and its view that aesthetic education, rather than concerning itself with aims and attainments peculiar to the arts, became an instrument for something vaguely defined as 'personal development'. The teacher, he said, 'was admonished not to interfere with the very personal process of the child's artistic creativity,' 'not to inflict her adult view on the child's developing conception of reality.'[76] Rejecting this for its evident unreality, he reformulated the aims of art education to encompass a range of objectives not highly valued by progressivist writers: the training of visual perception and awareness, provision for active and systematic instruction by the teacher, and a highly developed appreciation of the traditions of art. Rejecting the notion of the child as artist, he called for a deepening of artistic understanding and a cultivation of the intellective and affective capacities necessary to foster that unique form of understanding. To that end he put forward a model for art education in the primary school which was based on classroom research monitored from his curriculum research unit at Stanford University. The aims defined for the project exemplify the balance of cultural, historical, critical and expressive elements which can be realistically accommodated even in an art curriculum for the elementary school:

> This project . . . is based upon the assumption that artistic learning is not an automatic consequence of maturation, that it can be facilitated through instruction and that a curriculum developed with clarity and with in-instructional support for the elementary school teacher working in the self-contained classroom can be used effectively to enable even the very young child to obtain both competence and satisfaction in the visual arts.
>
> One of the first tasks that needed to be undertaken was that of identifying some of the domains which constitute the visual arts and which were teachable and learnable for children at so tender an age. Although there are a variety of ways of staking out the field, we arbitrarily decided to identify three that seemed to us to be reasonably wide in scope and yet flexible enough so that we could alter our plans if that seemed appropriate. These three domains are the *productive*, that domain dealing with the formulation of objectives having expressive and aesthetic quality; the *critical*, that domain dealing with the perception of qualities constituting art; and the *historical*, that domain dealing with the evolution of art in human culture. Within each of these domains we have attempted to identify those concepts and principles that appear both significant and useful for handling the material within the domain.[77]

Peter Abbs, in *English within the Arts*, similarly asserts the need for a balance between productive, critical and historical responses to art. He condemns 'progressivist' educators for their excessive indulgence of individual impulses. 'I think,' he says, 'it is just to say that they possess an effusive concept of the child, at once intolerably vague and highly indulgent. In their minds the poet and the child become synonymous; yet the poet expresses his culture in a way no child can possibly do.'[78] Two of the defects of progressivist theory which he particularly sought to rectify were:

> (i) its failure to stress the dependence of expression on a mastery of the formal and structural conventions of the relevant art-form;
> (ii) its failure to combine imaginative expression with a sensitive appreciation of the cultural heritage.[79]

Through his notion of an arts workshop Abbs has devised a highly impressive pedagogy for the implementation of these aims. A particular strength of the workshop strategy is its emphasis on the teacher's active and purposeful involvement in the whole process. The methods described for the teaching of English writing, for example, involve close and continuous assistance from the teacher in the planning and structuring of the writing, in the techniques of paragraphing, sentence-construction, grammar, punctuation, spelling and the various ordering processes necessary for the shaping of the writing into clear, mature, well-ordered prose. Similar methods are developed to achieve a close and meaningful relationship between expressive activities and literary studies. And there is no pretension by Abbs that the writing workshop is a nursery for young artists. Some indeed may emerge from it, but for the great majority the experience is intended to provide a deepened awareness of the aesthetic potentialities of language, an awareness which is further enriched through the simultaneous development of literary sensitivities.[80]

It is in this context of identifying the balance of expressive-productive and critical-historical potentialities in the sphere of aesthetic creativity that Buber's ideas become relevant to the debate I have attempted to describe. With Eisner and Reid he shares a deep concern for the interrelation and simultaneous development of these potentialities. His affinities with Abbs and Holbrook are closer again since both writers have drawn directly on his aesthetic theories in support of their own view of the growth and development of the creartive imagination. Holbrook explicitly acknowledges his dependence on Buber's philosophical anthropology in *English For Meaning* (see Chapter 5, 'The Heavenly Bread of Self-Being').[81] Both writers have taken the foundation principles of their aesthetic theories from Buber. Their indebtedness to his philosophy is particularly evident on issues such as the relational nature of the creative act, the intentional character of symbolic meaning-making, and the tension and balance occurring between the activities of origination and response. Yet close comparison between their work and Buber's points to a deep divergence between them on certain issues also, and these hold deep implications for the formulation of aims for a sound and balanced linguistic pedagogy.

To understand the nature of these differences it is necessary first to consider some further controversies in the field of vernacular language education that have been occurring mainly since the publication of the Bullock Report, *A Language For Life*,[82] in Great Britain in 1975. The publication of the Bullock Report marked a further stage in the redefinition of the aims of language education that had been proceeding since the 1960s. The debate generated by Bullock on what should constitute a vernacular language curriculum has resulted in the publication of several further reports, one of which, an H.M.I. Document, *English from 5 to 16*,[83] has become the focus of most current discussions on the whole matter because of its attempt to provide a definitive and comprehensive specification of aims for first language education. The H.M.I. Document begins by asserting the responsibility of all teachers for the development of linguistic competence. It then identifies the specific responsibilities of English teachers and the aims they are expected to achieve. It insists that those who teach English are 'explicitly concerned. with *every aspect* of the growth of their pupils' command of language';[84] it calls for a progressive growth in the range and variety of purposes for which pupils can understand and use language and a corresponding growth in their command of the appropriate forms, techniques and styles of language that they can respond to and use. These principles are applied to the four fundamental modes of linguistic usage — speaking, listening, reading and writing — and the Inspectors emphasize the importance of interrelating all four modes. They reiterate the words of the Bullock Report: 'Language grows incrementally, through an interaction of writing, talk, reading and experience, the body of resulting work forming an organic whole.'[85] The primary aim of English teaching, they say, is the promotion of this interaction. On this principle they base their specification of aims which is sufficiently concise to quote in its entirety:

> Education in the spoken word should aim: to develop the pupils' ability to speak with confidence, clarity, fluency and in appropriate forms of speech, in a variety of situations and groupings for a variety of audiences, for a range of purposes of increasing complexity and demand; and correspondingly to develop their capacity to listen with attention and understanding in a similar variety of situations and for a similar range of purposes.
>
> In the area of reading, the aims should be to enable pupils: to read fluently and with understanding a range of different kinds of material, using reading methods appropriate to the material and the purposes for which they are reading; to have confidence in their capacities as readers; to find pleasure in and be voluntary users of reading, for information, for interest, for entertainment, and for the extension of experience and insight that poetry and

fiction of quality afford; to see that reading is necessary for their personal lives, for their learning throughout the curriculum, and for the requirements of living and working in society.

As to writing, the aims should be to enable pupils: to write for a range of purposes; to organize the content of what is written in ways appropriate to the purposes; to use styles of writing appropriate to the purposes and the intended readership; to use spelling, punctuation and syntax accurately and with confidence.

There is a fourth aim which applies over all the modes of language. This is to teach the pupils about language, so that they achieve a working knowledge of its structure and of the variety of ways in which meaning is made, so that they have a vocabulary for discussing it, so that they can use it with greater awareness, and because it is interesting.[86]

This definition of aims has an obvious ancestry. It is clearly based on the socio-linguistic, communication model for English associated with the research of Bernstein, Britton, Barnes, Halliday, Doughty and others[87] — research which was given official endorsement in the Bullock Report of 1975. While it is important to acknowledge the many positive advances in English teaching that must be attributed to all these sources — not least their recognition of the importance of oracy, their concern for social as well as individual uses of language, their concern for functional literacy and the pedagogic methods necessary to achieve it — it is essential also to consider the criticisms directed at their approach to English teaching. The more usual criticisms point to their naive conception of linguistic growth, their diminished sense of the place of imagination in the development of linguistic competence, their limited awareness of the cultural heritage, their neglect of emotional development, their poor sense of the relation of literature to everyday linguistic usage, and of the place of the aesthetic and the poetic in the process of linguistic growth. This comment from Peter Abbs is fairly typical of the disillusionment felt by many at the kind of thinking associated with Bullock and other theorists of similar orientation:

> Yet literature, in many of the arguments for linguistics, became reduced to being little more than just another manifestation of language, a manifestation that was even dying out, that was, perhaps, in no way essential to the functioning of materialist civilization. Peter Doughty, in characteristic vein, declared that the new English teacher should be committed *to language in all its complexity and variety and not merely the highly idiosyncratic form of literature.* The highly idiosyncratic form of Homer, Shakespeare and D.H. Lawrence! Halliday, in the same light, or, more truly, in the same darkness, insisted that the true discipline for the English teacher was no longer literature — that idiosyncratic version of language destined to die out in the T.V. metropolis — but linguistics. It was as if F.R. Leavis

and David Holbrook and countless others never lifted their pens. Earlier traditions of English teaching had been, with alarming efficiency, simply erased. In the numb space buzzed the small insects 'communications', 'skills', 'strategies', 'language operates'; the drone of a new technicism. Curiously, the word 'communication' fell like lead from the lips of a thousand teachers, so there seemed less and less to say. What had been overlooked in the pathological obsession for communications was the elusive underground of the psyche, those preconceptual forces of latent formulation locked in the emergent impulses of the body and the unconscious. Only by maintaining contact with these deeper pre-verbal energies can language itself remain resonant, charged, rich, strange, compelling and worthwhile. Creativity exists prior to words. And words, if they are to have the power of authentic utterance, must return constantly to their non- verbal origins, back to the creative impulse. The rejection of psychoanalysis had, indeed, been premature. Without any sense of depth or inner mystery, 'communication' was destined to become confined to surfaces, growing ever thinner and ever more transparent until there was nothing left to say, except words.[88]

Abbs's views on these matters clearly reflect the influence of Holbrook and Leavis, though there are significant issues on which he differs from both. All three are agreed that the cultivation of the imagination is the primary purpose of English teaching. Holbrook, in his assessment of the Bullock Report, argued that English is concerned primarily with the development of the power of symbolization and that this is achieved through the training of the imagination. He spoke of the fallacious epistemology underlying the Report, in particular its view of language as essentially a medium of inter-personal and social communication which can be developed through the training of specified strategies and skills. He complained that Bullock dealt peripherally and superficially with literature and the whole cultural tradition, that it responded to pragmatic, material needs. Language, he argued, is developed through the fostering of symbol-making or meaning-making capacities that are rooted in the unconscious. Echoing Leavis' *The Living Principle*,[89] he stressed the intentional relationship that exists between mind, symbol, language and reality, and the deepened awareness of that relationship which experience of the symbolic provides. Since the study of literature and the cultivation of imagination through other such activities are the main ways of achieving this purpose, he insists they must occupy the primary and dominant position in any definition of the aims of first language teaching.[90]

The Holbrook argument has much to commend it, insofar as it recognizes the centrality of aesthetic consciousness in linguistic and cognitional development, and thereby points to a radical defect in the thinking of Bullock and its successors. One must ask, however, whether it claims too much for the place of aesthetic meaning in English as a whole. Abbs, for instance, and to some degree Holbrook also, sees English as being concerned essentially and exclusively with aesthetic development. While pointing, however, to the indivisibility and wholeness of linguistic experience they appear simultaneously to suggest a separation of aesthetic from non-aesthetic uses of language. To understand the possible scale of this contradiction we must look to its roots in Leavis's *The Living Principle*. Leavis argued for the centering of English studies on literature, on the grounds that literary and creative studies would ensure the training of intelligence and sensibility together and 'bring into relation a diversity of fields of knowledge and thought.' He called for the 'cultivation of sensitiveness and precision of response and a delicate integrity of intelligence.'[91]

It is necessary to consider the implications of this 'integrity of intelligence' more closely. One must ask, in particular, if it implies that the synthesizing powers described should be extended into spheres of meaning beyond the aesthetic. When Leavis speaks of the training of perception, judgement and analytic skills through the literary-critical discipline, and the training of a non- specialized intelligence, and when he speaks of the power of the literary-critical 'to lead constantly outside itself', is he not advocating the comprehension of a variety of sources of meaning, and of the linguistic powers appropriate to their development, within the framework of a single linguistic discipline? Does the goal of fashioning an integrity of intellect, in other words, not involve the simultaneous comprehension of aesthetic and non- aesthetic meaning and the fostering of aesthetic and non- aesthetic uses of language in terms of their essential indivisibility in everyday life? Should it not include mastery of the linguistic usages appropriate to general, descriptive, empirical, non-symbolic, unmediated, discursive and literal, as well as non-discursive, symbolic and metaphoric forms of meaning? The answer, if we are to judge from the standpoint even of writers, such as Abbs, who are sympathetic to Leavis's views, is that linguistic development has indeed to embrace all such varieties of language and meaning. But one must further question the practicality of the solution proposed by Abbs.

His solution, ironically, is the 'language across the curriculum' policy advocated by Bullock.[92] While recognizing the need for linguistic instruction in a variety of contexts, aesthetic and non-aesthetic, he would entrust this responsibility to teachers of all subjects in the curriculum. Taking the particular instance of comprehension and essay- writing, he argues that the habit of critical reading is crucial to all disciplines, as is the capacity to write critically and intelligently, and that these skills must therefore be developed in all the disciplines of the curiculum. 'Why,' he asks, 'should English teachers be specifically concerned with imparting the techniques of comprehension?' 'All academic disciplines,' he argues, 'must develop in the young the skills of reading (like skimming, scanning, use of an index, comprehension and evaluation) and the skills of writing (note-taking, ability to organize notes intro arguments, ability to organize arguments into essays)'. 'Through language across the curriculum,' he suggests, 'English is freed to find its own intrinsic shape as an arts discipline.'[93]

The argument certainly has its attractions and the emphasis on English as a corporate responsibility — which is not new in itself and may be traced at least to the early 1920s and to Sampson's *English for the English*[94] — is something that needs to be positively and explicitly formulated as a curriculum aim. But there are two basic flaws in the thesis. Firstly, it engenders once again the division in linguistic experience I have mentioned: a division which is rooted in a highly exclusivist conception of the range of aesthetic meaning and in a highly subjectivist theory of language. Secondly, in present circumstances the proposal is impossibly unrealistic. For its effective implementation it would require the willingness of science, mathematics, geography and history teachers to give systematic instruction in the linguistic aspects of their work. Equally, it would require pedagogic training for all these teachers in language teaching methodology, and specific provision for such instruction would have to be made in the curricula designed for all these disciplines. In the absence of such conditions at the present time the policy is almost certainly unworkable and the provision of comprehensive linguistic training must remain therefore the responsibility of the English teacher.

But underlying the 'aesthetic' model of English also is a philosophy of linguistic development which rightly identifies the roots of this development in the symbolizing processes of the unconscious but, in doing so, largely ignores the objective character of language as both an externally structured phenomenon and a medium for interpersonal and social communication. Out of concern for the literary, the symbolic and the metaphoric uses of language, Abbs, Holbrook and Leavis excessively emphasize its subjectivity to the virtual exclusion of those objective features manifested in its grammatical and syntactical forms and in its everyday usage as a medium for social communication. And this is the point where they diverge fundamentally from the wholistic theory of language put forward by Buber in 'The Word That is Spoken' and from the concept of aesthetic form put forward in 'Man And His Image-Work' and some related writings. It will be recalled that Buber stressed the interrelation of three modes of language — its modes of present continuance, potential possession and actual occurrence — and argued for the dependence of all modes of language on the dynamic of present spokenness. Implied in this conception is the radical integrity of all linguistic usages and their dependence ultimately on the spokenness of living speech — a spokenness which is most fully and most perfectly manifested in poetic speech. Implied, furthermore, is the need to accommodate this wholeness, integrity and relatedness of linguistic meaning within the unified framework of a single linguistic discipline. The dispersion of linguistic modes and usages across various disciplines — such as Abbs proposes in *English within the Arts* — would result in a structural fragmentation of the various elements which together constitute an indivisible linguistic unity. The clear implication of Buber's linguistic philosophy is that this radical indivisibility of linguistic meaning must be the primary reality determining the aims of first language teaching and the content and scope of the language curriculum. Ironically, the aims for English teaching cited earlier from sources such as the Bullock Report and the H.M.I. document, *English from 5 to 16*, are indeed based on this very principle but, unfortunately, fail to emphasize the cen- centrality of the poetic and aesthetic amongst all modes of language and fail to accord them a status in the discipline that would appropriately reflect their centrality.

The whole matter can be seen more clearly if we look at some of the specific issues on which Abbs and Holbrook diverge from the integrated conception of linguistic usage put forward by Buber. In their concern to emphasize the primacy of aesthetic and symbolic meaning-making they show scant regard, for instance, for the nurturing of linguistic capacities in the sphere of social communication. Abbs, in his proposal to 'reconstitute English as an art',[95] would relegate the responsibility for all social, pragmatic and functional uses of English to teachers of disciplines other than English i.e., to teachers unqualified in the methods of linguistic instruction. Holbrook's commentary on the Bullock Report is informed by a similar contempt for what he describes as an approach to language teaching which is founded on a concept of 'a machine man whose primary *functions* are communication, information and control *processes*.'[96] Buber, however, asserts the interdependence of personal, social and aesthetic uses of language. In 'What Is Common To All' he defines authentic communication as a genuine speaking and listening in the social interchange of community life and he grounds the social dialogic of the I-We in the mutuality manifested in the interchange of living speech.[97] A genuine spokenness in the speech addressed to the other, and a genuine listening by the other to the speech addressed to him, are the conditions defined in the essay for the creation of the authentic community spirit. The language of social communication is seen to be radically dependent on the speech of interpersonal dialogue and that speech is seen to attain its dynamic livingness in its own poetic and symbolic modes. It follows that this interdependence of the aesthetic, interpersonal and social modes of language must determine the aims of language teaching, the content of the language curriculum, and the teaching methods that are to be used to foster linguistic growth. The essential integrity of all linguistic modes demands that they be comprehended within the unified framework and integrated logical structure of a single discipline.

A second closely related issue concerns the teaching of the formal and technical aspects of language. Earlier I suggested that the views articulated by Leavis, Holbrook and Abbs were rooted in highly subjectivist theories of language and that this subjectivity was manifested particularly in their conception of English as exclusively an aesthetic discipline. One of the consequences of this view is that their treatment of the structural aspects of language pedagogy is confined almost entirely to the sphere of the aesthetic and the symbolic. Thus, Abbs, for example, argues that instruction in reading comprehension, summary and precis writing, and other such activities, be undertaken in disciplines other than English. 'Such a policy', he says, 'leaves English as a discipline free to assert its own nature, its existential, creative and imaginative propensities, its commitment to literature and myth, to metaphor and prophecy, its closeness to all the arts, its fundamental expressive and aesthetic nature.'[98] Some attention is given to structural features of language in the language workshop described by Abbs but is confined therein exclusively to imaginative uses of language. Such a policy would again be deeply in conflict with the dialogic integrity of the inter-personal, aesthetic and social uses of language described by Buber.

Holbrook devotes even less attention to the structural and technical aspects of literacy and proposes a model for English pedagogy that is not alone exclusively aesthetic but is confined to certain varieties of imaginative experience such as the teaching of literature and the fostering of creative writing abilities. Rarely in his work does one find recognition that English is concerned also with objective processes such as the structuring procedures by which writing, whether of the creative or functional varieties, is given order, refinement and shape. Holbrook himself concedes that self-expression as a concept of creativity is — to use his own words — 'woefully in-adequate'.[99] It is unfortunate that he has not fully considered the implications of this; in common with the 'creative writing' advocates of the 1960s — Pym, Langdon, Hourd, amongst others[100] — he has done much to foster the illusion that formal, structuring conventions are largely peripheral and subordinate aspects of writing, despite evidence available even in the 1960s that children instructed in the technical skills are able to write more confidently, both in imaginative and non-imaginative contexts.[101]

Even in the sphere of imaginative writing alone his neglect of structural principles would be radically at variance with the theories of aesthetic form put forward by Buber, despite his extensive reliance on Buber's philosophy for his analysis of the issues in the Bullock controversy. Buber's aesthetics emphasize the close interrelation of subjective and objective realities. Aesthetic potentiality or creativity is fulfilled, he says, as relational encounter and, specifically, as the encounter of the perceiving subject with the world of objective form. 'Form' is defined by Buber as the objectified, structured character of the reality which the subject perceives.[102] Applied to the sphere of the language arts, that objectified reality is the structural form which is inherent in language itself. Linguistic competence therefore requires not only the fostering of imaginative fluency in language usage but also the mastery of linguistic structure and of all the rules and conventions of usage dismissed so contemptuously by Holbrook in his comments on Bullock.

Buber's emphasis on the spokenness of living language is highly relevant also to these debates. Powerful support was provided for the fostering of oral-aural capacities both in the Bullock Report and previously in the research of scholars such as Barnes and Wilkinson,[103] whose pioneering studies have been largely responsible for demonstrasting the need to develop listening and speaking as well as reading and writing capacities. Traditionally, first language education has been concerned almost exclusively with reading and writing and this neglect of oracy and auracy is still evident in the writings of Holbrook and Abbs. Buber's work, as we have seen, asserts the primacy of living speech and insists that the spoken word is the root-source of all linguistic utterance. The development of speaking and listening powers must, by this conception of linguistic growth, become a central and continuing preoccupation for the language teacher. Significantly, however, Buber insists also that this is ultimately a *poetic spokenness*, that the living speech derives its force and vitality from the presence of the poetic in everyday life and reaches its highest accomplishment in the art of poetry. An adequate formulation of aims for speech education would have to give due attention, therefore, to the place of imagination in the spheres of oral and aural development. This latter principle, regrettably, has been insufficiently emphasized by Bullock, Wilkinson, Barnes and others, despite their concern for the importance of speech and its central place in the first language curriculum.

To sum up, therefore, Buber's aesthetic philosophy points to the need for a redefinition of aims for first language teaching that might seek to rectify the deficiencies of several contemporary approaches to this task. Such a redefinition would uphold the integrity of language studies as a unified discipline encompassing all fundamental modes of linguistic usage. It would reject the exclusivity of the aesthetic models put forward by Leavis, Holbrook and Abbs. Equally, while sharing with Bullock and others a deep concern for the interaction of all basic linguistic modes — the modes of speaking, listening, reading and writing — it would reassert the primacy of imaginative uses of language and a deepened experience of its symbolic modes in the crucial educational task of fostering the powers of literacy.

# VII
# Community and Adult Education

The basic principles of Martin Buber's philosophy of adult and community education can be identified both from his writings on social and educational theory and from the practical evidence of his work for adult education in Israel in the years preceding and following the creation of the new state. His conception of the aims of adult education is closely bound up with the philosophy of community socialism which he has developed in a range of theoretical writings in the sphere of social philosophy. But it has firm roots also in his writings dealing specifically with education, such as the essays in *Between Man and Man* and his commentaries on nineteenth century traditions in adult education. His convictions were profoundly influenced too by his active involvement in the training of adult tutors and the provision of tuition centres for immigrants in Israel in the 1940s and 1950s. This present attempt to define his views on the aims of adult and community education is focussed on each of these sources. The chapter is divided into five sections. The first examines the philosophical principles on which Buber's conception of the aims of adult education is based. The second considers the implications of his personal witnessing of the ideals of this philosophy. The third attempts to locate his views in the traditions of nineteenth century theories of adult education, especially those associated with the Scandinavian writers, Grundtvig and Kold. The fourth examines his work in the adult education movement in Israel and the fifth offers a brief commentary on his influence on twentieth century adult education theory.

## 1 Community Socialism: Its Aims and Ideals

Buber's social philosophy is firmly rooted in the traditions of Judaism and, specifically, in the social teachings and customs of the Jewish Hasidic communities of the eighteenth century. In several of the essays from his collections *On Judaism* and *Israel and the World*[1] he cites extensive Biblical support for his ideal of a community where material resources are justly distributed, where social divisions are minimized, where individuals seek to assist one another in their daily needs, and where the spiritual, cultural, ethical and social autonomy of all individuals is assured. In one of these essays, 'The Land and Its Possessors,'[2] he declares that the just distribution of material resources is part of God's purpose for man. The idea of God as the source and ultimate owner of all material wealth is the cornerstone of the Jewish concept of justice, he writes. In several other essays from these collections[3] he identifies various features of the social teachings of Judaism — their community orientation, their emphasis on individual responsibility, their concept of social praxis, their integration of spiritual, cultural and social ideals — and locates them firmly in the traditions of the Jewish scriptures.

The essential conditions for the realization of these ideals are set out more elaborately, however, in works such as 'Society and the State'[4] and *Paths in Utopia*[5] where he further locates his social theories in later traditions of socialist thought and, specifically, in the traditions of utopian socialism which were themselves derived ultimately from the social principles of Judaism. In *Paths in Utopia* he defines the basic principles of decentralistic socialism, the philosophy on which his community ideals are based. In the rigid political centralism typical both of capitalist and communist societies — though far more repressively manifested in the latter — he sees the major obstacle to the growth of community life. He points to the origins of state centralism in Marx's writings — despite some ambiguity on the issue as evidenced by Marx's correspondence with Vera Zasulich[6] — and the more rigid centralism advocated by Lenin, which led to the gigantic state structures of the USSR and other East European socialist states. These he dismisses as a 'tragic misdevelopment of the socialist revolution' initiated by utopian philosophers such as Proudhon, Kropotkin and Landauer and their pre-decessors in the socialist traditions of Judaism.

As a first step in the rediscovery of the true meaning of socialism Buber called for a re-examination of the works of these utopian theorists, stressing particularly the Jewish origins of their philosophy. In *Paths in Utopia* he adopts the Judaic prophetic-apocalyptic distinction[7] to differentiate the voluntaristic character of utopian socialism from the deterministic character of its marxist successor. Proudhon he particularly admired for his anti-centralist 'mutualism' or 'communalism': for his recognition that social transformation begins within the community — and is therefore primarily a social rather than a political objective.[8] Society is transformed, he writes, not primarily through the political process but through the renewal of social and community relationships. He praises Kropotkin also for his rejection of political atomism and for his vision of a free association between voluntary cooperative movements.[9] But he found more compelling evidence for the kind of internal transformation on which he based his own theories of social change in the writings of his fellow Jewish philosopher, Gustav Landauer.[10] He quotes extensively from Landauer's writings in support of his view that the seeds of the community exist in all societies in latent form and can be brought into being if the appropriate conditions are created. He writes of his enthusiasm for Landauer's concept of socialism as 'the continual becoming of community in mankind', as 'the attempt to lead man's common life to a bond of common spirit in freedom.'[11]

Before the implications of all this are considered more closely, it is important to say that, while Buber drew extensively on the utopian socialists for the construction of his own social philosophy, there were fundamental issues also on which he reconceived the principles of utopian socialism. While reiterating the attractions of a decentralised socialism, he was not advocating a reassertion of models for social change that have long since been eclipsed by history. Rather, he advocated the revitalization of societies — whether capitalist or communist — in the spirit of a community rather than a politically oriented socialism, many of the principles of which had their origins in the writings of Proudhon, Kropotkin and Landauer. He calls, not for a 'bringing back', but a 'rebirth' of the commune — an organic commonwealth in which humanity can be rescued from the degradation of collectivism.[12] Such a *consociatio consociatorum* could be created within a totalitarian state just as it could within a westernized democracy. It would have to be generated, however, not through political initiatives but by fostering the disposition towards community inherent in all societies: a disposition originating in the immediacy of interpersonal relationships. It is in this tracing of the process of social transformation to the level of the interpersonal that Buber's most radical reconception of the utopian socialists lies.

Just as his understanding of the religious relationship is based not on the conventions of ritualised religion but ultimately on the mutuality of interpersonal dialogue, so also must his community philosophy be traced to its roots in the I-Thou dialogic. The realm into which the I-Thou dialogic expands to embrace the communal and the social is designated the sphere of the I-We by Buber.[13] Just as the intimacy of interpersonal relation is rooted in the essential mutuality and reciprocation of the I-Thou, so the true spirit of community life is traced in his work to the dynamic plurality of the I-We. The quality of the community spirit thus created depends ultimately, as in the interpersonal dialogic, on the genuine address of the I and the genuine response evoked in the Thou. The plurality of this reciprocation is manifested in the I-We-ness of community life. The human cosmos, he writes, can be tranformed socially through I-We-ness, just as the interpersonal relation attains the maturity of genuine inclusion through the I-Thou dialogic. The need for such a transformation is made profoundly urgent by the collectivism of modern societies, both in its communist and its capitalist modes. 'Man,' Buber declares, 'will not persist in existence if he does not learn and persist in it as a genuine We.'[14]

Three conditions are set out by Buber for the generation of I-We-ness, each of which can be developed actively through the education of the community spirit. The first involves an authentic speaking, listening and communing within and between communities.[15] He adopts the term *logos* — borrowing from the language of Heraclitus — to designate the ontological presence of mutuality in the communal life of man. Communal life, he explains, springs in the first instance from the reciprocal speaking or listening of interpersonal dialogue. Where genuine communication occurs We-ness exists, either potentially or actually. The reciprocal flow of communication which begins in the interchange of speech attests to the existence of the living We. This 'speech-with-meaning', or logos, is the initial moulder of the social order; it is the mode of existence of people communicating with one another. A genuine spokenness in the speech addressed to the other, or conversely, a genuine listening to the voice of the other, are the essential conditions of its achievement.

The second condition is a deepening of personal conscience, the ground from which the individual's responsible answering to the needs of his community must spring.[16] Buber differentiates between the 'routine' or 'play-on-the surface' conscience and the 'unknown conscience' which originates in the 'ground-of- being' and is 'discovered ever anew'. Applying this notion in its social context, he instances the temptation to acquiesce in the judgements of the crowd as something which constantly endangers the freedom and responsibility of individual conscience, and warns that the tension and conflict of authentic disagreement is the life blood of a true community:

> Our age is intent on escaping from the demanding 'ever anew' of such an obligation of responsibility by a flight into a protective 'once-for-all.' The last generation's intoxication with freedom has been followed by the present generation's craze for bondage; the untruth of intoxication has been followed by the untruth of hysteria. He alone is true to the one Present Being who knows he is bound to his place — and just there free for his proper responsibility. Only those who are bound and free in this way can still produce what can truly be called community. Yet even to-day the believing man, if he clings to a thing that is presented in a group, can do right to join it. But belonging to it, he must remain submissive with his whole life, therefore with his group life as well, to the One who is his Lord. His responsible decision will thus at times be opposed to, say, a tactical decision of his group. At times he will be moved to carry the fight for the truth, the human, uncertain and certain truth which is brought forward by his deep conscience into the group itself, and thereby establish or strengthen an inner front in it. This can be more important for the future of our world than all fronts that are drawn to-day between groups and between associations of groups; for this front, if it is everywhere upright and strong, may run as a secret unity across all groups.[17]

The third condition is the individual's awareness and exercise of responsibility in his dealings with the community — an issue which Buber discussed in the context of his essay on Kierkegaard's supposed abdication of social responsibility.[18] He calls for an integration of religious, social and political ideals in the individual's assessments of the needs of his community and his response thereto. Should the social or political be separated from the realm of faith, the result, in Buber's view, would be a social or political reductionism. The individual is called on to respond with the 'totality of his life'. If the socio-economic sphere is to be informed by the dictates of faith — a faith, by Buber's conception, which is rooted not in conventional religion but in the life of dialogue — so must this faith be an all-embracing reality, extending its influence into every sphere of life. 'He who does not let his relation of faith be fulfilled in the uncurtailed measure of the life he lives, is trying to curtail the fulfilment of God's role in the world,' he writes.

## 2 Promoting Intercommunal Dialogue

Buber believed that all these ideals could be fulfilled through carefully designed programmes in adult and community education. The particular concern of these programmes would be the creation of the three conditions for the generation of a community which I have endeavoured to describe. He spoke of the need for an active commitment by educators to the promotion of community ideals. He repeatedly asserted the importance of the Jewish concept of praxis and, addressing himself particularly to Jewish educators, urged that they take active steps to create the community spirit. 'I repeat: not truth as idea, nor truth as shape or form, but truth as deed is Judaism's task,' he wrote. 'Its goal is not the creation of a philosophical theorem or a work of art but the establishment of true community.'[19]

He spoke also of the primary obligation of the educator to bear living witness in his own life to the reality of community ideals. Shortly before his death he advised a group of kibbutz educators in Israel on how they could create the community spirit in the kibbutzim. He stressed the influence they could exert through personal example: 'Real influence is slow,' he said. 'A man lives and actualises what he intends to teach others. Sometimes he must devote the whole of his life to this but such a life is worth living.'[20] Some years earlier in correspondence with a Benedictine monk, Father Caesarius Lauer, he warned of the danger of dialogical philosophizing in place of lived dialogue. 'The talk about dialogue takes from men the living experience of dialogue. In dialogue it is the realisation that is decisive since it is working reality, that means life.'[21]

It seems appropriate, in the light of all this, that some instances of Buber's personal commitment to the advancement of community ideals be provided so that an authentic personal context be established for the further elucidation of his theoretical writings on community and adult education. Three instances may be cited for this purpose: his endeavours to promote dialogue, firstly, between Jews and Christians; secondly, between Jews and Germans in the aftermath of the Holocaust, and thirdly, between Jews and Arabs before and after the partition of Palestine in 1948.

Several commentators — particularly those writing from a Christian standpoint — have spoken of the value of Buber's contribution to the promotion of Jewish-Christian dialogue. Leonhard Ragaz, a Christian theologian deeply committed to this cause, considered that Buber's contribution to this dialogue was the most notable of those made from the Jewish standpoint.[22] In a memorial address on Ragaz in Jerusalem in 1945, Buber responded with an impassioned assertion of the importance of Christ's teachings in the traditions of Judaism. 'I firmly believe,' he declared, 'that the Jewish community, in the course of its renaissance, will recognise Jesus; and not merely as a great figure in its religious history, but also in the organic context of a messianic development extending over millennia whose final goal is the redemption of Israel and the world.[23] There were several instances of Buber's practical commitment to this cause. His biographer cites lectures on the continuity of the Old and New Testaments he delivered in Jerusalem synagogues in the 1940s, several meetings he held with Quakers in Great Britain and the United States, and correspondence on Christian teachings he conducted with several notable thinkers such as Dag Hammerskjold, Albert Schweitzer and Patriarch Athenagoras.[24] Buber's most enduring contribution to Jewish-Christian understanding, however, is *The Two Types of Faith*, his scholarly exploration of the two traditions.[25] In this work he makes an impassioned call for the rediscovery of the radical Hebraic content present in both the Jewish and the Christian traditions.

A further instance of Buber's personal witness to intercommunal dialogue was his work to promote reconciliation between the Jewish and German peoples in the aftermath of World War II and the Holocaust. For some time immediately following the war he had declined a number of invitations to visit Germany. 'I have proclaimed publicly my undiminished interest in Germans of good will,' he said, 'but I cannot bring myself to take part in the activity of German public institutions for this demands a degree of association which I do not feel myself capable.'[26] One of his invitees, the evangelical theologian, Karl Rengstorf, argued that what was needed in this tension-charged situation was some positive expression of understanding and love.[27] Another German theologian told Buber: 'The monstrous blood-guilt of my people weighs on me daily as a heavy burden.'[28] Buber responded: 'Without love man cannot live — not truly, not as man. But love today more than ever seems to be grace — felt out of grace, received out of grace.'[29] Shortly afterwards he travelled to Germany to receive the Goethe Prize at the

University of Hamburg, though he realised this gesture would be considered offensive to Jews. He accepted the prize, he said, 'as one of the first few signs of a new humanity arising out of the anti-human chaos of our time.'[30] Later he accepted the Peace Prize of the German Book Trade at St Paul's Church in Frankfurt and donated the prize money to the cause of Arab-Jewish understanding. On that occasion he delivered an important paper, 'Genuine Dialogue and the Possibilities of Peace,' in the presence of the President of the West German Republic.[31] These visits provoked an intensely hostile reaction in Israel. Buber was personally vilified in several Israeli newspapers, was ostracised by most of his colleagues at the Hebrew University, and was denounced in the Israeli parliament. He defended himself with these words: 'I cannot condemn a people as a people as the Christian Church has so often done in branding the Jewish people as murderers of the Messiah.'[32]

Buber's work for the improvement of Arab-Jewish relations is yet another remarkable example of his practical commitment to intercommunal dialogue, though his efforts in the course of more than two decades to promote good relations between the two races were far less successful than his work for the Jewish-Christian and Jewish-German causes. He was a leading figure in the Ihud movement set up in 1942 to advocate a Federation of Near Eastern States and to facilitate peaceful coexistence bertween Arabs and Jews. He proposed that immigration be controlled to ensure population parity between the two communities in Palestine and called for a binational political settlement.[33] These policies again caused him to be isolated politically and socially — he was opposed particularly by David Ben-Gurion — and he experienced great personal hostility for his views. He forecast (correctly) that Ben-Gurion's demand for uncontrolled immigration and the creation of a Jewish majority in Palestine would lead to partition and the creation of a small Jewish state that could only be maintained through militarization. Insisting that it was crucial to accord equality of treatment to the Arabs, Buber called for a full restoration of their civil and political rights and demanded that all discrimination against them be ended.[34] As a measure of the depth of his commitment to this cause he lived with his family in an Arab suburb of Jerusalem and took a particular interest in the welfare of Arab students at the Hebrew University. After partition he continued to advocate a Near Eastern Confederative Union and worked for the development of Arab-Jewish fellowship through the adult education movement.

All three examples I have given will illustrate Buber's personal application of dialogic ideals in the context of communal, racial and sectarian conflict. They have relevance therefore far beyond that of the local situation in Israel. They point to the ultimate goal towards which Buber insisted community education must be directed: the active promotion of peace, through the resources of interpersonal and communal dialogue. Effective and open

communication, the exercise of social responsibility, and fidelity to individual conscience, were identified earlier as the three conditions laid down
by Buber for the fostering of the community spirit. Their purpose ultimately
is the creation of peace, in the contexts of community, national and international life. Much of Buber's social philosophy is concerned with the origins
of conflict; while considering the great ethnic, cultural and political conflicts
of his time he looks for their roots at the level of intercommunal relations,
and identifies therein the only stable, long-term possibilities for enduring
peace. In 'Education and World View' he examines the problems posed by
conflicting traditions, beliefs and differing world views (Westanschauung )
within the community or group.[35] He recognizes the importance of diverse
viewpoints: 'Community,' he says, 'is the overcoming of otherness in living
unity.' But he advises careful interpretation of the convictions held, a
'rooting' of viewpoints in the problematics of everyday life, and 'their
constant authentication in the light of lived conscience and experience.'[36]

The goals of communal, racial and international peace can be promoted
actively through various social agencies, but particularly through education.
Its aim, as defined by Buber in essays such as 'Education and World View'
and 'Genuine Dialogue and the Possibilities of Peace', is ultimately the
creation of trust, the only enduring foundation for peace.[37] In the latter essay
he addressed himself to the youth of Germany shortly after World War II and
reminded them that the demonry set loose amongst their people was simply
the contra humanitas present in all men. The voice of demonry, he said,
should be countered with the humane voice of the spirit, a voice awakened
through mutual dialogue.[38] Peace, he writes, is not simply the absence of
conflict; it is achieved through the speech of genuine conversation. The
presupposition of this conversation is mutual trust, a willed entering into
interpersonal and communal dialogue. Maurice Friedman, citing Buber's
words in this essay, wrote of him: 'If I had to choose one sentence to
summarise the whole message of Buber's life and thought it would be this:
"Let us dare, despite all, to trust".'[39]

It is important, before considering the educational implications of all this,
that Buber's thoughts on the question of peace be located accurately in the
context of contemporary peace philosophies. There were several occasions
when he identified closely with various peace movements. He had strong
affinities with the Quakers, for instance, and in 1952 he visited Haverford
College, a centre for Quaker studies in the USA. While there he addressed
Quaker students on the subject of peace and joined their discussions and
prayer meetings.[40] Later he found that he shared many of the views of Andrei
Sakharov on the prevention of nuclear warfare and endorsed the doctrine of
peaceful coexistence put forward in *Progress, Coexistence and Intellectual
Freedom*.[41] Again he expressed admiration for the beliefs of Martin Luther

King and traced the origins of King's teachings on civil disobedience to the writings of Henry David Thoreau.[42] At the height of the Cuban missile crisis he echoed the sentiments of Thoreau by declaring that young people were fully justified in disobeying the State's injunction to take arms. And on the occasion of the Eichmann trial in Israel he insisted that the state was bound by the Biblical injunction: 'Thou shalt not kill.'[43] Despite all this, however, he declared on several occasions that he was not a pacifist. He wrote to his biographer in 1952: 'I am not a pacifist; for I do not know at all whether in a given situation in which fighting had been necessary I would not fight.'[44] He rejected pacifism on the same grounds as he rejected all 'isms' — as an abstraction — and insisted that all situations should be judged existentially and responded to in a manner consistent with the judgements of conscience, while stressing the individual's responsibility nonetheless to do all in his power to create the dialogic conditions for the resolution of conflict and the creation of trust.

## 3 The Influence of Grundtvig and Kold

The primary aims of adult and community education, as envisaged by Buber in his philosophical and educational writings, are the promotion and practical realisation of the social ideals I have endeavoured to describe. It remains now to examine the specific pedagogic and curricular policies necessary for the implementation of these ideals. There are a number of essays in which Buber explicitly located his thinking on these issues within the traditions of adult education which originated with Bishop Grundtvig and Christian Kold in Denmark during the nineteenth century. The circumstances of Grundtvig's emergence as an educationalist were particularly interesting to Buber in view of the former's deep reservations on political nationalism – reservations which were similar to those expressed by Buber himself on the excesses of chauvinistic Zionism. He strongly endorsed Grundtvig's view that Denmark's defeat at the hands of the Russians in 1864 revealed not only the military weakness of Denmark but a more fundamental weakness in the spiritual character of its people. Buber wrote admiringly of the way Grundtvig, in the wake of the Russian defeat, turned to the rural communities, and set out to revive the spiritual and cultural traditions of the country through the new folk schools he had founded:

> He knew that society itself could not create a way of life nor an image of life without an affinity for tradition, and yet, such a society could not exist without a renewal of tradition to suit the demands of the new reality. He saw the tradition from a unique point of view. He made the teachings and laws of Christianity as part of the people's education, and he enveloped them in the ancient powers of the imagination, dormant in the people. Grundtvig

revived and renewed those powers which in ancient days received such
strong expression in Scandinavian mythology.[45]

In Grundtvig's writings Buber found a powerful precedent for his view
that the curriculum of the adult school should give adequate recognition to
the cultural traditions of the people. Grundtvig considered the 'annotated'
reading of classical literature, particularly the heritage of Scandinavian
literature, should be promoted enthusiastically in his folkschools.[46] In his
own essay, 'On National Education,' Buber argues in similar fashion that
Jewish literature — and especially the scriptures — should be the mainstay
of the community school curriculum. He proposed that an intensive
programme in the Hebrew language and literature, the history and geography
of Palestine, and the Jewish scriptures should constitute the core of the
curriculum to be taught in these schools: 'We should teach the students the
reality of life,' he writes, 'but we should open their eyes and hearts to see
that it is only a means to the spiritual truth and its way in the world.'[47]

Even more importantly, however, Buber found a precedent in Grundtvig's
work for his belief in the central importance of the relationship between
teachers and students, and between the students themselves, within the adult
learning community. In language echoing his previously quoted description
of dialogue as 'living speech' he writes approvingly of Grundtvig's belief
that 'living conversation' is the dynamic informing the whole process of
teaching and learning:

> The conversation between the teacher and his students, composed of the
> students' questions on what they do not understand and what they desire to
> learn, and of the teacher's answers to these questions, will be completed by
> a discussion between the students themselves under the guidance of the
> teacher whose main topic will be the students' own past experiences. Both
> of these forms embody the basic principle of Grundtvig's method, which I
> call the principle of dialogue in education.[48]

Additionally, Buber borrowed from Grundtvig the concept of a specially
created environment for the education of adult students. (We shall see
presently that he extended this concept into his training scheme for adult
tutors also). Arguing that the special requirements of the task of educating
adults made it necessary to devise special forms of pedagogy for them, he
spoke of the attractions of boarding institutions such as those Grundtvig had
founded for the Danish farmers. If the aim were simply to transmit certain
types of knowledge, this could be achieved through lectures attended by the
students outside their working hours. Since the purpose of the adult courses,
however, was to 'get hold of a man as a whole and influence him completely,'
then it would be necessary to take him out of his daily occupation for some

time — as Grundtvig did — and have him join a study group oriented primarily towards the assimilation of cultural and community ideals.[49]

Buber further cites the work of Christian Kold and the people's school movement in support of his conception of adult education as a process of cultural and spiritual formation. He relates a parable on Kold's response to a farmer who complained that he had forgotten much of what he heard at lectures. 'When we sow wheat,' Kold replied, 'we have no need to mark the place as the wheat will sprout in its season.' He assured the farmer that the message he heard would return in time. He stressed the need, however, to achieve an organic relation between knowledge and the reality of everyday life:

> In order for this to happen, however, adult education as a whole must be directed to develop the man as a whole and not to merely maintain his brain. He should learn to think, not only with his mind, but with all his spiritual-physical essence, with all his limbs and senses. His thinking should not be a special department, separate from the rest of his existence, his eyes, his ears and his fingers must participate in it as well. That trend in the movement of adult education, which is Grundtvig's real inheritor, set as its aim the education of man for the fostering of a renewed organic character of the spirit.[50]

In the course of his discussion of the Danish folkschools Buber made an important distinction between the role of the adult education institute and that of a conventional institute of higher education, such as a university. The historical function of the university, he said, is to train students to think systematically in specialized fields, whereas the adult institute aims to train students to serve as citizens in their society. Unlike the university, which subordinates its social and cultural to its primary academic responsibilities, the adult institute is mainly a place where community responsibilities are promoted and these determine all its functions and policies — its curriculum, teaching methods and everyday activities.[51]

Of the community responsibilities developed in the adult institute, Buber, like Paulo Freire several decades later, pays particular attention to the development of a high level of critical consciousness amongst the adult students. And this has a significant bearing on the styles of teaching and the nature of the teacher/learner relationship he advocates. He writes of the importance of encouraging the student to question and clarify his own ideas and convictions: to expose his prematurely developed beliefs to the critical appraisal of his colleagues and teachers. Much of the work of the adult school he envisages would be devoted to the evaluation of various social influences, particularly propagandist influences and all matters associated with the political and economic life of the community. In this Buber draws heavily on his own dialogic conception of teaching to conceive the kind of relationship which is most conducive to the critical sharing of ideas in the complex circumstances of the adult school. He particularly stresses the personal integrity of the teacher. Taking the example of Socrates as the kind of teacher who embodied the qualities he describes, he differentiated between the teacher as a person and the activity of teaching. Socrates, he says, did not exert his decisive influence by what he taught, but rather by his personality; so the student is educated not by the teacher's 'teaching' but by the reality, presence and truth of his personhood. A remarkable passage from Buber's long paper, 'Adult Education,' describes the nature of this encounter:

> A good teacher educates when speaking as well as when silent, during the lessons as well as during recess, during an occasional conversation, through his own behavior, provided he really exists and is really present. He is an educator by touch. The people's school is based upon the encouragement of contact between teacher and students — upon the principle of dialogue; dialogue of questions from both sides, and answers from both sides, of joint observation of a certain reality in nature, or in art or in society, dialogue of joint penetration into one of the problems of life, dialogue of true fellowship, in which the breaks in conversation are no less of a dialogue than speech itself.[52]

But while claiming support from Socrates for his explanation of the dialogic relationship, Buber had some reservations about the incessant activity of questioning traditionally associated with 'Socratic learning'. In some discussions with another theorist on adult education, Robert Maynard Hutchins, he warned of the danger that this might degenerate into a dialectical game, a scoring of points, rather than a dialogue, the essence of which is personal encounter and the gradual sharing by each of the becoming existence of the other.[53]

It is interesting to learn from Buber's biographer that Buber himself lived out these ideas in his own teaching. Discussing Buber's work as a tutor at the Adult Education Centre he founded in Jerusalem, Maurice Friedman writes: 'He gave every pupil an opportunity to interrupt and ask questions . . . his influence on the students was very great, not because of the content of his teaching but because of his personality. He himself embodied the aim of the whole school which was primarily addressing the wholeness of the person.'[54] When Buber went to Israel he had ample scope for the implementation of his convictions on adult education in the demanding situation presented by the steady flow of immigrants from the Jewish Diaspora coming into the new state in the aftermath of World War II.

We can look finally, therefore, to the period of Buber's work in Israel for some further witness — in this instance in his capacity as a professional educator — to his convictions on the aims and ideals of adult education. In some essays written after his arrival in Israel he discusses the problems of adult educators, faced with the challenge of meeting the needs of the masses of immigrants pouring into Israel in the years immediately preceding and following the creation of the state. The particular need of Israel was to find a strong cultural identity for these teeming masses coming to the country from a great diversity of ethnic backgrounds. Buber speaks of the unprecedented difficulties arising from the socio-cultural and economic differences amongst the peoples of the Diaspora. Despite their common Jewishness, they differed greatly from one another in character, language and lifestyle. He called for the creation of a new elite of adult educators, imbued with the traditions of Jewish culture, well educated in the scriptures, the Hebrew language and literature and the history of Israel, to meet the needs of this complex and highly challenging situation.

Looking at the wider aspects of the problems facing Israeli adult educators at this time, Buber speaks of a malaise and despair of the soul amongst the immigrant masses that strongly echoes his comments in an essay, 'The Prejudices of Youth,' where he attributes a universal sickness of the spirit amongst the young to the forces of rationalism and scientism dominating the culture of the present time.[55] Of the Jew coming from the Diaspora he writes: 'His soul is eaten by despair; despair of mankind, of human society and of the truthfulness of the spiritual values of mankind ... it penetrates and pierces to the very bottom of the soul and even the reality of the Jewish state does not succeed in overcoming it.'[56] Indeed, the emergence of the new state created the further problem of chauvinistic nationalism, prejudice and intolerance which Buber considered to be deeply in conflict with the spiritual/cultural essence of the genuine national spirit. The new pioneering educator would seek to restore the original character and identity of the nation.

Buber was given a practical opportunity to put these thoughts into action in 1948. Since his arrival in Palestine in 1938 he had insisted that adult education be a major part of the work of the Hebrew University and he was a member of the university's planning committee on education which drew up a nationwide programme of lectures and courses in cities, villages and kibbutzim throughout Israel. In furtherance of his belief that a pioneering elite of adult tutors was the key to the whole enterprise, he proposed in 1947 that a special centre for the training of adult tutors be set up in the old Mount Scopus campus of the Hebrew University. The Beth Midrash C'Mores Am or School for the Education of Teachers of the People came into being, with

Buber as president and Dr Gideon Freudenberg as the director with responsibility for the daily administration of the Centre.

In a paper published in *Molad*, the Hebrew monthly, in 1951, Buber gives a succinct definition of the aims and methods he adopted for the work of the Centre. Using a term borrowed from Ferdinand Lasalle, he described the tutors as 'teachers for the people'. They were not volunteer or part-time tutors, he said, but 'full time professionals' who regarded the work of the adult educator as a 'calling of primary importance'. Their work, he said, was more exacting than that of the conventional educator; it claimed the person's entire being. Recalling his experience at the Frankfurt Lehrhaus, he spoke of the importance of small group, seminar tuition. Each tutor was expected to know all his students personally. 'Contact,' he wrote, 'is the root and basis of education':

> It means that the connection between teacher and student is not merely on an intellectual plane — the influence of a developed mind upon one that has not yet fully matured — but a connection between personalities, so that one human entity confronts another. In other words, the teacher should not be on a higher plane than the student; he should not speak down from the platform to the desk. What is wanted is true reciprocity, through the interchange of experiences between the matured mind and the mind that is still in the process of formation; for the experiences of the latter are also of importance. It is not enough for the student to ask questions from below and the teacher to reply from above. Nor is it enough for questions to be asked and answered on either side. What is sought is a truly reciprocal conversation in which both sides are full partners. The teacher leads and directs it, and he enters it without any restraint. I call this the 'dialogue principle' in education.[57]

Reviewing the progress of the whole venture in *The Torch*, another Jewish monthly, in June 1952, Buber recalled that some of the best 'teachers for the people' came from the ranks of the immigrant communities themselves.[58] He spoke of the highly heterogenous character of the group: their ages ranged from 17 to 50, some had a complete high school education, others were university graduates; some knew little about Judaism, others were deeply rooted in its traditions. All were destined to teach new immigrants in camps, settlements or in ulpanim (intensive short courses in Hebrew organized by the government in special tuition centres). The training programme lasted for one year, though students were required to work up to fourteen hours daily as a condition of their acceptance. Buber spoke of the value of having all students accommodated under the same roof; apart from its educational advantages, this helped them to overcome differences associated with age, cultural background, economic disadvantage and educational attainment. On Buber's own evidence, the methods appear to have been remarkably successful. 'In the course of my life,' he wrote, 'I have not seen such intensity of nothing but learning from morning until midnight.'[59]

Buber's 'Centre for the Education of Teachers of the People' remained in existence for four years. There are plans currently in preparation to bring it into being once again. Seven years after Buber's death the Hebrew University announced the establishment of the 'Martin Buber Centre for Adult and Continuing Education'. The Institute has adopted many of Buber's ideas in its programmes for continuing education. Its declaration of aims, for instance, is heavily indebted to Buber's social philosophy, especially his thinking on the promotion of community fellowship. The Centre's brochure begins with these words: 'Keenly conscious of the negative consequences of operating an institution of higher learning as an ivory tower, the Hebrew University has always been a pioneer in the field of adult education, opening its doors to members of the community from all walks of life.'[60] It conducts a broad and rapidly expanding range of programmes that encourage the notion of life as 'a learning process'. On the role of the university as a centre for community education, the Centre's chairman, Professor Saul Patos writes: 'In the last decade there has been a tendency for universities to adopt a more diverse role. Universities seek to get nearer to the public and they are no longer the preserve of youngsters who spend three years there, and an academic elite of research and teaching staff.'[61]

Of the various study programmes offered by the Centre, one which seems particularly close to Buber's ideals is the Ma'ale Study Programme for Older Students. Initiated in 1978, the programme is intended for students over fifty years of age who wish to study for a degree. Starting with an initial enrolment of twenty students, the course now has 250 participants. The students come from all walks of life — they include clerks, social workers, blue and white collar workers, businessmen, soldiers, secretaries, lawyers, teachers, doctors and nurses — ages range from fifty to eighty and more than two thirds are over sixty years old. The pedagogical director, Kalman Yaron, a student of Buber's and a graduate of the School for Teachers of the People, writes: 'I suspect that the chance to come here invigorates many who might otherwise struggle to fill the vacuum that retirement leaves in their lives and which often leads to premature mental and physical deterioration.'[62] Students on the Ma'ale programme take the same courses as regular undergraduates, though usually on an extended time scale and, in accordance with Buber's pedagogic principles, are taught mainly through seminar instruction.

## 5 Conclusion: Buber's Influence on Adult Education Theory

Buber's influence on adult education, however, extends far beyond the immediate Israeli situation in which he was involved for the last two decades of his life. There are some interesting parallels, for instance, between his views and those of a notable figure in American adult education, R.M. Hutchins. Hutchins' argument in *The Learning Society* that lifelong education is necessary to realize the full potential of the human subject strongly echoes Buber's views on the aims of the whole enterprise.[63] Several fruitful exchanges on the subject occurred between Buber and Hutchins. An encounter which is recorded in *Philosophical Interrogations* indicates the closeness of their views on some matters; Hutchins on that occasion expressed great admiration for Buber as an educator and for his work in preparing adult tutors in Israel.[64] They differed, however, on many issues and Hutchins' rather elevated, hierarchical concept of intelligence as the distinguishing characteristic of humanness could hold little attraction for someone who had sought for the greater part of his life to demonstrate the primacy of dialogue, mutuality and the potential for reciprocation as the all-encompassing reality of human existence.[65]

No such dichotomy is evident, however, between Buber and two Third World educationalists — Helder Camara and Paulo Freire — who have drawn extensively on his dialogic philosophy. Camara, in *Race Against Time* and *The Desert is Fertile* identifies universal selfishness as the root cause of poverty and social conflict, and advocates a process of social renewal that bears a striking resemblance to Buber's community socialism. Camara's vision of community renewal is based, like Buber's, on the promotion of interpersonal and intercommunal fellowship or brotherhood. But he is a good deal more explicit than Buber in identifying Christianity as an alienating force in history, because of its fatalistic acceptance of the political or social status quo and its supposed political neutralism.[66] He counsels a transformation of society which will be achieved through social praxis and sees education — especially adult and higher education — as key agencies in achieving the envisaged renewal of individual and social consciousness.[67] He further echoes Buber through his strongly asserted faith in the power of moral pressure exerted by committed minorities and, significantly, he adopts a term derived from Jewish tradition ('abrahamic') to describe their deep sense of social commitment and brotherhood.[68]

Freire's debt to Buber is acknowledged explicitly in *Pedagogy of the Oppressed* and is clearly apparent in all his major writings.[69] Chapter 3 of the *Pedagogy* elaborates his own dialogic philosophy and defines the foundation principles of the radical pedagogy he has designed to meet the needs of the oppressed. His terminology, like Camara's, is strongly reminiscent of Buber's : he writes of the dialogic encounter as an 'existential necessity', embodying a 'profound love for the world and for mankind'.[70] In *The Politics of Education* he calls again for a radical reconception of educational methodology and describes the educator as a knowing subject, experiencing the act of knowing together with his students.[71] He emphasizes the critical reflective element in dialogue as the means of developing awareness amongst the oppressors and oppressed, and again applies the critical process to the alienating traditions of historical Christianity. His notion of education as 'action for freedom', in which he emphasizes its creative potential for historical transformation, is an extended formulation of Buber's concept of praxis. But Freire has advanced significantly on Buber in identifying the universal phenomenon of illiteracy as both a root cause and a symptom of mass alienation: as a condition consigning the oppressed masses to a marginalized and dehumanizing status amongst their fellowmen.[72]

The widespread impact of Freire's writings in the whole sphere of contemporary adult education suggests that this is one of the practical issues on which the socialist ideals he shares with Buber can be most profitably focussed in the immediate future. There are other issues, such as those relating to interracial and sectarian conflict, economic and social exploitation and the myriad forms of social discrimination and injustice that are evident in most modern societies, that can equally become the focus of the vision of community renewal developed by Buber, Camara and Freire. The conditions necessary to bring about such a renewal — the fostering of interpersonal and communal dialogue, the awakening of critical consciousness and individual responsibility, the promotion of cooperation and trust - are identified with compelling force and clarity in their writings. In those writings also this ideal of social and community renewal is located firmly in the practical context of a dynamic and potentially transformative vision of the aims, practice and pedagogic methodology of the adult education process.

# VIII

# Towards the Future: The Relevance of Buber's Educational Philosophy

The appearance in recent years of a number of studies purporting to redefine the 'aims of education' indicates a widespread contemporary concern for the directions in which education is likely to, or ought to, proceed in the future.[1] Buber's writings, being essentially philosophical formulations of educational principles and ideals, represent yet another contribution to the 'aims-defining' exercise. It becomes necessary, in the first instance, therefore, to indicate the ways in which his writings might be said to make a *distinctive* contribution to this whole process. Initially, it can be said there are two fundamental respects in which they differ from other contemporary attempts to reconceive the aims of education. Firstly, Buber attributes much of the confusion and uncertainty which exists on this issue to the ideological character of the standpoints adopted by most educational theorists. In his own work he adopts a supra-ideological approach to the definition of educational aims: rather than attempting to offer alternatives to existing definitions, he offers a radically reconceived methodology for the purpose of identifying these aims. Recognizing that education, like all other human enterprises, is centrally concerned with relationships, he focusses his work primarily on the nature of such relationships. He looks particularly at the fundamental educational relationships of teaching and learning, of believing and knowing, of expressing and creating, of loving and responding. Through their basic methods of critical enquiry and description, his writings present complex, penetrating and sophisticated insights into all such relationships, each of which is defined within the all-encompassing framework of the ultimate educational relationship: the interpersonal dialogue between man and man.

The method of his thought is characterized, secondly, by its recognition of the truth that educational change proceeds normally by way of synthesis and assimilation, and that a stable process of innovation is one which is firmly grounded in a renewed understanding of the received traditions of education. From the various theoretical conflicts precipitating educational change new formulations emerge which can simultaneously retain and reject certain aspects of the traditions they replace. Buber's work exhibits to a remarkable degree this principle of assimilative continuity. It exhibits it in his evaluation both of the specific traditions of educational theory and of the cultural traditions on which they are founded. He argued eloquently for a *rebirth* of tradition, insisting that received values and truths are themselves dynamic phenomena that need to be reinterpreted to accommodate the processes of historical change. Thus, while he rejected both the rigid authoritarianism of what he called the 'old traditions' in education and the relativist instabilities of the 'new', he praised the former for their effective transmission of inherited truths and the latter for their liberation of education from the excesses of repressive authoritarianism. Similarly, while he argued forcefully for the propagation of traditional culture, he called simultaneously for a radical reappraisal of that culture in terms of its contemporary meaningfulness and relevance. Thus he writes of a Jewish tradition renewed by the democratic impact of the Hasidic reforms; of a Christian tradition reinterpreted in the light of its Hebraic roots and its continuity with Judaism; and of a socialist tradition revitalized through a restatement of its religious roots both in Christianity and Judaism and in the community ideals articulated by the nineteenth century utopians. To these must be added the three thousand year old Jewish traditions in teaching and learning, the existentialist traditions of the pre-Socratic Greek philosophers and the Hebrew prophets of the fifth century B.C.E., and the later existentialist thought of the nineteenth century writers, Kierkegaard, Nietzsche and Dostoievsky — on all of which he drew extensively for the formulation of his educational theories. There are few instances in modern times of a philosophy of education exhibiting such a remarkable degree of continuity with the inheritance of human culture.

The specific relationships on which Buber's educational philosophy is focussed are deeply informed, therefore, by his attention to the need for innovation and change and by his profound sense of the traditional cultural and theoretical foundations on which change and innovation must be based. This may be illustrated firstly from his treatment of the central relationship in education: the relationship between teacher and learner. It is important, in the first place, to emphasize his concern for the inseparability of the two elements in this relationship, since many of the defects in modern education to which he addressed himself could be attributed to the separation of teaching from learning — a separation manifested, for instance, in certain forms of developmentalist learning theory, with their diminished sense of the impact of teaching on classroom learning and their failure, as a consequence of this, to emphasize the importance of pedagogic efficiency in the advancement of learning. Buber's conception of the teaching-learning relationship shows a deep sense of the moral and personal integrity by which the relationship is ultimately informed and defined. Seeing it as essentially a dialogue conducted between teacher and learner, he considered that the quality of its dialogic reciprocity, far from being diminished or impeded, is greatly strengthened and enhanced by the formative and decisive impact which the teacher can exert over the learning process. Thus he spoke of teaching as a confirming of individual potentiality, a notion that differs radically from the 'facilitator' model of teaching associated with 'progressive' education, but which differs also from the authoritarianism of older traditions of teaching, by virtue of its conception of teaching and learning as a freely chosen activity of collaborative meaning-making. He emphasized the openness of the meaning-making activity, and insisted that the learner appropriate meaning freely and determine its relevance subjectively. But he insisted also that knowing in its most mature forms is a highly disciplined, reflective, culturally informed activity; he envisaged a decisive role for the teacher, therefore, in enabling the learner to acquire those habits of critical reflection that would make the free search for meaning more effective and more fruitful.

Thus, he rejected the 'growth-oriented' model of learning on the grounds that it radically misconceived the notion of personal freedom, that it falsely identified personal fulfilment with self-fulfilment, and that it severely limited the teacher's potential impact upon the learning process. His own notion of freedom is rooted in his anthropological conception of man as essentially a relating, loving, reciprocating being: one who fulfils himself in his capacity to love and whose freedom is most completely fulfilled in exercising that capacity. He rejected the idea of development as self-fulfilment, therefore, as an indulgence of selfish tendencies and called for a focussing of all learning on the the altruistic tendencies inherent in man's nature. The child's freedom is fulfilled, he said, not through his capacity for self-expression, but through the 'instinct for communion'; his freedom is a means towards an end beyond itself, the end of personal fulfilment through love. Both teaching and learning are concerned, therefore, with the nurturing of relational encounters: encounters with persons, with the heritage of culture and thought, with the world of nature — with all those realities that are external to the perceiving subject. In developing these relational propensities in his pupils, the teacher can exercise a highly formative role by initiating them into the cultural traditions in which all their encounters are ultimately rooted, by fostering their innate disposition to appropriate meaning freely and subjectively, and by instructing them in the discipline of critical reflection which makes the search for meaning more purposeful. An effective balance is maintained, therefore, between the notion of learning, on the one hand, as a freely oriented activity of personal enquiry, and the concept of *childhood* learning, on the other hand, as an undeveloped, immature, haphazard activity which requires the decisive intervention of a teacher, if it is to proceed effectively towards its goal of genuine meaning-making.

The teacher-learner relationship is the central concern of Buber's philosophy and his most significant contribution to modern educational theory consists in his radical and detailed reformulation of that relationship. Some further areas in which he could be said to have made substantial contributions include moral and religious education, aesthetic education, language education, adult and community education. Behind much of what he had to say on all these matters, however, lies a recurrent and emphatic adherence to a principle that has since become almost an obsessive preoccupation of twentieth century educationalists. That principle is the non-relativist character of religious, moral and epistemic truths. The scale of the problem of relativism may be illustrated by these comments from a recent, widely acclaimed publication, *The Closing of the American Mind*. Its author, Allan Bloom, writes: 'There is one thing a professor can be absolutely certain of: almost every student entering the university believes, or says he believes, that truth is relative. . . . The students' backgrounds are as various as America can provide. Some are religious, some atheists; some to the left, some to the right; some intend to be scientists, some humanists or professionals or businessmen; some are poor, some rich. They are unified only in their relativism and in their allegiance to equality. And the two are related in a moral intention. The relativity of truth is not a theoretical insight but a moral postulate, the condition of a free society, or so they see it.'[2]

The relativizing processes described here by Bloom are rejected at every level in Buber's philosophy, but particularly at the levels of moral, religious, aesthetic, social and epistemic truth. It is ironic, perhaps, in view of his emphasis on the ultimately *relational* nature of all truth that this should be the case. But all the relational modes of existing he described — particularly those of loving, knowing, believing and creating — are directed ultimately towards the absolute truth of the infinite, intemporal, unconditioned reality of Thouness. The reality of *absolute relation* is the truth to which all other values and truths are ultimately referrable. Thus, while he affirms that knowing is a free process of meaning-making and an appropriation of all meaning into the realm of the subjective and the personal, he insists that all knowing is directed finally towards the absolute truth of the interpersonal in its unconditioned, intemporal and non-finite forms. And since man's sense of a personal relation to that final reality is what Buber designates the religious dimension of his existence, he places all other forms of relation within the all-encompassing framework of the religious relationship.

Thus he rejects the commonplace separation of morality from religious faith as a violation of an integrity already present in the nature of man. He particularly rejected the formulation of value-systems in terms exclusively of social, pragmatic or utilitarian needs and warned of the catastrophic consequences that would follow from this. Yet he warned also of the dangers of defining ethical principles in accordance with abstract, depersonalized axioms and norms. His ethics are founded on the complementary, if paradoxical, principles of the absolute character of moral truth, on the one hand,

and the radical freedom of ethical choice and decision-making , on the other. The intrinsic value of human action is determined, he declared, by the absolute criteria of dialogic truth and is known to the individual in his authentic awareness of what essentially he is: a being potentially capable of loving, reciprocating responses in all the situations with which his existence presents him. His ethical decision-making consists in his appraising every such situation in terms of the possibility it presents for a genuine dialogic response. That appraisal, in turn, is dictated by the inner imperatives of his own conscience: imperatives he is free to follow or to reject. Ethical behaviour is primarily, therefore, the responsible exercise of personal freedom. But the dictates of conscience, while emanating spontaneously from the depth of man's nature, are strengthened, deepened and clarified by various self-illuminating processes, such as the study of the received traditions of moral truth and the collaborative search for ethical meaning, which Buber saw as the main concerns of the moral educator.

The aims he proposes for moral education, therefore, involve the affirmation of certain absolute criteria of moral truth, together with a clear emphasis on the free nature of ethical choice, the personal character of moral decision-making and the uniqueness of every situation in which such decisions are made. Buber has proposed a highly practical pedagogy for the realization of these goals, and the educator is seen to have a highly influential role in the whole process. While the main responsibility of the educator is to assist the individual student in the illumination of his own conscience — and the self-illumination sought is disclosed ultimately in the depth of individual personhood — the search for moral meaning is itself seen again as a collaborative activity in which teacher and student explore the ethical implications of every choice and decision confronting them. But in this instance again the educator exercises a *confirming* influence on his pupil. Through his advice and guidance, through the struggles and conflicts that may occur between them, he confirms his pupil's potentiality to determine moral meaning and freely exercise his capacity for moral choice and decision-making. Secondly, the process is seen by Buber as an exercise of *critical* meaning-making and is to be conducted in the same spirit of disciplined reflection as all the learning activities that are part of the educational process. In that context the traditions of moral truth (e.g the Judaeo-Christian scriptures) become highly relevant and serve as important sources for the illumination of ethical meaning in terms of its traditional formulations. They are subjected, however, to the same action of critical scrutiny as all the other sources that may be uitilized in the search for moral illumination And thirdly, the confirming role of the educator is extended into the function of pastoral counselling, by virtue of which the healing of anxiety, guilt, disbelief, despair or any of the myriad symptoms of a disturbance of the spirit the educator encounters in his students, becomes part of the whole activity of moral self-improvement in which they are jointly engaged. The pastoral concern which is frequently seen as the specialized function of trained 'counsellors' is seen by Buber as an integral function of all teaching and one necessarily bound up with the interpersonal character of the teaching-learning dialogic.

In devising aims and pedagogical guidelines for moral education, therefore, Buber avoids the instabilities of relativism, on the one hand, and the impersonal tyranny of dogmatism, on the other. He offers a non-prescriptive, freely oriented ethical pedagogy that has the combined attractions of accommodating the uniqueness of personal needs and the contingencies of existential circumstance and change, while being firmly rooted in, and continuous with, the received heritage of moral truth. Recognizing the complexity of contemporary moral needs, especially amongst the young, he sought to respond to those needs with the sensitivity, openness and realism they require. Behind a widely felt need for moral assurance and stability, however, he detected a deeper but closely related need to which he insisted educators had a further obligation to respond. He believed that the need for faith is keenly felt, even at a time (perhaps, especially at a time) when the conventional forms and rituals of religion are widely rejected. For the educator struggling with a widely expressed scepticism regarding the dogmas and practices of institutionalized religion, Buber's philosophy has the merit of identifying the nature of that faith independently of the religious conventions with which it is commonly linked. His recommendations for the renewal of religious faith through education are based on the radical proposition that that faith originates at the common level of interpersonal experience, and that it can be nurtured, therefore, not primarily through the teaching of religious doctrines, but through the fostering of the relational potencies of existence, and particularly the relational potency of love. He sees the restoration of faith and of a sense of the meaningfulness of existence as a crucial exercise once again of the teacher's function of confirming personal potentiality. Buber defined that potentiality as the capacity for meaning-giving faith which is inherent in man's nature. The teacher, he declared, can assist his pupils in that free process of self-illumination and self-healing through which they can learn to make their lives meaningful and purposeful. His position is similar to that of Dostoievsky's Father Zossima who advises the mother of Lise that she will recover her lost faith if she 'strives to love her neighbour actively and indefatigably'.[3] In addition to emphasizing the relational character of religious faith, Buber's proposal has the further merit of bridging the common dichotomy between the sacred and the secular and ensuring that, far from being a specialized province of life, a weekly ritual celebration, that faith is applied existentially to the contingencies of everyday life and is the spirit permeating every facet of that life. The quest for faith, therefore, becomes a quest for an organic spirituality within which all facets of experience can be integrated. Essentially, it is the individual's pursuit of the synthesizing resources of the spirit which are present in his own nature.

By insisting that faith is rooted in the universal and self-transforming realities of human freedom and love, Buber felt he had responded to the major causes of the disillusionment with religion he had observed amongst the young. Yet his understanding of the nature of faith remains broadly compatible also with the traditions of religion, and especially those on which his work is most directly focussed. The central concern of his religious teaching is the principle that man loves God by loving God's creation. This is simply the principle of immanence for which strong support can be found both in the Jewish and in the Christian traditions. But the Jewish and Christian traditions that Buber describes differ radically also from the conventional orthodoxies that are normally assumed to represent those traditions. He himself had advocated a rediscovery of the meaning of the Jewish and Christian traditions in terms of their original scriptural, or mythic, simplicity. The pedagogy he proposed for *religious* education, therefore, would include methods of fostering a critical reading of scriptural texts, in accordance with the same principles of reflective meaning-making described earlier in the context of learning as a whole. He advised close attention to the Biblical text, a genuine openness to textual meaning, and a personal evaluation of all that the text conveys. In the scripture narrative, he said, the student could discover the traditional evocations of that organic spirituality he would more immediately seek to attain in the everyday circumstances of his life.

It is highly significant, from an educational standpoint, that Buber so strongly emphasized the place of imagination in the process of religious education. He wrote frequently of the essentially symbolic character of religious meaning and, equally, he warned of the dangers that symbols become outworn or objectified, and spoke of the need for a continuous process of reinterpreting or reformulating symbolic religious meaning. That function of symbolic reformulation has been served traditionally by religious literature, music and art, where the images and symbols of scripture are consistently reinterpreted and the language of scripture is constantly re-vivified. The religious orientation of the arts is underlined again in the conception of aesthetic symbol as a penetration of the transphenomenal, the unconditioned, infinite and intemporal which Buber put forward in his aesthetic writings. Both conceptions — the idea of religious art as a regeneration of the language and imagery of the scriptures or as a religiously oriented, transcendent activity — point to the need to explore the potentially complementary relationship between aesthetic, moral and religious education.

From the standpoint of the modern educator, therefore, Buber's approach to religious education has the attraction primarily of locating religious faith in the everyday experience of the interpersonal. It was in that context he believed that modern youth would find it personally meaningful. But he was equally aware of the sterility of a faith divorced from religious tradition, was deeply contemptuous of new religious cults, and insisted that religious experience should be rooted in the received religious traditions. He called, however, for a radical rediscovery of the meaning of those traditions, and provided the theoretical foundations for a highly imaginative pedagogy for the realization of that purpose. The same synthesis of innovative and traditionalist principles, therefore, informs his thinking on religious education as has already been identified in the sphere of moral education and in his entire conception of the nature of teaching and learning. A similar synthesis can be identified in his treatment of two highly problematic issues in modern education: the issues of creativity and literacy.

Few issues have become so contentious in modern education as the nature of creativity and, amongst the various formulations put forward, few can be potentially so damaging as the expressive concept associated with pragmatist philosophy and the 'progressive' movement. The identification of creativity with self-expression was seen by Buber as leading, firstly, to a debased conception of the nature of artistic creation, and thence to a debased understanding of the aims and purposes of aesthetic education as a whole. Secondly, in the particular sphere of linguistic development he considered it would lead to an impoverished appreciation of the literary arts, a diminished command of symbolic language and consequently to diminished standards in literacy. In his Heidelberg lecture he identified the drive for self-expression in the name of 'creativity' as an aspect of the general thrust towards self-growth and self-fulfilment in progressivist educational theory. Since his main response to this was a reassertion of the fundamentally relational character of human existence, he argued for a similar orientation in the conception of the nature of creativity and in the aims and methods of aesthetic and linguistic education.

Buber's Heidelberg lecture and his essay, 'Man and his Image-work', through their mature formulation of a relational aesthetic, provide a firm theoretic foundation for a definition of aims for aesthetic education. Both works emphasize the notion of creativity as an aesthetic potentiality manifesting capacities for interpersonal encounter — in this instance encounters with the existential evidence of beauty — that are comparable to other forms of dialogic encounter, such as loving, knowing and believing. Both essays also stress the universal character of aesthetic dialogue and insist that it is a potentiality which is present in all men. But the aesthetic encounter is seen, crucially, to combine both the functions of origination and response and there is the clear assertion that the first function exists exceptionally in the rare instances when aesthetic potentiality finds fulfilment as art.

Buber conceives an approach to aesthetic education that takes full account of the universal presence of aesthetic potentialities and that recognizes the complex interdependence that exists between *aesthetic* and *artistic* propensities. The key to this complex relationship lies in his conception of aesthetic origination and response as intentional, meaning-conferring activities. The principle of meaning- conferring straddles both the artistic and aesthetic functions: the artist, specifically through his evocation of the reality of form, *intends* aesthetic meaning through the act of artistic creation; the reader/listener/viewer *intends* the meaning of that creation through the act of critical appreciation. In both instances the focus of the act of meaning-conferring is their common origin in the interpersonal dialogic of the I-Thou; both emerge from the depth of human encounter — from man's relation to fellowman, to the surrounding universe, to the heritage of religion, culture and art.

The fruits of this finely balanced formulation are to be seen particularly in the sphere of language education. The importance of literacy is only gradually becoming apparent to western educators, though socialist and Third World educators have long seen it as the key to human advancement, and define it in a fundamental and radical fashion as the means to educability and ultimately, therefore, as the basis of human freedom. Recently, Fernando Cardenal, the organizer of the phenomenally successful literacy campaign in Nicaragua, commented: 'It must be remembered that literacy, the ability to read and write, is not simply a collection of academic skills. Literacy is what separates human beings from the beasts of the field and empowers them not only to understand but also to change the world around them.'[4] That illiteracy is not exclusively a Third World problem but one which is tragically evident in developed countries as well — and especially amongst their disadvantaged populations — is gradually being acknowledged by western educators. Studies such as Hirsch's *Cultural Literacy* indicate the scale of the problem in the U.S., but there is little evidence there of the kind of commitment to tackling the problem that was evident in the Nicaraguan Campaign of 1980 and earlier in the Cuban, Tanzanian and Soviet literacy campaigns.[5] It would seem that a serious concern for this most fundamental of human rights is still largely confined to socialist states where the waste of human potential and the denial of human freedom is directly linked with illiteracy.

Buber, a socialist himself, was fully aware of the importance of literacy and conveyed this in essays such as 'The Word that is Spoken' and 'What is Common to All'. There are two crucial assertions in these works: one, that literacy is founded on the dynamic spokenness of living speech, and two, that this is rooted, in turn, in the cultivation of imaginative and symbolic modes of language. Like Eliot in 'The Music of Poetry',[6] Buber asserted that all modes of language are rooted in its living, spoken forms and are constantly sustained and enlivened by their relation to those forms. He insisted that mastery of oral-aural capacities was the key to the whole process of linguistic growth. That conviction was powerfully strengthened by his own immersion in the Hasidic traditions of oral folklore and in the richness of the culture that was derived from those traditions. The importance of his views has been spectacularly borne out recently in the experience of Israeli educators with the thousands of Falasha Ethiopian Jews airlifted into Israel. Their extraordinary powers of learning ability have been attributed directly to the richness of the oral culture passed on to them by generations of their own people.[7] The same truth has been confirmed in the above mentioned literacy campaigns in Nicaragua, Cuba, Tanzania and the U.S.S.R.

Buber, however, while stressing the primacy of speech and its importance as the source of linguistic fluency, further affirmed the essentially dialogic, interpersonal character of spoken language. All language, he declared, originates in encounter; its ultimate source is the 'betweenness' or 'being-with-others' in which its radically dialogic character is manifested. The dialogic of language, he further explained, is made manifest as the poetic or symbolic element in all speech and this, in turn, finds its most accomplished expression in the various literary art-forms. The mastery of oral speech, therefore, entails a concomitant need to master the poetic and symbolic elements of language, if true literacy is to be achieved. The pedagogic implications are clear enough: a comprehensive and balanced language pedagogy is one which gives due attention to oral-aural capacities and to the symbolic uses of language made available through the study of its various literary and aesthetic forms.

Yet the absence of such a balance is sadly evident in much of the pedagogic theory currently influencing approaches to vernacular language instruction. In some instances, most notably amongst writers drawing their insights mainly from sociolinguistics, one finds clear recognition of the importance of oracy, but a failure to acknowledge sufficiently the place of imagination in the nurturing of all forms of linguistic fluency. One also finds amongst them a highly commendable concern for pragmatic and functional uses of language, but without due regard for the dependence of such usages on the primary fluency engendered by encounters with the poetic and aesthetic. On the other hand, amongst writers such as Holbrook and Abbs, one finds a sensitive application of the dialogic principle to the sphere of literary studies, but a general neglect of oracy and auracy, together with a limited sense of the importance of language as *social* dialogue. There is clearly a need to formulate aims for a language pedagogy that will give due attention to its oral-aural, imaginative, symbolic and social dimensions. Buber's work provides significant pointers on how such an undertaking might be conceived.

Buber's views on language education are drawn from the combined resources of his aesthetics and his dialogic and social philosophy. Their combined impact is evident again in his views on adult and community education. In these he anticipated some major initiatives that occurred subsequently in a number of Third World socialist states. What may now be called the classic aims of socialist education — promoting universal educability, providing for high levels of pedagogic efficiency, equalizing opportunity through consistency in curriculum provision — all these are clearly underlined in Buber's educational writings. He recognized, however, that appropriate educational provision at adult level would be necessary to achieve the ultimate goals of a just and equitably organized society. His work provides an elaborately developed and highly coherent articulation of aims for the achievement of those goals through education. Because it links the specific aims and instructional procedures of adult education with broader issues in the spheres of moral, religious and aesthetic education, his treatment of the whole adult education process is far more comprehensive than that provided by other contemporary theorists, even those of the calibre of Freire and Hutchins.

Not surprisingly, in view of his experience as a tutor at the Frankfurt Lehrhaus and as the founder of a training centre for adult tutors in Palestine, his most notable contribution lies in the sphere of practical pedagogy. What was most significantly innovative in his pedagogic theory was, firstly, his recognition that the most pressing responsibility of the adult tutor was to induce in his students the predisposition to learn, and secondly, his further insistence that this was a matter chiefly of creating the relational conditions conducive to that end. Buber's dialogic conception of the role of the adult tutor is his main response to the complex and highly challenging demands that each of these represents. It is combined with a strong emphasis on the need for substantial cultural content in the curriculum taught to adult students. His view that developing educational potential — which initially means developing the powers of literacy — is itself an inadequate measure for the promotion of true cultural liberation, unless that initial process is followed by culturally and intellectually enriching programmes, has profoundly influenced approaches to adult education in underdeveloped countries. It has not generally been adopted, however, in the developed nations of Europe and North America where adult education is frequently conceived as a leisurely recreation rather than a means to the practical realization of educational equity. Freire's argument that Third World conditions exist also in developed nations — especially in their urban ghettoes and rural wastelands — and that they require equally radical solutions,[8] has gone largely unheeded by educational policy-makers in those countries.

Underlying Buber's definition of a radical dialogic pedagogy for adult education, and his concern that curricula for adult courses should have substantial content, is his all-embracing vision of the whole process as a means to community transformation, and thence, to the realization of the ideals of religious socialism. He believed the transformation of relationships that education could promote at the level of the interpersonal could be brought about also at the level of the communal and the social, and he considered that properly designed educational programmes, such as those he introduced in Germany and Palestine, could achieve that goal. Adult education, he felt, should be provided not just for the disadvantaged but for all communities and should be directed towards their total cultural, social and spiritual renewal. Once again, there is considerable evidence of the practicality of this view from the Base Communities movements organized in several Latin American countries in accordance with principles that strongly resemble those defined by Buber. There is little indication, however, that the same much needed process of renewal has been undertaken in the developed nations of Western Europe and North America where the stresses of poverty, unemployment, drug culture, delinquency, crime and a myriad other social abuses require similarly radical provision for social reform. The first step in such a process would be to reexamine policies on adult and community education — which at present are hopelessly inadequate — with a view to utilizing their potential for community renewal. A crucial requirement for the success of such initiatives would be the formulation of aims and the structuring of programmes in accordance with firmly established theoretical principles. Buber's philosophy of adult and community education could be a most fruitful source for the identification of the principles on which such a venture would be based.

It is important in this context also to reiterate Buber's conviction that community education may provide mankind's best hope for survival at a time when the threat of nuclear annihiliation is an everpresent reality. Throughout his life he argued that all human conflict originates at the immediate level of interpersonal and social relationships and therefore must be confronted at that level to prevent its escalation into its more dangerous forms. On this principle he based a lifetime of activity to promote good relations between the various communities amongst whom he lived. The community education methods he pioneered and put into practice were based on a simple objective — the elimination of fear and mistrust. He believed that objective could be achieved through genuine communication: through a genuine speaking and listening with a view to achieving a true understanding of differences in belief and outlook and with a view to creating the conditions in which dialogue could take place. It is highly significant that he should have been supported in this viewpoint by internationally prominent figures in the cause of peace, such as Hammerskjold, Schweitzer, Luther King and Sakharov. At a time when courses in peace education have become so contentious — to the point where they have been prohibited by certain governments fearing the impact of pacifist ideas[9] — it might be appropriate that Buber's ideas on the subject be given more attention in the construction of both school and adult education programmes.

Buber's contribution to modern educational theory, as I said at the outset, lies in his reformulation of educational aims in accordance with the dialogic principles that are central to his entire philosophy. Those aims lie in the various spheres I have endeavoured to describe. What remains to be emphasized are the two principles that seem to pervade all his thinking on education. The first is that education is necessarily a unified and a unifying process: that whatever one's particular concern, or however specialized one's involvements as an educator, they must ultimately be related to the spiritual, religious, social, cultural, aesthetic, moral and other elements which together constitute its essential integrity. The second principle is his constant assertion of the radical *importance* of education itself — of its immense potential for the cultivation of human capacities and for the enrichment and transformation of human existence. That principle was compellingly exemplified for Buber in the extraordinary history of his own people and their survival as a race. In *Israel and the World* he explains all this with a simple parable from the *Midrash:* 'Delegates of the other nations were once dispatched to a Greek sage to ask him how the Jews could be subjugated. This is what he said to them: "Go and walk past their houses of prayer and study. . . . So long as the voice of Jacob rings from their houses of prayer and study, they will not be surrendered into the hands of Esau. But if not, the hands are Esau's and you will overcome them".'[10]

# Notes

CHAPTER I
In this chapter I have drawn extensively on the abundance of autobiographical and biographical sources which exist for the study of Buber's life and work. I have made considerable use, for instance, of Buber's own autobiographical writings, such as *Meetings* (La Salle, Illinois: Open Court Publishing, 1973); *A Believing Humanism: My Testament, 1902-1965*, ed. Maurice Friedman (New York: Simon and Schuster, 1967); and 'My Way To Hasidism' from *Hasidism and Modern Man* (New York: Horizon Press, 1958). I have also drawn heavily on the three volumes of Buber's letters, *Briefwechsel aus sieben Jahrzehnten*, ed. Grete Schaeder (Heidelberg: Verlag Lambert Schneider, 1972-1975). Of the biographical sources which exist I am especially indebted to the monumental three volume study by Maurice Friedman, *Martin Buber's Life and Work* (London: Search Press, 1982; New York: E. P. Dutton, 1983 and 1985) and to *Encounter with Martin Buber* by Aubrey Hodes (Harmondsworth: Penguin Books, 1975)

1    Martin Buber, *Meetings*, p. 18.
2    Ibid., pp. 18-19.
3    Ibid., pp. 19-20.
4    Ibid., pp. 20-21.
5    Ibid., p.24.
6    Ibid., pp. 22-23.
7    Ibid., pp. 26-27.
8    Ibid., pp. 28-29. Steven Katz has carefully analysed the Kantian influence on Buber. He sees Kant's philosophy, with its distinction between the phenomenon and the noumenon as providing the basis for Buber's distinction between the 'I-It' and the 'I-Thou' realms. See S. Katz, 'Martin Buber's Epistemology: A Critical Appraisal,' *International Philosophical Quarterly* (1981) 21, pp. 133-158.
9    Ibid., pp. 29-30.
10   Ibid., p.30.
11   Ibid,., pp. 31-32.
12   See Friedman, *Martin Buber's Life and Work*, Vol. I, p.50.
13   Buber's views on the Christian mystics were published subsequently in *Ekstatische Konfessionem* (Jena: Eugen Dietrichs Verlag, 1909).
14   See Chapter 3, Section I.
15   Martin Buber, *The Tales of Rabbi Nachman*, trans. M. Friedman, (London: Souvenir Press, 1974).
16   Ibid., p.12.
17   Martin Buber, *The Legend of the Baal Shem* (New York: Schocken Books, 1969).
18   e.g. S.Y. Agnon, *A Guest For the Night* (New York: Schocken Books, 1968). See especially descriptions of religious worship, pp. 123, 127, 132-5, 180-181, 191-8, 259-262, and portraits of zaddikim, pp. 198-202, 458. See also Isaac Bashevis Singer, *In My Father's Court* (Penguin Books, 1980) for some colourful vignettes of Hasidic customs.

19    Martin Buber, 'Die Duse in Florenz', *Die Schaubuhne*, I, 15, Dec. 1905; 'Drei Rollen Novalis', *Die Schaubuhne*, 11, 2, Jan. 1906.

20    Martin Buber, *On Judaism*, ed. N. Glatzer (New York: Schocken Books, 1972).

21    M. Friedman, *Martin Buber's Life and Work*, I, p. 145.

22    Martin Buber, *Daniel: Dialogues on Realization*, trans. M. Friedman (New York: McGraw-Hill, 1965).

23    See Note 19.

24    Martin Buber, *Pointing the Way* (London: Routledge and Kegan Paul, 1953), pp. 67-74).

25    Ibid., pp. 63-67.

26    Aubrey Hodes in *Encounter With Martin Buber* (pp. 10 ff.) suggests that Mehe committed suicide. 'I asked Buber at our next meeting what happened to the young man', he writes. 'Buber closed his eyes for a moment, as if in pain. Then he said quietly, He went and afterwards he took his own life.' Friedman dismisses Hodes' account as 'a journalistic attempt to make his portrait more intimate' and claims the conversation quoted by Hodes did not in fact take place. Hodes' version, he says, is an elaboration of a spurious account of the Mehe episode given by Meyer Levin in *The New York Times Magazine*, December 3, 1960. Friedman quotes a letter from Buber to himself in which the former confirmed that Mehe died at the front in World War I (*Martin Buber's Life and Work*, I, p.188).

27    Martin Buber, *Between Man and Man* (London: Fontana Books, 1969), pp. 31-32.

28    Maurice Friedman, *Martin Buber's Life and Work*, I, p.201.

29    Buber was appointed a lecturer in Jewish religious philosophy at Frankfurt University in 1925.

30    Friedman, *Martin Buber's Life and Work*, I, p.222.

31    Ibid., p. 229.

32    Martin Buber, *On Judaism*, ed. Nahum Glatzer (New York: Schocken Books, 1967), pp. 108-148.

33    Ibid., pp. 149-174.

34    Friedman, *Martin Buber's Life and Work*, I, p.255.

35    Ibid., pp. 267-274.

36    Ibid., p. 277.

37    Ibid., p. 279.

38    See 'The Task', *A Believing Humanism*, pp. 10I ff.

39    Martin Buber, *Between Man and Man*, pp. 109-131.

40    Franz Rosenzweig, *The Star of Redemption*, trans. W. Hallo (New York: Holt, Rinehart and Winston, 1970).

41    See Nahum Glatzer, 'Buber as an Interpreter of the Bible' in Paul A. Schillp, *The Philosophy of Martin Buber* (London: Cambridge University Press, 1967), pp. 360 ff.

42    Martin Buber, *Israel and the World*, (New York: Schocken Books, 1963), pp. 89-102, 119-135.

43    Buber, *A Believing Humanism*, pp. 144-152.

44    Buber, *The Origin and Meaning of Hasidism* (New York: Horizon Press, 1960), pp. 142-143.

45    Friedman, *Martin Buber's Life and Work*, 11, p. 29.

46    Buber, *Between Man and Man*, pp. 109-131.

47    Florens Christian Rang was a former Lutheran pastor and lawyer who advocated ecumenical dialogue between different religions. Rang had adopted a highly nationalistic stance in support of Germany during the war , but later regretted this and worked to improve relations between Germany and other European nations. Rang died

in 1924. Buber dedicated *The Kingship of God* to him in 1932.

48 Leonhard Ragaz was a Christian socialist whom Buber met in the early 1920s. Ragaz believed in a non-violent, state-free community socialism. Buber shared his disenchantment with the legalism and dogmatics of Orthodox Judaism and the Christian churches.

49 Buber, *Pointing The Way* (London: Routledge and Kegan Paul), pp. 112-114.

50 Buber, *The Two Types of Faith*, (New York: Harper Torchbooks, 1961).

51 Buber, *Between Man and Man*, pp. 17-59.

52 Buber, *Der Jude und Sein Judentum* (Cologne: Millzer Verlag, 1934), pp. 674-684.

53 Buber, *Israel and the World*, pp. 146-7.

54 Ibid., pp. 78 ff.

55 Friedman, *Martin Buber's Life and Work*, 11, p.167.

56 Ibid., p. 205.

57 Buber, *Pointing the Way*, pp. 98-108.

58 Buber, *Israel and the World*, pp. 137-145.

59 Ibid., pp. 173-182.

60 Friedman, *Martin Buber's Life and Work*, 11, pp. 225 ff.

61 For correspondence between Buber and Trub see *Briefwechsel*, 11, pp. 568, 573, 596, 597, 611, 615, 618. See also 'Healing Through Meeting', *Pointing the Way*, pp. 93-97.

62 For Buber's assessment of Trub see 'Healing Through Meeting', *Pointing the Way*, pp. 93-97.

63 *Briefwechsel*, 11, pp. 613 ff.

64 Buber, *Between Man and Man*, pp. 60-107.

65 Ibid., p.15.

66 Buber, *Israel and the World*, pp. 41-52.

67 Buber, *Die Stunde und die Erkensis* (Berlin: Schocken Verlag, 1936).

68 Buber, *Between Man and Man*, pp. 148 ff.

69 Buber, *The Knowledge of Man* (New York: Harper Torchbooks, 1965).

70 Buber, *Between Man and Man*, pp. 132-146.

71 Friedman, *Martin Buber's Life and Work*, 11, p. 287.

72 *Harijan*, November 26, 1938, pp. 39-44.

73 Buber, *Pointing the Way*, pp. 126-138.

74 Friedman, *Martin Buber's Life and Work*, 11, pp. 298 ff.

75 Buber, *The Prophetic Faith* (New York: Harper Torchbooks, 1960), pp. 155 ff.

76 Buber, *For the Sake of Heaven*, trans. Ludwig Lewishon (Philadelphia: Jewish Publication Society, 1949).

77 Isaac Bashevis Singer, *The Family Moskat* (Penguin Books, 1981).

78 Buber, *Israel and the World*, pp. 197-213.

79 Ibid., pp. 240-252.

80 Ibid., pp. 113-116.

81 Friedman, *Martin Buber's Life and Work*, 11I, pp. 18-21.

82 Ibid., pp. 18-19.

83 Ibid., p.81.

84 Buber, *Tales of the Hasidim: The Early Masters* and *Tales of the Hasidim: The Later Masters*, trans. Olga Marx (New York: Schocken, 1948, 1975).

85 See *Briefwechsel*, 111, p. 184 (letter from Hesse to Buber).

86 Buber, *Paths in Utopia* (London: Routledge and Kegan Paul, 1951).

87 Buber, *Eclipse of God* (New York: Humanities Press, 1979).

88 Abraham Joshua Heschel, *God In Search of Man* (Philadelphia: Jewish Publ. Soc., 1956); *A Passion For Truth* (London: Secker and Warburg, 1974).

89    Sidney and Beatrice Rome (eds.), *Philosophical Interrogations* (New York: Harper Torchbooks, 1964). See pp. 6I ff.
90    Buber, *Elija* (Heidelberg: Verlag Lambert Schneider, 1963).
91    Buber, *The Knowledge of Man*, pp. 149-165.
92    Buber, *Pointing the Way*, pp.192-207.
93    Buber, *A Believing Humanism*, pp. 55-56.
94    Ibid., p. 56. Buber's tribute to Schweitzer is highly illuminating both on his own view of Christianity and his wholistic concept of medical care.
95    Buber,*The Knowledge of Man*.
96    Ibid., pp. 132-3.
97    Ibid., pp. 166-184.
98    Buber, *Israel and the World*, pp. 253-257.
99    See 'Spirits and Men', A Believing Humanism.
100   'Autobiographical Fragments' in Schillp, *The Philosophy of Martin Buber*.
101   Rome, *Philosophical Interrogations*.
102   Buber, *Pointing the Way*, pp. 220-229.
103   For Buber's description of his meetings weith Hammerskjold in New York and Jerusalem see *A Believing Humanism*, pp. 57-59.
104   Friedman, *Martin Buber's Life and Work*, 11I, p. 324.
105   Ibid., pp. 337-8.
106   Buber, *Israel and the World*, pp. 258-263.
107   Hodes, *Encounter with Martin Buber*.
108   See *Time*, 23 March 1962, 13 April 1962, 15 June 1962 and *Newsweek*, 25December 1961 and 6 June 1962.
109   Friedman *Martin Buber's Life and Work*, 111, pp. 356 ff.
110   *New York Times*, June 5, 1962.
111   *Encyclopedia Hinuchit* (in Hebrew) (Hebrew University of Jerusalem, 1960).
112   Buber, *The Knowledge of Man*, pp. 110-120.
113   Prize named after the Hebrew poet, Hayyim Bialik (1873-1934).
114   Friedman, *Martin Buber's Life and Work*, 11I, p.385.
115   Ibid.
116   Ibid., pp. 398-9. See also Hodes, *Encounter with Martin Buber*.
117   Buber, *A Believing Humanism*, pp. 117-122.
118   Ibid., p. 229
119   Friedman, *Martin Buber's Life and Work*, 11I, pp. 420-421.
120   *Jerusalem Post*, 14, 15 June 1965.
121   *New York Times*, 14 June 1965.
122   *Newsweek*, 17 June 1965.

CHAPTER II

1    Buber, *Between Man and Man*, p. 158.
2    Schillp, *The Philosophy of Martin Buber*, p. 693.
3    For Buber's view of St. Augustine see *Between Man and Man*, pp. 159 and 163, and for his view of Pascal see *Eclipse of God*, p. 49. For some further comment on Heraclitus see *Eclipse of God*, pp. 30, 100.
4    Buber, *Between Man and Man*, pp. 148-247.
5    This view is disputed by Philip Wheelwright who points in his essay, 'Buber's Philosophical Anthropology', to the centrality of the question of man's essential nature in Socratic and Aristotelian philosophy. (Schillp, *The Philosophy of Martin Buber*, pp. 69-96).

6    Buber, *Eclipse of God.*, p. 100.
7    Buber, *Meetings*, p.28.
8    Buber, *Between Man and Man*, p. 150.
9    Buber, *Eclipse of God*, p.51.
10   Buber, *On Judaism*, p. 158.
11   Buber, *Eclipse of God*, p. 54.
12   Buber, *Between Man and Man*, p. 168.
13   Rosenzweig had written his doctoral thesis on Hegel. It was published in 1920.
14   Buber, *Between Man and Man*, p. 170.
15   Buber, *Eclipse of God*, p. 19.
16   Buber, *Between Man and Man*, p. 176.
17   Ibid., p. 173.
18   Buber, *Pointing the Way*, p. 201.
19   For a detailed analysis of Feuerbach's critique of Christianity see Max W. Wartofsky, *Feuerbach* (Cambridge University Press, 1977).
20   Buber, *Between Man and Man*, p. 180.
21   See Maurice Friedman, *The Worlds of Existentialism* (University of Chicago Press, 1964), pp. 50-53 for some passages from Feuerbach of particular relevance to Buber's analysis.
22   Buber, *Between Man and Man*, p. 182.
23   Ibid., p. 177.
24   Ibid., p. 179.
25   Buber, *Paths in Utopia*, pp. 99 ff.
26   Ibid., p. 91.
27   Buber, *Eclipse of God*, pp. 103 ff. The word 'suspension' has two connotations in this essay. The first is that of the temporary suspension of the ethical by God himself, as in his command to Abraham to sacrifice his son, Isaac. This is the sense in which the word is used by Kierkegaard in *Fear and Trembling*. But the word is used also by Buber in its ordinary meaning of dispensing with, or rendering inoperable, the traditionalist Judaeo-Christian ethic.
28   Buber, *Meetings*, pp. 27-30.
29   Ibid.
30   Ibid. Buber was so enthused with *Thus Spake Zarathustra* that he translated part of it into Polish.
31   Buber, *Meetings*, p 30.
32   Buber, *Between Man and Man*, p. 189.
33   Ibid., p. 188.
34   ibid.
35   Ibid., p. 170.
36   Ibid., p. 73.
37   Ibid., p. 78.
38   Soren Kierkegaard, *Works of Love*, trans. D.F. Swenson (New York: Kennikat Press, 1946), pp. 15-74.
39   e.g. *Attack upon Christendom*, trans. W Lowrie (Princeton University Press, 1972), p. 285. Also *Christian Discourses*, trans. Lowrie (Princeton University Press, 1972), p. 285. See Josiah Thompson, *Kierkegaard* (London: Gollancz, 1974) for the text of a letter from Kierkegaard to Regine explaining why he was ending their engagement (p. 207).
40   See R.D. Laing, *The Divided Self* (Penguin Books, 1969) and Andrew Collier, *The Philosophy and Politics of Psychotherapy* (London: Harvester Press, 1973), p. 20.

41    Kierkegaard, *Christian Discourses*, p. 4.
42    *The Gospel of St Matthew*, 22: 39.
43    Buber, *Between Man and Man*, p. 82.
44    Ibid., p.87.
45    Ibid., p. 89.
46    Ibid., p. 92.
47    See Kierkegaard, *Christian Discourses*, p. 385 and editor's note.
48    Buber, *On Judaism*, Chapters 3, 5 and 8.
49    Buber, *Between Man and Man*, p. 89.
50    ibid., p. 94.
51    Ibid., p. 103.
52    Ibid.
53    Karl Marx and Friedrich Engels, *On Literature and Art* (Moscow: Progress Publishers, 1979), p. I.
54    Buber, *Between Man and Man*, p. 105.
55    Ibid., p. 108.
56    Ibid., p. 195.
57    Jean-Paul Sartre, *Situations I* (Paris, 1947). See section entitled 'Un Nouveau Mystique'.
58    Sartre, *Being And Nothingness* (London: Methuen, 1976), p. 222.
59    Buber, *Eclipse of God*, p. 67.
60    Ibid., p. 70.
61    Ibid., p. 66.
62    Buber, *Between Man and Man*, p. 203.
63    Martin Heidegger, *Being and Time* (Oxford: Blackwell, 1973), pp. 157 ff.
64    Buber, *Between Man and Man*, p. 215.
65    Ibid., p. 217.
66    e.g. *Poetry, Language, Thought* (New York: Harper Books, 1971).
67    e.g. Jean Wahl. See Schillp, *The Philosophy of Martin Buber*, pp. 475-511.
68    e.g. Karl Rahner.
69    Buber, *Eclipse of God*, p. 76.
70    Ibid.
71    Heidegger, *Being and Time*, pp. 153-168.
72    See *Between Man and Man*, p. 82.
73    Ibid., p. 215.
74    The term 'logicized' is used by Buber for all rationalistic concepts of God. It is applied particularly to the theology of Herman Cohen. For a comparison of Buber's and Cohen's religious writings see R.N. Seltzer, *Jewish People, Jewish Thought* (New York: Macmillan, 1980).
75    Buber, *Eclipse of God*, p. 28.
76    Ibid., p. 31.
77    Ibid., p. 35.
78    Buber, *I and Thou*, trans. W. Kaufmann (Edinburgh: Clark, 1970), pp. 87-89.
79    Franz Rosenzweig, *Understanding the Sick and the Healthy* (New York: Noonday Press, 1953).
80    Buber, *Pointing the Way*, pp. 87-92.
81    Ibid., p. 9.
82    Ibid.
83    Schillp, *The Philosophy of Martin Buber*, p. 69.
84    Ibid.

85 Ibid.
86 Ibid.
87 Nathan Rotenstreuch, 'Buber's Dialogical Thought' in Schillp, *The Philosophy of Martin Buber*, pp. 132 ff.
88 H.W. Schneider, 'The Historical Significance of Buber's Philosophy', Schillp, pp. 470 ff. The word 'experience' has clear connotations of objectification in *I and Thou* and is identified with knowledge of the 'I-It' variety. 'Empiricism' seems a particularly inappropriate term therefore to describe Buber's philosophy.
89 Buber, *Daniel*, p. 173.
90 Grete Schaeder, *Martin Buber* (Gottingen: Vandenhoeck, 1966) p. 29.
91 Maurice Friedman, *Martin Buber's Life and Work*.
92 Schillp, *The Philosophy of Martin Buber*, pp. 689 ff.
93 Ibid, p. 689. See also *Eclipse of God*, pp. 25-46.
94 Buber, *The Legend of the Baal Shem*, p. 13.


CHAPTER III
1 Buber, *Eclipse of God*, p. 34.
2 Buber, *Israel and the World*, p. 19.
3 Buber Centenary Commemoration Broadcast, BBC Radio 3, February, 1978.
4 See Maurice Friedman, 'The Bases of Buber's Ethics' in Schillp, *The Philosophy of Martin Buber*, for a discussion of the relationship between Buber's anthropological and religious writings.
5 e.g. *On Judaism*, pp. 79-94.
6 Further information on the historical evolution of Hasidism will be found in the following:
S.W.Baron, *A Social History of the Jews* (Columbia University Press, 1955).
S.M. Dubnow, *A History of the Jews in Russia and Poland* (Philadelphia: Jewish Publ. Soc., 1916).
Solomon Grayzel, *A History of the Jews* (New York: Mentor, 1968).
S. Horodetsky, *Leaders of Hasidism* (London, 1928).
J.S. Minikin, *The Romance of Hasidism* (New York: Macmillan, 1935).
G. Sholem, *Major Trends in Jewish Mysticism* (New York: Schocken, 1954).
R. M. Seltzer, *Jewish People, Jewish Thought* (New York: Macmillan, 1980).
E. Wiesel, *Souls on Fire: Portraits and Legends of Hasidic Leaders* (New York: Random House, 1973).
7 Jews originating in Northern and Central Europe were traditionally known as 'Ashkenazim' Originally, Jews from North Africa and the Middle East who settled in Spain in medieval times were known as 'Sephardim'. The terms 'Ashkenazic' and 'Sephardim' are now generally used to distinguish Jews of European origin from those of North African or Middle Eastern origin.
8 Seltzer, *Jewish People, Jewish Thought*, p. 476.
9 Ibid.
10 A detailed description of the curriculum followed in the Polish academies is given in Seltzer, p. 478.
11 Ibid. p. 482.
12 The word literally means 'tradition' in Hebrew.
13 Buber, *The Origin and Meaning of Hasidism*, p. 117.
14 The Haskalah was the Jewish Enlightenment, the cultural and philosophical move-

ment of the eighteenth and nineteenth centuries which was opposed by traditionalist believers as a secularization of Judaism, but was represented by its advocates, the *maskilim*, as a modernization of Jewish teaching. The word 'haskalah' is derived from the Hebrew 'sechel' which means 'intelligence' or 'understanding'.

15    Hillel Zeitlin (1871-1942), poet and essayist. The philosophical pessimism of his early essays is transformed into religious hopefulness in his later Hasidic writings. Clad in prayer-shawl and tefellin, Zeitlin was killed by the Nazis on the way from the Warsaw Ghetto to Treblinka in 1942.

16    Abraham Joshua Heschel (1907-1972) was born in Warsaw and educated in Poland and Germany. He succeeded Buber as Head of the Frankfurt Lehrhaus. Heschel adopted the phenomenological method of Husserl in his religious writings and drew heavily also on Hasidic traditions. His principal works are *God In Search Of Man* (Philadelphia: Jewish Publ. Soc., 1956) and *A Passion for Truth* (London: Secker and Warburg, 1974). Some interesting parallels with Buber's interpretations of Kierkegaard and with his treatment of Hasidic themes will be found in chapters 1, 2 and 5 of the latter.

17    e.g. *Hasidism and Modern Man*, pp. 47-73; *Meetings*, pp. 19-20, 38-41; *Between Man and Man*, pp. 223-224.

18    Buber, *Between Man and Man*, p. 224.

19    Buber, *Hasidism and Modern Man*, p. 56.

20    Ibid., pp. 52-53.

21    Buber, *Meetings*, pp. 27-30.

22    Buber, *Hasidism and Modern Man*, p.53.

23    Buber, 'Uber Jakob Boehme', *Wiener Rundschau*, V, 12, pp. 251-253.

24    Landauer's interest in mysticism was an important factor in directing Buber towards Boehme, Eckhart and other German mystics.

25    Buber, 'Gustav Landauer', *Die Zeit*, XXXIX, 506, p.127.

26    Buber, *Ekstatische Konfessionen* (Jena, 1909).

27    Buber, *Pointing the Way*, pp. 25-30.

28    Ibid., p.28.

29    Friedman, *Martin Buber's Life and Work*, I, p. 93.

30    Buber, *Pointing the Way*, p. 29.

31    Ibid., p. 27.

32    Buber, *Hasidism and Modern Man*, p. 58.

33    Ibid., p. 59.

34    Friedman, *Martin Buber's Life and Work*, I, p. 101.

35    e.g. *Tales of the Hasidim: The Early Masters; Tales of the Hasidim: The Later Masters.*

36    Friedman, *Martin Buber's Life and Work*, I, p. 102.

37    Buber, *The Legend of the Baal Shem*, p. 10.

38    Buber, *Die Legende des Baalschem* (Frankfurt: Rutten and Loening, 1907).

39    Friedman, *Martin Buber's Life and Work*, I, p. 119.

40    Buber, *Hasidism and Modern Man*, pp. 42, 233.

41    Buber, *The Origin and Meaning of Hasidism*, p. 140.

42    See *Between Man and Man*, pp, 132-147.

43    Buber, *Hasidism and Modern Man*, pp. 30, 49.

44    For a more detailed definition of avoda see *Hasidism and Modern Man*, p. 84.

45    Ibid., pp. 200-201.

46    Ibid., p. 180.

47    A sixteenth century religious writer whose simplified interpretations of the Kabbala were adopted by the Hasidim. For a detailed discussion of Lurian Kabbalism see

Friedman, *Martin Buber: The Life of Dialogue* (London: Routledge and Kegan Paul, 1955), pp. 16-23.

48  See *Hasidism and Modern Man*, p.98. *Kavanot* could be defined simply as the intentional striving for redemption.

49  Buber, *The Origin and Meaning of Hasidism*, p. 136.

50  Buber, *For the Sake of Heaven* (New York: Meridian Books, 1958), p. 102.

51  See *The Origin and Meaning of Hasidism*, pp. 133-7.

52  Ibid.,, p. 134.

53  See Note 47 above.

54  Buber, *The Origin and Meaning of Hasidism*, p. 185.

55  Ibid., p. 186.

56  See *Hasidism and Modern Man*, pp. 217 ff.

57  Buber, *The Origin and Meaning of Hasidism*, pp. 198-9.

58  Buber, *Hasidism and Modern Man*, p. 138.

59  Ibid., p. 75.

60  Ibid., p. 78.

61  See Chapter 2, Section 1.

62  Buber, *The Origin and Meaning of Hasidism*, p. 27.

63  Ibid., pp. 148-9.

64  See *The Two Types of Faith* for a full discussion of this issue.

65  Buber, *The Origin and Meaning of Hasidism*, p. 129.

66  Buber, *Hasidism and Modern Man*, pp. 98 ff.

67  Buber, *The Origin and Meaning of Hasidism*, p. 111.

68  Ibid., p. 179.

69  Ibid.

70  Friedman, *Martin Buber's Life and Work*, I, p. 108.

71  Buber, *Between Man and Man*, p. 223.

72  Seltzer, *Jewish People, Jewish Thought*, p. 746.

73  Schillp, *The Philosophy of Martin Buber*, pp. 403-435.

74  Ibid., p. 405.

75  Ibid., p. 407. Gnosticism was a religious movement blending Christian teaching with esoteric pagan philosophy that flourished in the first century A.D. Its defining characteristic was a sharp distinction between the 'good' spiritual world and the 'evil' material world. The term 'gnostic' is used generally therefore to signify a belief in the world as intrinsically evil.

76  Schillp, *The Philosophy of Martin Buber*, p. 416.

77  *Buber Commemorative Broadcast*, BBC Radio 3.

78  Schillp, *The Philosophy of Martin Buber*, pp. 689-744.

79  Ibid., p. 731.

80  Ibid., pp. 732 ff. The reference is to Sholem (see above).

81  John MacQuarrie, *Existentialism* (Penguin Books, 1972). See especially pp. 270-274.

82  Rudolph Bultmann, *Jesus Christ and Mythology*, trans. Fuller (New York: Scribner, 1958).

83  Ludwig Ebeling, *Word and Faith*, trans. Leitch (SCM Press, 1963). See especially chapter 9.

84  Paul Ricoeur, *Essays on Biblical Interpretation* (Philadelphia: Fortress Press, 1980).

85  Martin Buber and Franz Rosenzweig, *Die Schrift und ihrer Verdentschung* (Berlin: Schocken Verlag, 1936).

86  Buber and Rosenzweig had translated the Old Testament from Genesis to Isaiah when Rosenzweig died in 1929. Buber continued with the work until 1961. A four volume

translation was published in 1962.
87    Schillp, *The Philosophy of Martin Buber*, p. 364.
88    Amos 4: 13. For comment see *On Judaism*, p. 216.
89    Amos 9: 7.
90    See *On Judaism*, p. 220.
91    e.g. Psalm 19.
92    e.g. The Song of Solomon.
93    Buber, *The Prophetic Faith* (New York: Harper Torchbooks, 1960), p. 5.
94    Buber, *Israel and the World*, p. 119.
95    Buber, Moses (New York: Harper Torchbooks, 1958). See pp. 162-171.
96    Buber, *The Two Types of Faith*, p. 8.
97    Ibid., pp. 12-13.
98    Ibid., pp. 11-12, 14, 20-21.
99    Mark, 9: 14-29.
100   John, 20: 25.
101   Hebrews 11: I.
102   Galatians 3: 6.
103   Romans 8: 26.
104   Matthew 5: 17.
105   Buber, *The Two Types of Faith*, p. 34.
106   Buber, *On Judaism*, p. 44.
107   Matthew 5: 17.
108   Leviticus 19: 2.
109   Buber, *The Origin and Meaning of Hasidism*, p. 251.
110   Buber, *On Judaism*, p. 127.
111   Corinthians 11, 5: 21. See also Romans 8: 2, I: I-6; Ephesians I: 15-23; Peter I, 3: 22.
112   Buber, *On Judaism*, pp. 127-128
113   See beginning of chapter.
114   Buber, *Eclipse of God*, p. 135.
115   Buber, *Hasidism and Modern Man*, p. 24.
116   Buber, *The Two Types of Faith*, p. 162.
117   The reference is to Franz Kafka's novel, *The Castle*. Buber and Kafka met in Berlin
      in 1911. It is highly probable that Kafka encountered Hasidism through Buber's
      translations of the legends. See Friedman, *Martin Buber's Life and Work*, I, pp.
      140-141.
118   Buber, *The Two Types of Faith*, p. 143.
119   See *Eclipse of God*, pp. 78-92 and 131-138.
120   Buber, *Israel and the World*, p. 234.
121   Buber, *On Judaism*, p. 158.
122   Ibid.
123   Buber, *Israel and the World*, p. 234.
124   The term atheoi was used by the Greeks to signify those who denied the traditional
      gods. Buber uses it in this sense also. See *Eclipse of God*, p. 46.
125   Buber, *Israel and the World*, pp. 95-96.
126   See *Eclipse of God*, pp. 113-120.
127   Ibid., p. 98.
128   Ibid., p. 120.
129   Buber, *Hasidism and Modern Man*, p. 27.
130   Ibid.
131   Ibid.

132   Ibid., pp. 38-9.
133   Ibid., p. 30.
134   Buber, *On Judaism*, pp. 80-81.


CHAPTER IV
1     Buber, *Israel and the World*, pp. 149-50.
2     G.H. Bantock, *Education in an Industrial Society* (London: Faber, 1963), pp. 24-57;
      *Dilemmas of the Curriculum* (Oxford: Robertson, 1980, pp. 37-49; R.S. Peters, *John
      Dewey Reconsidered* (London: Routledge and Kegan Paul, 1974), pp. 102- 123;
      *Perspectives on Plowden* (London: Routledge and Kegan Paul, 1969), pp. I-20;
      Jacques Maritain, *Education at the Crossroads* (Yale University Press, 1974), p. 32;
      P. Hirst, *Knowledge and the Curriculum* (London: Routledge and Kegan Paul, 1974),
      pp. 121-2, 127-9.
3     Buber, *Between Man and Man*, p. 115.
4     Ibid., p. 112.
5     Ibid., p. 114.
6     Ibid., pp. 117-118.
7     Ibid., p. 121.
8     Ibid., pp. 117, 122.
9     Ibid., p. 121.
10    Ibid., pp. 120-121.
11    Ibid.
12    Ibid., p. 123.
13    Ibid.
14    Buber, *Israel and the World*, pp. 149-50.
15    Buber, *Between Man and Man*, p. 130.
16    Ibid., pp. 129-130.
17    Buber, *Meetings*, p. 18.
18    Buber, *I and Thou*, p. 76.
19    Buber, *Israel and the World*, p. 138.
20    Buber, *Between Man and Man*, pp. 125-6.
21    Buber, *The Origin and Meaning of Hasidism*, pp 26, 44.
22    Ibid.
23    Ibid., pp. 44, 130-131.
24    e.g. Friedman, *Martin Buber's Life and Work*, 11, p. 21.
25    Buber, *The Origin and Meaning of Hasidism*, p. 42.
26    Buber, *Israel and the World*, p. 41-52.
27    Buber, *The Knowledge of Man*, p. 78.
28    Ibid., pp. 181-2.
29    Buber, *Between Man and Man*, p.117
30    Ibid., p. 128.
31    Ibid., p. 117.
32    Ibid.
33    Ibid., p. 117.
34    Buber, *The Knowledge of Man*, p. 112.
35    Buber, *Israel and the World*, p. 42.
36    Buber, *The Knowledge of Man*, pp. 62-3.
37    Buber, *Israel and the World*, pp. 45-6.

38    Ibid.          3.
39    Ibid
40    Ibid
41    Buber, *Pointing the Way*, pp. 152-5.
42    Buber, *Pointing the Way*, p. 181.
43    Ibid.
44    T.S. Eliot, *After Strange Gods* (London: Faber, 1934).
45    Ibid., p. 62.
46    Buber, *On Judaism*, p. 11.
47    Ibid., p. 18.
48    Ibid., p. 19.
49    Ibid., p. 17.
50    Buber, *Israel and the World*, p. 146.
51    Ibid., p. 138.
52    Ibid.
53    Ibid., p. 139.
54    Ibid., p. 152.
55    Ibid., p. 148.
56    Ibid., p. 140.
57    Ibid.
58    Ibid., pp. 141-2.
59    B. Curtis, *Phenomenology and Education* (London: Methuen, 1978), pp. 80-99.
60    Ibid., p. 80.
61    Ibid., p. 85.
62    Ibid., pp. 87-88.
63    David Holbrook, *English for Meaning* (Windsor: NFER, 1979), p. 115.
64    Ibid., p. 96.
65    Ibid., p. 99.
66    Ibid., pp. 96-98.
67    Bernard T. Harrison, *Learning through Writing* (Windsor: NFER, 1983), pp. 7-8.


CHAPTER V
1     Buber, *Israel and the World*, p. 43.
2     Ibid., p. 44.
3     Ibid., p. 49.
4     Buber, *On Judaism*, pp. 158-9.
5     Ibid., p. 80.
6     Ibid., p. 240.
7     Ibid., pp. 161-2.
8     Buber, *Israel and the World*, p. 50.
9     Ibid., pp. 50-51.
10    Buber, *Eclipse of God*, pp. 7I-2.
11    Buber, *On Judaism*, p. 150.
12    Ibid., p. 80.
13    Ibid.
14    Ibid., p. 149.
15    Ibid., p. 151.
16    Ibid., pp. 160-16I.

17    Buber, *Israel and the World*, p. 42.
18    Buber, *I and Thou*, p. 123.
19    Ibid., p. 150.
20    Buber, *Israel and the World*, p. 49.
21    F. Dostoievsky, *The Brothers Karamazov* (London: Landsborough Publications, 1958), p. 31.
22    Buber, *Eclipse of God*, p. 43.
23    Buber, *On Judaism*, pp. 161-2.
24    Buber, *Israel and the World*, pp. 175-6.
25    Ibid., p. 181.
26    Ibid., p. 176.
27    Buber, *I and Thou*, pp. 123-4.
28    Buber, *Israel and the World*, pp. 94-5.
29    Ibid., p. 42.
30    Ibid., pp. 97-8.
31    Buber, *On Judaism*, p. 95.
32    Ibid., pp. 103-4.
33    Buber, *The Knowledge of Man*, p. 156.
34    Buber, *On Judaism*, pp. 104-5.
35    Ibid., p. 97.
36    Ibid., pp. 105-6.
37    Ibid., p. 154.
38    Buber, *Israel and the World*, p. 87.
39    Buber, *On Judaism*, p. 164.
40    Buber, *Israel and the World*, p. 89.
41    Ibid., p. 93.
42    R. Wagner, 'Religion und Kunst' in John Chancellor, *Wagner* (London: Granada, 1980), p. 275.
43    B. Pasternak, *Doctor Zhivago* (London: Fontana Books, 1969), p. 105.
44    Osip Mandelstam, *The Complete Critical Prose and Letters* (Ann Arbor: Ardis, 1980), pp. 91 2.
45    Buber, *Eclipse of God*, pp. 93-112.
46    Ibid., p. 95.
47    Ibid.
48    Ibid., pp. 96-97.
49    Ibid., pp. 98-99.
50    Ibid., p. 99.
51    Ibid., pp. 119-20.
52    Buber, *Between Man and Man*, p. 119.
53    Ibid., p. 91.
54    Ibid., p. 95.
55    Ibid., pp. 91-92.
56    Buber, *Hasidism and Modern Man*, pp. 42, 233.
57    Ibid., p. 140.
58    Ibid., pp. 30, 49.
59    Buber, *On Judaism*, pp. 46-7.
60    Buber, *Between Man and Man*, p. 92.
61    Ibid., p. 93.
62    Ibid., p. 93.
63    Buber, *The Knowledge of Man*, p. 132.

64    Ibid., pp. 135-6.
65    Ibid., 131-3.
66    Ibid., pp. 135-6.
67    Ibid., p. 147.
68    Ibid., pp. 147-8.
69    Buber, *Between Man and Man*, pp. 140-I.
70    Buber, *Israel and the World*, pp. 137-45; *Between Man and Man*, 132-47.
71    Buber, *Israel and the World*, p. 142.
72    Georg Kerschensteiner (1854-1932), a German educational theorist and reformer who
      wrote extensively on physical and vocational education.
73    Buber, *Between Man and Man*, p. 147.
74    Ibid., p. 141.
75    Ibid., pp. 139-140.
76    Ibid., pp. 132-3.
77    Ibid., p. 134.
78    Ibid., p. 134.
79    Ibid., p. 135.
80    Ibid.
81    Ibid., p. 136.
82    Ibid., pp. 142-3.
83    Buber, *The Knowledge of Man*, p. 134.
84    Buber, *Between Man and Man*, pp. 143-4.
85    Buber, *Israel and the World*, p. 143.
86    Ibid., p. 83.
87    Ibid., p. 144.
88    Buber, *Between Man and Man*, p. 139.
89    Ibid., pp. 146-7.


CHAPTER VI
1     Buber, *Between Man and Man*, p. 112.
2     Ibid., p. 110.
3     Ibid.
4     Ibid., p. 112.
5     Ibid., p. 114.
6     Ibid.
7     Buber, *I and Thou*, p. 61.
8     Buber, *The Knowledge of Man*, pp. 150-151.
9     Ibid.
10    Ibid., p. 152.
11    Ibid., p. 153.
12    Ibid., p. 154.
13    Ibid.
14    Ibid., p. 155.
15    Ibid., p. 156.
16    Ibid., p. 159.
17    Ibid.
18    Ibid., p. 160.
19    Ibid.

20   Ibid., p. 162.
21   Ibid., pp. 164-5.
22   Ibid., p. 165.
23   Buber, *Between Man and Man*, p. 44.
24   Ibid.
25   Buber, *The Knowledge of Man*, p. 67.
26   Buber, *I and Thou*, p. 91.
27   Ibid., p. 173.
28   Ibid., p. 60.
29   Ibid., pp. 60-61.
30   *The Knowledge of Man*, p. 111.
31   Ibid.
32   Ibid.
33   Ibid., p. 112.
34   Ibid., pp. 115-116.
35   Ibid., pp. 117-118.
36   Ibid., pp. 114-115.
37   Ibid., p. 118.
38   Ibid., p. 161.
39   Ibid., pp. 161-2.
40   Ibid., p. 118.
41   Ibid., p. 119.
42   Ibid., p. 120.
43   Buber, *I and Thou*, p. 116.
44   Ibid.
45   Friedman, *Martin Buber's Life and Work*, I, p.19.
46   Buber, *Pointing the Way*, p. 79.
47   Ibid., pp. 79-80.
48   Friedman, *Martin Buber's Life and Work*, I, p. 21.
49   Buber, *The Knowledge of Man*, p. 109.
50   Ibid.
51   Buber, *Pointing the Way*, p. 63.
52   Ibid.
53   Ibid., pp. 63-4.
54   B. Pasternak, 'Il Tratto di Apelle', *Prose and Poems*, ed. Schimanski (London: Benn, 1959), pp. 129-54.
55   Buber, *Pointing the Way*, p. 64.
56   Ibid., pp. 65-66.
57   Buber, *The Knowledge of Man*, p. 146.
58   Ibid.
59   Buber, *Pointing the Way*, p. 77.
60   Ibid., pp. 77-8.
61   Herbert Read, *Education through Art* (London: Faber, 1963), p. 8.
62   Ibid.
63   Ibid.
64   M. Langdon, *Let the Children Write* (London: Longman, 1965); D. Pym, *Free Writing* (University of Bristol Press, 1966); M. Hourd, *The Education of the Poetic Spirit* (London: Heinemann, 1949).
65   M. Peel, *Seeing to the Heart* (London: Hart-Davis, 1967); B. Maybury, *Creative Writing in the Primary School* (London: Batsford, 1967).

66   B. Owens and M. Marland, *The Practice of English Teaching* (Edinburgh: Blackie, 1970), p. 38.
67   D. Holbrook, *English for Maturity* (Cambridge University Press, 1967).
68   D. Holbrook, *English for the Rejected* (Cambridge University Press, 1972), p. 113.
69   e.g. M. Peters, *Spelling: Caught or Taught* (London: Routledge and Kegan Paul, 1967).
70   G.H. Bantock, *Education in an Industrial Society* (London: Faber, 1963), p. 14.
71   D. Murphy, 'Comparative Trends in Post-Primary Curriculum Reform', *Studies in Education*, Spring, 1983, pp. 7-35.
72   Mary Warnock, *Schools of Thought* (London: Faber, 1978).
73   Mary Warnock, *Imagination* (London: Faber, 1976), p. 207.
74   Louis Arnaud Reid, 'The Concept of Aesthetic Development' in *The Development of Aesthetic Experience* (ed. Ross) (Oxford: Pergamon, 1982); E. Eisner, 'Building Curricula for Art Education' in R.A. Smith, *Aesthetics and Problems of Education* (University of Illinois Press, 197I), pp. 387-401; P. Abbs, *English Within the Arts* (London: Hodder and Stoughton, 1982); B. Harrison, *Learning Through Writing* (Windsor: NFER, 1983).
75   Reid, *The Development of Aesthetic Experience*, p. 99.
76   Eisner, *Aesthetics and Problems in Education*, p. 389.
77   Ibid.
78   Abbs, *English Within the Arts*, p. 11.
79   Ibid.
80   Ibid., pp. 38-83.
81   David Holbrook, *English For Meaning* (Windsor: NFER, 1979).
82   A. Bullock, *A Language For Life* (London: HMSO, 1975).
83   Department of Education and Science, *English from 5 to 16* (London: HMSO, 1984).
84   Ibid., pp. 2-3.
85   Ibid.
86   Ibid., p. 3.
87   e.g. B. Bernstein, Class, *Codes and Control* (London: Routledge and Kegan Paul, 1977); J. Britton, *Language and Learning* (Penguin, 1972); D. Barnes, *Language, the Learner and the School* (Penguin, 1969); P. Doughty, *Exploring Language* (London: Arnold, 1972).
88   Abbs, *English Within the Arts*, p. 21.
89   F. R. Leavis, *The Living Principle* (London: Chatto and Windus, 1975).
90   D. Holbrook, *English for Meaning*, pp. 75-120.
91   Ibid., pp. 9, 34.
92   Abbs, *English Within the Arts*, p. 23.
93   ibid., p. 27.
94   G. Sampson, *English For The English* (Cambridge University Press, 1975).
95   Abbs, *English within the Arts*, p. 27.
96   D. Holbrook, *English for Meaning*, p. 36.
97   Buber, *The Knowledge of Man*, pp. 89-109.
98   Abbs, *English Within the Arts*, p. 30.
99   Holbrook, *English For Meaning*, p. 36.
100  See Note 64 above.
101  See Note 69 above.
102  Buber, *Between Man and Man*, pp. 112-114.
103  D. Barnes, *Versions of English* (Heinemann, 1984); A Wilkinson, *Assessing Language Development* (Oxford University Press, 1980).

CHAPTER VII

1   Buber, *On Judaism* (New York: Schocken Books, 1972); *Israel and the World (New York: Schocken Books, 1963)*.
2   Buber, *Israel and the World*, pp. 227-34.
3   e.g. 'Teaching and Deed', 'Israel and the Command of the Spirit', 'Judaism and Mankind', 'Renewal of Judaism', 'Judaism and Civilization', 'The Silent Question'.
4   Buber, *Pointing the Way* (London: Routledge, 1957).
5   Buber, *Paths in Utopia* (London: Routledge and Kegan Paul, 1957).
6   Ibid., p. 90.
7   Ibid., p. 10.
8   Ibid., pp. 27 ff.
9   Ibid., pp. 38 ff.
10  Ibid., pp. 46 ff.
11  Ibid., p. 52.
12  Ibid., pp. 129 ff.
13  Buber, *The Knowledge of Man*, pp. 89-110.
14  Ibid., p. 108.
15  Ibid., pp. 89-91.
16  Buber, *Between Man and Man*, p. 93.
17  Ibid., p. 94.
18  Ibid.
19  Buber, *On Judaism*, p. 113.
20  Friedman, *Martin Buber's Life and Work*, 11I, p. 393.
21  Ibid., p. 193.
22  Ibid., p. 47.
23  Ibid.
24  See Henry P. Van Dusen, *Dag Hammerskjold: The Statesman and his Faith* (New York: Harper and Row, 1967), pp. 215-219; Friedman, *Martin Buber's Life and Work*, 11I, p. 387.
25  See *The Two Types of Faith*, pp. 13-14.
26  Friedman, *Martin Buber's Life and Work*, 11I, p. 105.
27  Ibid., p. 106.
28  Ibid.
29  Ibid.
30  Ibid.
31  Buber, *Pointing the Way*, pp. 232-9.
32  Friedman, *Martin Buber's Life and Work*, 11I, p. 123.
33  See Buber, *Towards Union in Palestine* (Westport, Connecticut: Greenwood Press, 1947).
34  Friedman, *Martin Buber's Life and Work*, 11I, pp. 24-32.
35  Buber, *Pointing the Way*, pp. 98-108.
36  Ibid.
37  Ibid.
38  Ibid.
39  Friedman, *Martin Buber's Life and Work*, 11I, p. 307.
40  Ibid., pp. 154-5.
41  Ibid., p. 321.
42  Ibid., pp. 327-8.
43  Ibid., pp. 356-64.
44  Ibid., p. 159.

45    Buber, 'Adult Education', *Molad* (Tel Aviv, 1951) (translation by Martin Buber Center for Adult Education, The Hebrew University of Jerusalem).
46    Ibid.
47    Ibid., p. 12.
48    Ibid., p. 4.
49    Ibid.
50    Ibid., pp. 5-6.
51    Ibid., p. 6.
52    Ibid., p. 7.
53    Rome, *Philosophical Interrogations*, pp. 64-8.
54    Friedman, *Martin Buber's Life and Work*, 1II, p. 77.
55    Buber, *Israel and the World*, pp. 41-53.
56    Buber, 'Adult Education', p. 12.
57    Ibid., pp. 14-15.
58    Buber, 'Adult Education in Israel', *The Torch* (June, 1952), pp. 7-11.
59    Ibid., p. 8.
60    The Hebrew University of Jerusalem, *Education for All* (Jerusalem, 1983), p. 1.
61    Ibid.
62    Ibid., p. 2.
63    R. M. Hutchins, *The Learning Society* (Penguin Books, 1972).
64    Rome, *Philosophical Interrogations*, pp. 64-68.
65    Helder Camara, *Race against Time* (London: Sheed and Ward, 1971); *The Desert is Fertile* (London: Sheed and Ward, 1971).
66    Camara, *Race against Time*, p. 79.
67    Ibid., pp. 73 ff.
68    Camara, *The Desert is Fertile*, pp. 6 ff.
69    P. Freire, *Pedagogy of the Oppressed* (Penguin Books, 1972), p. 151.
70    Ibid., pp. 61-62.
71    P. Freire, *The Politics of Education* (London: Macmillan, 1985).
72    Ibid., pp. 47-49.


CHAPTER VIII
1     e.g. John White, *The Aims of Education Restated* (London: Routledge and Kegan Paul, 1982).
2     Allan Bloom, *The Closing of the American Mind* (New York: Simon and Schuster, 1987), p. 25.
3     Dostoievsky, *The Brothers Karamazov*, p, 31.
4     P. Zwerling and C. Martin, *Nicaragua: A New Kind of Revolution* (Westport, Conn., Lawrence Hill, 1985), p. 76.
5     See Harvey J. Graff, *National Literacy Campaigns: Historical and Comparative Perspectives* (New York: Plenum Press, 1987).
6     T.S. Eliot, *Selected Prose*, ed. Hayward (London: Faber, 1955).
7     See *The Times Educational Supplement*, 18 January 1985 and 26 July 1985.
8     P. Freire, *The Politics of Education* (London: Macmillan, 1985), p. xviii.
9     See *The Times Educational Supplement*, 10 June 1983 and 24 June 1983.
10    Buber, *Israel and the World*, p. 44.

# Bibliography

Allentuck, M., 'Martin Buber's Aesthetic Theories: Some Reflections,' *Journal of Aesthetics and Art Criticism*, 30, I, Fall, 1971.

Balthasar, Hans Urs von. *Martin Buber and Christianity* (trans. A. Dru) (London: Harvill Press, 1961).

Beek, M.A. and Sperna, W.J. *Martin Buber: Personalist and Prophet* (New York: Newman Press, 1968).

Berkovits, E. *Studies in Torah Judaism: A Jewish Critique of the Philosophy of Martin Buber* (New York: Yeshiva University, 1962).

Berry, Donald J. *Mutuality: The Vision of Martin Buber* (Albany: State University of New York Press, 1985).

Borouity, E.B. 'Education Is Not I-Thou,' *Religious Education*, 66 (1971), pp. 326-331.

Breslauer, S.D., *The Chrysalis of Religion: A Guide to the Jewishness of I and Thou* (Nashville: Abingdon, 1980).

Buber, Martin. *At the Turning: Three Addresses on Judaism* (New York: Farrar, Strauss and Young, 1952).

___, *A Believing Humanism: My Testament, 1902-1965* (trans. Friedman) (New York: Simon and Schuster, 1967).

___, *Between Man and Man* (trans. Smith) (London: Fontana Books, 1979).

___, *Daniel: Dialogues on Realization* (trans. Friedman) (New York: Holt, Rinehart and Winston, 1964).

___, *Eclipse of God* (trans. Friedman) (New York: Humanities Press, 1972).

___, *For the Sake of Heaven* (trans. Lewisohn) (Philadelphia: The Jewish Publication Society, 1945).

___, *Good and Evil: Two Interpretations* (New York: Scribner, 1953).

___, *Hasidism and Modern Man* (trans. Friedman) (New York: Horizon Press, 1958).

___, *I and Thou* (trans. Smith) (Edinburgh: Clark, 1937).

___, *Images of Good and Evil* (trans. Bullock) (London: Routledge and Kegan Paul, 1952).

___, *Israel and Palestine: The History of an Idea* (trans. Godman) (London: East and West Library, 1952).

___, *Israel and the World: Essays in a Time of Crisis* (New York: Schocken Books, 1963).

___, *Kingship of G...* s. Scheimann) (London: Allen and Unwin, 1965).

___, *The Knowle... 'an* (ed. Friedman) (New York: Harper and Row, 1966).

___, *The Legend of the Baal Shem* (trans. Friedman) (London: East and West Library, 1955).

___, *Mamre: Essays in Religion* (trans. Hort) (Oxford University Press, 1946).

___, *Meetings* (ed. Friedman) (La Salle, Illinois: Open Court Publishing, 1973).

___, *Moses* (New York: Harper Torchbooks, 1958).

___, *On the Bible* (ed. Glatzer) (New York: Schocken Books, 1968).

___, *On Judaism* (ed. Glatzer) (New York: Schocken Books, 1967).

___, *The Origin and Meaning of Hasidism* (trans. Friedman) (New York: Horizon Press, 1960).

___, *Paths in Utopia* (trans. Hull) (London: Routledge and Kegan Paul, 1949).

___, *Pointing the Way* (trans. Friedman) (London: Routledge and Kegan Paul, 1956).

___, *The Prophetic Faith* (trans. Witton-Davies) (New York: Macmillan, 1949).

___, *Tales of Rabbi Nachman* (trans. Friedman) (Bloomington: Indiana University Press, 1962).

___, *Tales of the Hasidim: The Early Masters* (trans. Marx) (New York: Schocken Books, 1961).

___, *Tales of the Hasidim: The Later Masters* (trans. Marx) (New York: Schocken Books, 1961).

___, *To Hallow this Life* (Westport: Conn.: Greenwood, 1958).

___, *The Way of Man according to the Teaching of Hasidism* (London: Routledge and Kegan Paul, 1951).

___, *The Way of Response* (ed. Glatzer) (New York: Schocken, 1966).

Buber, M. Magnes, J and Simon, E. (eds.) *Towards Union in Palestine* (Westport, Conn,: Greenwood, 1947).

Cohen, Adir. *The Educational Philosophy of Martin Buber* (The Sarah F. Yoselof Memorial Publications on Jewish Affairs) (New Brunswick: Associated University Press, 1985).

Cohen, Arthur. *Martin Buber* (London: Bowes and Bowes, 1957).

Cohen, M. and Buber, R. *Martin Buber: A Bibliography of his Writings* (Jerusalem: The Magnes Press, 1980).

Curtis, B. and Mays, W. *Phenomenology and Education: Self-consciousness and its Development* (London: Methuen, 1978).

Diamond, Malcolm. *Martin Buber: Jewish Existentialist* (New York: Oxford University Press, 1960).

Downing, Christine. 'Guilt and Responsibility in the Thought of Martin Buber,' *Judaism*, 18, 1969, pp. 53-63.

Etscovitch, L. 'Religious Education as Sacred and Profane: An Interpretation of Martin Buber,' *Religious Education*, 64, 1969, pp. 279-286.

Fox, E. 'The Buber-Rosenzweig Translation of the Bible', *Response*, 5, 3, 1971, pp. 29-42.

Friedman, Maurice, *Martin Buber's Life and Work*, 3 vols. (London: Search Press, 1982; New York: E.P. Dutton, 1983, 1985).

___, *Martin Buber: The Life of Dialogue* (London: Routledge and Kegan Paul, 1955).

___, (ed.) *Martin Buber and the Theatre* (New York: Funk and Wagnalls, 1969).

___, 'Martin Buber's Concept of Education,' *Christian Scholar*, 40, 1957, pp. 109-116.

___, 'Martin Buber's Theology and Religious Education,' *Religious Education*, 54, 1959, pp. 5-17.

___, (ed.) *The Worlds of Existentialism* (University of Chicago Press, 1964).

Gordon, H. and Bloch, J. *Martin Buber: A Centenary Volume* (Jerusalem: Ktav Publishing, 1984).

Grayzel, S. *A History of the Jews* (New York: Mentor Books, 1968).

Greene, Maxine. *Existential Encounters for Teachers* (New York: Random House, 1967).

___, *Teacher as Stranger: Educational Philosophy for the Modern Age* (Belmont, California: Wadsworth, 1973).

Halio, J.L. 'The Life of Dialogue in Education,' *The Journal of General Education*, 14, 1963, pp. 213-219.

Hillard, F.H. 'A Re-examination of Buber's Address on Education,' *British Journal of Educational Studies*, 21, 1973, pp. 40-49

Hodes, Aubrey, *Encounter with Martin Buber* (Penguin Books, 1972).

Horowitz, R. *Buber's Way to I and Thou* (Heidelberg: Verlag Lambert Schneider, 1978).

Katz, S. 'Martin Buber's Epistemology: A Critical Appraisal,' *International Philosophical Quarterly* (1981), 21: pp.133-158.

Kohanski, A.S. *An Analytical Interpretation of Martin Buber's I and Thou* (New York: Barrons, 1975).

Kohn, Hans. *Martin Buber, sein Werk und seine Zeit* (Hellerau: Jacob Hegner Verlag, 1930).

Kurzweil, Z. E. *Modern Trends in Jewish Education* (New York: Thomas Yoseloff, 1964).

Lyon, J.K. 'Paul Celan and Martin Buber: Poetry As Dialogue,', *Publications of the Modern Language Association of America*, 86, 1971, pp. 110-120.

Martin, Bernard. *Great Twentieth Century Jewish Philosophers* (New York: Macmillan, 1970).

Moore, Donald J. *Martin Buber: Prophet of Religious Secularism* (Philadelphia: The Jewish Publication Society, 1974).

Mullins, James. 'The Problem of the Individual in the Philosophies of Dewey and Buber,' *Educational Theory*, 17, 1967, pp. 76-82.

Manheim, W. *Martin Buber* (New York Twayne, 1974).

Murphy, J.W. *The Social Philosophy of Martin Buber* (Washington D.C.: University Press of America, 1983).

Oldham, Joseph. *Real Life Is Meeting* (New York: Macmillan, 1974).

Oliver, Roy. *The Wanderer and the Way* (London: East and West Library, 1968).

Panko, S.M. *Martin Buber* (Waco, Texas: Word Books, 1976).

Petras, J.W. 'God, Man and Society: The Perspectives of Buber and Kierkegaard,' *The Journal of Religious Thought*, 27, 1966, pp. 119-128.

Pfuetze, Paul. *Self, Society, Existence* (New York: Harper and Row, 1961).

___, *The Social Self in the Writings of George Herbert Mead and Martin Buber* (New York: Bookman Associates, 1954).

Pritzkau, Philo T. *On Education For the Authentic* (New York: Preston, 1977).

Ramana, Murti V.V. 'Buber's Dialogue and Gandhi's Satygraha,' *Journal of the History of Ideas*, 29, 1968, pp. 605-13.

Read. Herbert. *Education Through Art* (London: Faber, 1948).

Reiner, J. 'Religion in the Secular World: Notes on Martin Buber and Radical Theology,' *Response*, 2, 1968, pp. 3-17.

Rome, S. and B. (eds.) *Philosophical Interrogations* (New York: Harper Torchbooks, 1964).

Rosenblatt, H.S. 'Martin Buber's Concepts Applied to Education,' *The Educational Forum*, 35, 1971, pp. 215-228.

Rudovsky, David. 'Martin Buber's Existentialism: Sources, Influences and Interpretations,' *Journal of Hebraic Studies*, I, 1969, pp. 41-59.

___, 'The Neo-Hasidism of Martin Buber,' *Religious Education*, 62, 1967, pp. 235-44.

Schaeder, Grete. *The Hebrew Humanism of Martin Buber* (trans. Jacobs) (Detroit: Wayne University Press, 1973).

Schilpp, Paul A. *The Philosophy of Martin Buber* (London: Cambridge University Press, 1967).

Seltzer, R.M. *Jewish People, Jewish Thought* (New York: Macmillan, 1980).

Simon, C.M. *Martin Buber: Wisdom in our Time* (New York: Dutton, 1969).

Simon, Ernst. 'Jewish Adult Education in Nazi Germany as Spiritual Resistance,' *Leo Baeck Institute Year Book, 1965* (London: East and West Library, 1965), pp. 68-104.

Sloyan,Gerald. 'Buber and the Significance of Jesus,' *The Bridge*, 3, 1958, pp. 209-33.

Smith, R.G. *Martin Buber* (Richmond, Va., John Knox Press, 1967).

Stewart, D. *Theodor Herzl* (London: Quartet books, 1974).

Streiker, L.D., *The Promise of Buber*, (Philadelphia: J.P. Lippincott, 1969).

Tillich, Paul. 'Martin Buber and Christian Thought: His Threefold Contribution to Protestantism,' *Commentary*, 5, 1948, pp. 515-21.

Vermes, P. 'Martin Buber, A New Appraisal,' *Journal of Jewish Studies*, 22, 1971, pp. 78-96.

Vogel, M. 'The Concept of Responsibility in the Thought of Martin Buber,' *The Harvard Theological Review*, 63, 1970, pp. 153-82.

Winetrout, K. 'Buber: Philosopher of the I-Thou Dialogue,' *Educational Theory*, 13, 1963, pp. 53-7.

Wolf. E.M. 'Martin Buber and German Jewry: Prophet and Teacher to a Generation in Catastrophe,' *Judaism*, I, 4, 1952, pp. 346-52.

Wood, Robert E. *Martin Buber's Ontology: An Analysis of I and Thou* (Evanston: Northwestern University Press, 1969).

Zeigler, L. 'Personal Existence: A Study of Buber and Kierkegaard,' *Journal of Religion*, 40, 1960, pp. 80-94.

# Index